THIRTY MINOR UPANIṢADS

The publication of this book is sponsored by

Shri Azad Shivdasani

THIRTY MINOR

UPANIṢADS

Translated by

K. NĀRĀYĀṆASWĀMĪ AIYAR

Edited by

MADHU KHANNA

Foreword by

DR. KARAN SINGH

Introduction by

SWAMI VEDA BHARATI

2011

TANTRA FOUNDATION

NEW DELHI

First Published in 1914
Revised Edition 2011

Published by Tantra Foundation
Hari Bhari Farm, New Delhi - 110074

ISBN : 81-208-1565-3

Price : Rs.950=00

Typset and Printed by Neographics
K-2071(first floor), Chittaranjan Park, New Delhi - 110019

Contents

***

Editor's Note

It is a great privilege for the Tantra Foundation to present before the public the revised edition of the Thirty Minor Upaniṣads, translated by E. Narayanaswami Aiyar. This work was published as early as 1914 by the Adyar Library in Madras. For nearly eight decades after the publication of its first edition the book lay in abeyance and did not see the light of day. The present revised translation is an attempt to place the sublime teachings of the Thirty Minor Upaniṣads for the benefit of scholars and lay readers. These little known but important works are of later origin than the ancient classical Upaniṣads, 108 in number. They form a very important segment of the medieval sectarian Upaniṣads. The idea of preparing a revised edition of the Thirty Minor Upaniṣads is significant for several reasons. Firstly, the teachings of the Minor Upaniṣads are truly representative of the growth and development of the Hindu philosophical thought. They mark a certain remarkable continuity of philosophical ideas while introducing various transformations. Secondly, many Upaniṣads in the present collection contain several esoteric details on yogic practices that are seminal to the understanding of the yogic practices inherent in the Śaiva and Śākta Tantras.

The renewed interest in the area of consciousness studies and transpersonal psychology today makes the study of the Upaniṣads especially significant. The search for meaning of personal truths is still exerting today a tremendous influence on the cultural life of humanity on a global scale. For all these reasons the Upaniṣads are the profoundest importance for the future. They are a grand outpouring of religious fervour and contemplative spirituality, that is to say, a scripture that speaks of metaphysical varieties for all races and all times.

The original book has undergone several copious revisions for which I am alone responsible. However, a revisionistic venture, such as the current enterprise of this book suffers from many limitations. From the several editions that were found namely, *108 Upaniṣads in Telugu Characters*, edited by Siddhāntin Subrahmaṇya Śāstri, Madras, 1883; *Minor Upaniṣads*, critically edited by F. Otto Schrader, Madras Adyar Library, 1912; *Īśādi-aṣṭottara Upaniṣadaḥ* by Tukaram Tatya, Bombay Nirnaya Sagar Press, (n.d.); the author has adopted for his translation the afore mentioned South Indian editions. In a few places the author has referred to the Calcutta edition, namely, *The Atharvāṇa Upaniṣads with the Commentary of Narayaṇa*, edited by Rāmamaya Tarkaratna, Calcutta: Asiatic Society of Bengal, 1872-74. The Upaniṣads translated in this volume give a representative section of i. Vedanta; ii. Philosophical; iii. Mantra; iv. Sannyāsa and v. Yoga Upaniṣads from the several classes of Upaniṣads that exist. However, the selection of these texts is based on the author alone who has not given any rationale behind the selection of these texts. We have, as far as possible retained the original translation except in cases where the sentences were long-winded, outmoded or terse. In those places an attempt has been made to give a reader-friendly translation, retaining the sense of the original. Unfortunately, owing to paucity of time we, were unable to present the translations along with the original Sanskrit. In the revised edition diacritics are used with the transliterated Sanskrit following the standard usage. We have followed the conventions in the Roman and italics and have made some exceptions in certain places (eg. p.17 etc.). Sanskrit words now familiar in the current day usage (such as mantra, guru) and technical concepts (such as *ātman*, Brahman) for which there are inadequate equivalents in English have gone untranslated. A glossary of technical terms has been provided at the end of the book for a more accurate reading of concepts underlying the text passages.

The present work would not have taken shape without the generous grant from Mr. Azad Shivdasani, London. We most sincerely thank him for his good will and empathy to publish Indic scriptures that have a value for us today. Dr. Karan Singh very kindly consented to write a Foreword, and in several ways provided an inspiration for the auspicious beginning for the inaugural volume of the foundation.

I would like to record my deep sense of gratitude to Swami Veda Bharati, for his very perceptive and erudite Introduction "Continuous Revelation". We are blessed by his illuminating ideas to this inaugural volume of the foundation.

The editor wishes to express her special appreciation to all those who have helped in the arduous process of revisions. Smt. Keerti Ramachandran assisted me in the early drafts of the work. Pandit Satkari Mukhopadhyaya undertook the tedious but important task of proofreading the final draft of the revised manuscript. I am, personally beholden to all of them for their kind help and inspiration.

Last but not the least, I am thankful to Sri Ramashis Mukhopadhyaya for the fine production of this book.

PROF. MADHU KHANNA

Foreword

The Upaniṣads undoubtedly represent a high watermark of world wisdom, and remain a perennial source of inspiration and guidance down to the present day. The fact that they deal with perennial questions such as the relationship of the Ātman and Brahman (man and God in the Semitic tradition), the several pathways to the union (yoga) of the two, the importance of the Guru and the essential requirements of being a worthy student are of perennial significance, and retain their importance age after age down through the long and tortuous corridors of time.

Reading the words of inspired sages is, for me, one of the great joys of life. In memorable words, the Upaniṣads reveal to us a world of spiritual striving and realization, a world to which all human beings can have access regardless of their caste or creed, religion or nationality. It is for this reason that the Upaniṣads have had such a profound influence around the world. We may recall Schopenhauer's much quoted remarks: "From every sentence deep original and sublime thoughts arise, and the whole is pervaded by a high and holy and earnest spirit. In the whole world... there is no study ... so beneficial and so elevating as that of the Upaniṣads. They have been the consolation of my life, and will be the consolation of my death. They are destined sooner or later to become the faith of the people."

It is not known exactly how many Upaniṣads existed, but it is believed that the number was well over 200. Of these the great Adi Shankaracharya wrote commentaries on 11 of them, which have therefore been looked upon as the major Upaniṣads. These are the Iśa, Kena, Kaṭha, Praśna, Muṇḍaka, Māṇḍukya, Taittiriya, Aitareya, Chāndogya, Bṛhadāraṇyaka and Śvetāśvatara. In addition, there are several other Upaniṣads which, somewhat unjustly, have been labelled as 'minor'. They may not have attracted so much attention, but the truths that they contain are no less significant than those in the major ones.

It is, therefore, useful that some of the 'minor' Upaniṣads also become available to lovers of philosophy. In the context I welcome the publication of 'Thirty Minor Upaniṣads' which were translated by Shri K. Narayanaswami Aiyar almost a century ago and re-edited and updated by Prof. Madhu Khanna, a well known scholar. They carry an erudite introduction by Swami Veda Bharati, a reputed Vedantic scholar. In the complex and convoluted world in which we live, full of conflict and tension, the study of the Upaniṣads represent a gateway of a different reality illuminated by spiritual truths. I am sure this publication will help to popularize the comparatively lesser known texts, and thereby prove to be of help not only to scholars but to spiritual seekers in India and abroad.

DR. KARAN SINGH
MEMBER RAJYA SABHA
NEW DELHI

...lly, there is no study so beneficial and so elevating as that of the Upanisads. They have been the consolation of my life, and will be the consolation of my death. They are destined sooner or later to become the faith of the people.

It is not known exactly how many Upanisads were composed, but it is believed that the number was well over 200. Of these the great Adi Shankaracharya wrote commentaries on 11 of them, which have therefore been looked upon as the major Upanisads. These are the Isa, Kena, Katha, Prasna, Mundaka, Mandukya, Taittiriya, Aitareya, Chandogya, Brhadaranyaka and Svetasvatara. In addition, there are several other Upanisads which, somewhat unjustly, have been labelled as minor. They may not have attracted so much attention, but the truths that they contain are no less significant than those in the major ones.

It is, therefore, useful that some of the minor Upanisads also become available to lovers of philosophy. In this context I welcome the publication of 'Thirty Minor Upanisads' which were translated by Shri K. Narayanaswami Aiyar almost a century ago and revised and updated by Prof. Madhu Khanna, a well known scholar. They carry an erudite introduction by Swami Veda Bharati, a popular Vedantic teacher. In the complex and turbulent world in which we live, full of conflict and tension, the texts of the Upanisads represent a gateway to a different reality illuminated by spiritual truths. I am sure this publication will help to popularize the comparatively lesser known texts and thereby prove to be of help not only to scholars but to spiritual seekers in India and abroad.

DR. KARAN SINGH

INTRODUCTION

CONTINUOUS REVELATION

Swami Veda Bharati

One of the major fruits of spiritual progress is that the mind field *(citta)* and consciousness *(cit, caitanya)* become clear mirrors into which divine knowledge may reflect as revelation. In the Vedic tradition that has continued for uncountable aeons sacred revelation remains a common thread: the seers see the perennial truths anew:

> It is said to be perennial and yet today it is again new. The days and nights appear each in the same form as any other.[1]

It is simply impossible to determine the age and date of the composition of the Minor Upaniṣads of which there are over 200 to be found in the published compendiums, not to include the yet unpublished ones. Furthermore, it is not possible to determine as to what exactly makes a text worthy of the title 'Upaniṣad'. The

---

1. *sanātanam enam āhur utadya syāt punar navaḥ*
aho-ratre prajāyete anyo anyasya rūpayoḥ.
Atharva Veda 10.8.23

aupaniṣadika chapter of Kauṭalya's Arthashastra (14.1.1) gives prescriptions for secret weapons such as poisonous gases to be used in the battles. Vatsyayāna's Kāma-sūtra similarly has an 'Upaniṣadic' chapter (7.1-51, 2.1-59). The Bhagavadgītā, a spiritual text par excellence, is completely different from all other Upaniṣads in style and language. Many Upaniṣads are independent compositions, yet others are fragments some with variants — of larger texts. The Bṛhad-araṇyaka Upaniṣad is simply the fourteenth Section of the Śatapatha Brahmaṇa. The correct title of the Bhagavad Gita is Bhagavad Gita Upaniṣads (in plural), and it is a small part of the great epic Mahābhārata.

Furthermore, when we look at the subject matter of the Upaniṣads, major and minor, only a few have their contents organized in some kind of a logical sequence. Praśna Upaniṣad answers six questions on *prāṇa* in sequence. Śvetāśvatara begins by asking five or six questions in the first verse and giving seven propositions about reality in the second. But, thereafter it breaks into verses that seem to be extemporaneously organized as to their topics. It would be a gigantic task to take all the over 200 Upaniṣads and organize them in any logical sequence of their age, language, style or subject matter with regard to their relationship with one another, and with regard to the subject matter internally. Not only the titles, but even the dates of the Upaniṣads are hotly debated. The relative ages of each of the Upaniṣads can not be systematically evaluated. Although, at the face of it each Upaniṣad may appear as a reasonably homogeneous textual unit a closer textual analysis reflects a "more complicated histories of composition, with textual additions at various time periods adding new prospectus and ideas to these important texts".[1] The Upaniṣads constitute a "fluid textual genre" Some older Upaniṣads incorporate parts of larger texts, others like the Kaṭha, Muṇḍuka, are self-contained. The classical eleven Upaniṣads are quoted from Śaṅkarācārya.

---

1. Cohen, Signe Marie, *The Relative Chronology of the Older Upaniṣads: A Metrical and Linguistic Approach*. A Dissertation in Asian and Middle East Studies, University of Pennsylvania 1999, p. ii.

The classical idea of the identity of Brahman and ātman have been interpreted throughout the medieval periods, down to the modern times.[1] The Minor Upaniṣads were composed sometime between the medieval and post medieval period. Culled from the Arṇaya portion of the Vedas, these Upaniṣads are so called because they were studied in the forest dwellings of the sages, by the renunciate who had given up the life of a householder.

The Thirty Minor Upaniṣads translated here broadly fall into three groups. The first fourteen fall under the heading of Vedanta Upaniṣads. The second group falls under psychophysical Upaniṣads as they deal with the esoteric aspects of the physical and subtle body. The last group comprising fourteen are the Yoga Upaniṣads.

The ancient sages had proclaimed that the worthy adept *(adhikārī)* had to satisfy the preceptor to some degree about the four means *(sādhana-catuṣaṭaya)*. He had to be convinced about the truth of the identity of ātman and Brahman, be free of the ephemerality of the world; he should be indifferent to material life, and finally, must have fair mastery over the body, and firm control upon the fluctuations of the mind. The Thirty Minor Upaniṣads touch on all these aspects and are not so minor at all.

The scholars try to apply their linguistic and other tools to determine the exact authors and dates of scriptural texts. A seeker of spiritual knowledge is neutral to this delving. He/she seeks an inner truth that will guide his/her life towards becoming yet another channel for revealing the perennial knowledge. Hence we shall avoid here the temptation to get into the scholarly missions as to the dates and authors and such of the Upaniṣads.

Scholarship alone will often speculate but will not be able to give a final satisfactory solution to the problems of textual analysis of the Upaniṣads. All we can do is resort to the traditions passed on by the yogis whose texts these truly are. When a preceptor of the states of consciousness is in *samādhi*, the knowledge comes bubbling up in his/her ocean of fullness. It has its own internal sequence not commonly visible on the surface. It will take

1. Cohen cites the "Cakṣuṣā Upaniṣad, according to the colophone was completed in 1946", *op. cit.*, p.2.

a major volume to attempt to unravel the mystery of the intuitive sequences of thought patterns presented in the texts. We had better not attempt that here.

When one reads inspired texts, certain sections and statements draw our attention, according to the quest of our individual spirit, and the particular purification or guidance needed at a given level of our spiritual development. Other texts and segments, however deep, simply may not attract our attention at that time. It seems probable that this might have been the factor in the translator K. Narayanaswami Aiyar's choice of the thirty out of 200. Similarly, the sequence of the thirty is arbitrary and does not conform to the one seen in the published compendia. For example, the Muktika Upaniṣad is the last in the Section of one of the collections published by Motilal Banarasidass[1], but the author has it as the first in the translation of his selections. The Muktika Upaniṣad contains the lists of 108 Upaniṣads, each one's affiliation with a specific Veda, and the importance of studying these. In the tradition of Sanskrit classics such information normally comes at the end. But Shri Aiyar has chosen to reverse this custom.

Gaining access to the true meaning of inspired texts requires not only a thorough knowledge of the etymology and the grammatical construction of each word but to what state of spiritual experience the text may be referring. Shri Aiyar rightly observes:

> In order to expound the Upaniṣads, especially those that bear upon Yoga, someone who is a specialist in Yoga—better still, if he is an adept should undertake the task of editing and translating them...

We are gratified that Shri Aiyar's wish has been fulfilled by the Tantra Foundation which has undertaken to publish a revised edition of his work. The Vedic texts and their words contain layers upon layers of depths of meaning. Thus, each text may be translated in dozens of different ways. Each of those translations is correct but it can only be made complete by bringing together

1 The page references are to the edition of Upaniṣad-sangraha, ed. Jagadisha Shastri, Motilal Banarasidass, Delhi 1980.

all the layers in one—this is not an easy task. For example, let us look at the first few sentences of the Sarvasāra Upaniṣad. In the original it reads:

> How [does] the bondage [occur]? How liberation? What is nescience? What is knowledge? Thus. How wakefulness, dream, sleep and the fourth [state] [happen]?...

After stating six questions about twenty-three categories of reality, the Upaniṣad then proceeds to answer all the questions in four long paragraphs. Shri Aiyar does not follow that sequence. He states one question at a time and pulls out from the Sarvasāra Upaniṣad the appropriate answer. It makes for an easier reading. This device does no violence to the text but the reader may need to remind himself that the translation does not reflect the original text exactly even though his device makes the text more accessible to an average reader.

Translating is a complex task, (a) a three-line paragraph in Sanskrit may require six or more long ones in English; (b) the multilaterality of the meanings of words may need attention, for example, *apoha*[1]; (c) the verb root meanings (*yaugika*) become concealed under the thick layer of the conventional meaning (*ruḍhi*). These need to be unravelled for example, the word *parmeśṭhin* in the verse quoted below. (d) The poetic conventions and prosodial form of Sanskrit get lost in the thick English prose unless we make a diligent effort to present the original poetic value. (e) The experiential knowledge gets lost in the hands of the grammarian if he has not had the relevant spiritual experience to which the text is referring. Much of English translation of Sanskrit poetic works suffers from these deficiencies.

As we have said above, a text may be translated in numerous ways and all the translations are accurate. Let us take the first five lines of the Kaivalya Upaniṣad. The reader is asked to read Shri Aiyar's translation first. Then, here is an alternative rendering, thus:

---

1. *Apohya*. *Apoha* is a special principle in logic on which there is much debate between the Hindu and Buddhist logicians.

> Now, Aśvalāyana approached the Lord (Bhaga-vatī), Dweller in the Supreme State (*parameṣṭin*)[1], and said: Lord, do teach me the Brahman-knowledge, the excellent, concealed, ever resorted to by the noble (*sat*)[2]
> Whereby, a learned wise one[3]
> Refuting, negating and removing all sin,
> reaches the consciousness principle *(puruṣa)* that is transcendent beyond the transcendent.

To him he, the grandfather, replied:

> Obtain that through faith *(śraddhā)*, devotion *(bhakti)* and the yoga of meditation. Not by acts[4], nor by progeny or wealth, but through renunciation alone do some enjoy the immorality. Concealed in the cave[5] that shines brilliant one-world heaven, that shines brilliant beyond heaven, which the ascetics enter.

If the above illustration is helpful to the reader in formulating a methodology for the study and understanding of those highly complex texts, one may follow the same system as above and complete our task. Quite often one will need the help of other Upaniṣads and supplementary literature to fully grasp the implication of the passages under study. For example, how would one reconcile the fifteen *aṅgas* of *nididhyāsana* (Tejabindu Upaniṣad 1.15-37) with the eight limbs (*aṅgas*) of yoga in the Yoga Śūtra, also included among the fifteen metioned in the former work.

1. Commonly translated as Brahma, the Progenitor. That is a *ruḍhi,* conventional meaning. The *yaugika* meaning given by us suggests a level of divine universal consciousness.
2. Related to the Hindi word *sant,* saintly person. The alternative reading is based on the edition brought out by Motilal Banarasidass, Delhi (see note, p. XVI).
3. *Vidvān*, commonly translated as erudite but in the Upaniṣads it almost invariably means 'one who has got to know' the supreme reality as a personal experience.
4. *Karma*, ritual acts as well as the regular endeavours.
5. Many paths of meditation contain techniques and initiations for entering the cave of the heart, *dahara*.

Such are the questions to be answered by scholar-saints and the accomplished ones (*siddhas*). Even without taking the discipleship of such a preceptor an average reader cannot but be amazed at the originality of thought found on every page. For example, one cannot but be fascinated by such definitions (*ārthī-niruktis*) of *recaka, pūrka* and *kumbhaka* as given in the Tejobindu Upaniṣad (1.32, 23.):

> Refuting the world-systems is *recaka*."I am Brahman alone" this mental operation is *pūraka*. Then remaining stabilized in that awareness is *kumbhaka*.

Irrespective of what mode of translation one may undertake or study, one must not attempt the practices taught in the text without a very personal guidance from a preceptor. Initially one may not realize the harm and the hurt one might cause to oneself and then it will be too late. Nor should one attempt to understand intellectually the profundities of works like the Maṇḍala Brahmaṇa Upaniṣad and explore the experiential secrets of which even a partially realized spiritual guide will have no access. If one has not been initiated even into the shallowest level of *dahara-vidyā*, for example, how would one begin to comprehend what might be the five spaces, (*ākāśas*), one within another, taught in two groups: *ākāśa, parākāśa, mahākāśa, tattvākāśa, sūryākāśa* (Maṇḍala Brahmaṇa Upaniṣad 1.2), and *ākaśa, parākśa, mahākāśa, sūryākāśa*, and *paramākāśa* (op. cit., 4.1). We shall leave these questions for another time, till we meet someone who can show us "*etad vai tat*".

No matter how many translations one may read, or even read the original text fluently, yet for a true understanding he/she will need to learn and practise the art and science of *dhyāna-yoga*, as the Kaivalya Upaniṣad (1.3) says, to gain the knowledge concealed in the cave, one has to enter that which is beyond even the transcendent, the one that ascetics enter and settle in.

I

The Upaniṣads are often known as texts of philosophy. In the live tradition of the yogis they are studied as *pra-yoga-śāstra*, texts of sciences to be practised. All the other discussions and inspirational statements are complementary and supplementary, introductions and prologues to such practices. The word Upaniṣad has been clarified variously. The Western scholars, according to Max Muller have agreed in deriving *upa-ni-ṣad* from the Sanskrit root *sad*, to sit down, preceded by the prepositions, *nī*, down and *upa* expressing an idea of an assembly of pupils at the feet of the teacher to listen to his instructions. The commentators of the East (*bhāṣyakāras*), however, conceive it from the root *sad*, in the meaning of that which destroys ignorance by revealing the knowledge of the supreme reality. However, Patañjali goes a step further by highlighting the experiential dimension. They are called Upaniṣads, *upa-ni-sad*, sessions of sitting very close and near. Sitting close and near can be in physical proximity but in the case of yogis and their very close and near disciples the word has a completely different meaning which is illustrated by Patañjali in the Yoga Sūtra (1.37). It is a state of deep meditation when the guru's presence reflects in the mind of the disciple. That is how the Himalayan yogis explain it in the minds of their disciples in the latter's experiential moments.

This writer's preceptor[1] would ask the disciple to sit in his presence to learn. He would have the disciple recite a verse from the Upaniṣad. Immediately the disciple would go into an entranced state, different from any previous ones. Then the preceptor would have the disciple open his eyes and say to him/her: this is what it is (this state of meditation is the meaning of the verse). The first time that happened, the disciple realized the meaning of: This indeed is That (*etad vai tat*)[2]

Obviously, when the sages of the Upaniṣad sat his disciple down in meditation and study the (*nididhyāsana*) level of the study and led him/her into the desired level of meditative state, the preceptor—having shown what it was about—said: *etad vai tat,* this is what the verse means.

So the true translation of the Upaniṣad is not exchanging words of one language for those of another. That is not the

1. Swami Rama of the Himalayas, author of the classic, *Living with Himalayan Masters*.
2. Kaṭha Upaniṣad (2.1.3, 5, 6, 7, 8, 9, 12, 1.).

meaning. The Sanskrit word for an object or reality is *padārtha*, 'the meaning of the word' (*padasya arthaḥ*). The meaning of the word *jala* is not water, nor *wasser*, nor *de leau*, nor *ap*, nor *aqua*, nor *ague*. It is the object that is drunk. Not by reading, but by drinking does one find the *pada-arthaḥ*, the meaning of the word *jala*. Simply pronouncing a word in the place of another is no meaning; both are words, neither is the meaning. *Kham* of the Upaniṣad is the experience of *śūnya* in *samādhi*, not the word 'space', as often translated. Hence Śaṅkarācārya advises the teacher to help the student realize the meaning of the words *tat* and *tvam, tat-padārtha* and *tvam-padārtha*. Realization is the meaning, not translating *tat tvam asi* as 'thou art that'.

This is the essence of the *vidyās* given in the major Upaniṣads. The *dahara-vidyā* taught in Chāndogya (8.1) cannot be translated. It can only be known by those who have been initiated into the entry in the cave of the heart centre by a meditation preceptor, following the methods taught by Patañjali and Vyāsa in Yoga Sūtra (1.36). Then one will see within the meaning of the Chāndogya Upaniṣad (3.12.9; and 3.13.1-7). The *madhu-vidyā* taught in Chāndogya Upaniṣad (3.1.ff.) is to be translated by an adept, not merely a scholar of language and grammar, into the realization of the *madhu-pratika-bhūmi* of meditation as suggested by Patañjali and Vyāsa in Yoga Sūtra. (3.51).

It is thus that the Bhagvadgītā and the Upaniṣads speak of *jñāna* and *vijñana* as two distinct states of knowledge. Śaṅkarācārya consistently distinguished between the two on such verses as Muṇḍaka Upaniṣad (1.2.12, 2.2.7, 3.2.6) and Bhagvadgītā (6.8 *jñāna-vi-jñana tṛptatma* and 9.1 *jñānam vi-jñāna-sahitam*). Knowledge is only of the texts and the statements therein. Śaṅkara states:

> *Jñāna* is full learning of the categories taught in the texts; *vi-jñāna* is bringing to one's own experience the same way as has been learnt from the texts.[1]

1. *Jñānam śastrokta-padarthanam pari-jñānam*
vi-jñānam to śastrato jñātanam tathaiva
svānu-bhava-kāraṇam

Again on knowledge, distinguished in what way [by the prefix *vi* in *vi-jñana*] Accompanied with *vi-jñāna* [that is] endowed with [personal experience].[1]

This makes it obvious that the Upaniṣads are texts of yoga as guides to practices for personal experience, usurped by philosophers. The *ācāryas* were practitioners but many later commentators (*vṛtti-kāras*) not so, nor the modern translators. Many of the latter have not sat for five minutes of meditation and yet venture to translate these texts that have been exuded as fragrances from the flowers of profound spiritual experiences blooming within.

It is suggested that the reader be a seeker and read the Thirty Minor Upaniṣads presented here as texts that guide one to and through the states of experiential awareness (*vi-jñāna*). One should seek out the preceptor who has experienced the states described. There are indeed partial preceptors; they have experienced some of the stages (*bhūmis*). Then they can translate only the portions of the texts that refer to the realms of their personal experience. On the rest, they need to practise silence. The ideal is to be a scholar-saint like Śaṅkarācārya. But if a reader has to choose between a scholar and a spiritully accomplished person, a *siddha*, it is the *siddha* who will explain the true meaning by showing the *padārtha* of words (*jala*, ante) and will then say "*etad vai tat*"—This indeed is that.

Since the Upaniṣads, including the thirty here are revelations from within meditative states, they do not always follow a syllogistic logic in the patterns of their organization. They do not contradict each other but rather each specializes in one or more specific area(s) of spiritual experience. Spiritual experience means also defining the realities experienced for those who are word-bound, body-bound, and guidance for a code of conduct and discipline in areas of thought emotions and inter-relational behaviour. For example, the entire Vajra-sūci Upaniṣad is devoted to condemning the caste hierarchies on profound spiritual grounds.

The thirty Upaniṣads here cover many grounds. It will take a lifetime of study to compare their subject matter fully. The reader may undertake the *tapasyā* of *svādhyāya* and create his/her

1. *Jñānam kim-vi-śiṣṭm, vijñāna-sahitam anu-bhavayuktaṃ*

own more detailed chart in order to understand the text and to visualize the infinite span of spiritual ground the realization of which awaits one who is not a spiritual weakling (*bala-hīna*) but is spiritually virile (*virya-vān* and *viryavatī*).

May an aspirant not only to undertake a full analysis of the thirty Upaniṣads presented here. May s/he also give us notes on the actual processes of practices and the resultant spiritual experiences, knowing that these well-locked texts are composed in a manner so as to provide also the hidden keys to those who know how to seek.

As to those who find the keys, may the words they speak, today become the Upaniṣaḍs of tomorrow, thus perpetuating the lineage of continued revelation down the ages as those before us have done progressively and unceasingly through their times.

Sarvo muktim avapnuyāt-ity abyārthanāya,
Śrī-gurudeva-sevayam.

Oṃ

1
Muktika Upaniṣad of Śukla Yajurveda

ADHYĀYA I

Addressing with devotion and obedience Śrī-Rāma, the Lord Hari, at the end of his *samādhi*, who being himself changeless is witness to the countless fluctuations of the mind and who ever rests absorbed in the meditation of the Absolute while seated under the bejewelled dome of the palace in the lovely city of Ayodhyā, in the midst of Sītā, Bharata and Saumitri (Lakṣmaṇa) Śatrughna and others, eulogised day and night by Sanaka and hosts of other sages, as well as by Vaśiṣṭha, Śuka and other devotees of Viṣṇu—Hanūmān, after praising the gods asked, "O Rāma, thou art the supreme self, identical with Viṣṇu, who is being, consciousness and bliss *(saccidānanda)*. O foremost of the family of Raghu, I bow down to thee again and again. O Rāma, for the sake of emancipation I wish to know thy true nature. O Rāma, be thou gracious enough to tell me that by which I shall be easily released from the bondage of mundane existence and attain salvation."

[Śrī-Rāma replied] "O mighty-armed one, well asked. Listen then to the truth uttered by me. I am well established in Vedānta. Have you recourse to Vedānta as well?"

[Hanūmān again asked] "O foremost of Raghus, what are Vedāntas? Where do they abide? Pray enlighten me."

[Śrī-Rāma replied]"O Hanūmān, listen to me. I shall truly describe to you the nature of Vedānta. The Vedas were generated manifold through the exhalation of my breath as Viṣṇu. Like the oil in the sesamum seed, Vedānta is latent in the Vedas."

[Hanūmān asked again:] "O Rāma, how many are the Vedas and their branches? O Rāghava, what are the Upaniṣads? Please be gracious and tell me."

[Śrī-Rāma said:] "Through the division of Ṛgveda and others, the Vedas are said to be four in number. Their branches are many. So also the Upaniṣads. In Ṛgveda, there are twenty-one branches. O son of Vāyu, there are 109 branches in Yajurveda. O conqueror of enemies, there are 1,000 branches in Sāmaveda. O best of Monkeys, there are fifty branches in Atharvāṇaveda. In each branch, there is one Upaniṣad. Whoever, with devotion to me, studies even one of the hymns *(ṛks)*, attains the state of absorption, rare for even the sages to attain."

[Hanūmān asked:] "O Rāma, some excellent sages have said that there is one kind of salvation only, while others [state that salvation is attained] through the uttering of thy name or the initiation into *tāraka* (mantra) at Kāśī (Benaras); or declare it is through Sāṅkhya-Yoga, or through the Yoga of Devotion; other great sages, through meditation upon the meaning of the sacred sentences of the Vedas. Salvation is stated to be of four kinds through the divisions of *sālokya* and others."

[Śrī-Rāma replied:] "There is only one true emancipation. O Monkey, even a person addicted to evil practices attains the salvation of my world *(sālokya)* through the uttering of my name, but not of other worlds. Should one die in the street [named] Brahma-nāla (the Lotus-stalk) in Kāśī, he attains my *tāraka* (mantra). Such a person, freed from all sins, attains my real essence *(svarūpa)*. It is this that is termed *sālokya-svārūpya* salvation. The twice-born who is of virtuous conduct and who, without diverting his intelligence on any other, meditates upon me, the all-ātman, attains nearness (*sāmīpya*) to me.

"It is this that is termed *sālokya-svārūpya-sāmīpya* salvation. The twice-born who, according to the path opened by the teacher, meditates upon my immutable reality attains absorption (*sāyujya*) into me, like the caterpillar into the wasp. This is the *sāyujya* salvation which is productive of Brāhmic bliss and is auspicious. Thus these kinds of salvation arise through my worship (*upāsanā*).

"The only means by which the final emancipation is attained is through Māṇḍūkya Upaniṣad alone, which is enough for the salvation of all aspirants. If knowledge (*jñāna*) is not attained thereby, study the ten Upaniṣads; thou shalt soon attain *jñāna*, and then my seat. O son of Añjanā, if thy *jñāna* is not made firm, study well the thirty-two Upaniṣads. You shall get release. If you aspire for disembodied salvation *(videhamukti)*, study the 108 Upaniṣads. I will truly state in order the [names of the] Upaniṣads with their purificatory mantras (*śānti*). Listen to them. [They are:] Īśa, Kena, Kaṭha, Praśna, Muṇḍa, Māṇḍūkya, Tittiri, Aitareya, Chāndogya, Bṛhadāraṇyaka, Brahma, Kaivalya, Jābāla, Śvetāśvatara, Haṃsa, Āruṇi, Garbha, Nārāyaṇa, (Parama)-Haṃsa, (Amṛta)-Bindu, (Amṛta)-Nāda, (Atharva)-Śiras, (Atharva)-Śikhā, Maitrāyaṇī, Kauṣītakī, (Bṛhat)-Jābāla, (Narasimha)-Tāpanī, Kālāgnirudra, Maitreyī, Subāla, Kṣurikā, Mantrikā, Sarvasāra, Nirālamba, (Śuka)-Rahasya, Vajrasūcikā, Tejo-(Bindu), Nāda-(Bindu), Dhyāna-(Bindu), (Brahma)-Vidyā, Yoga-Tattva, Ātmabodhaka, Parivrāṭ (Nārada-Parivrājaka), (Tri)-Śikhī, Sītā, (Yoga)-Cūḍā-(Maṇi) Nirvāṇa, Maṇḍala-(Brāhmaṇa), Dakṣiṇā-(Mūrti), Śarabha, Skanda, (Tripādvibhūti)-Mahā-Nārāyaṇa, Advaya-(Tāraka), (Rāma)-Rahasya, (Rāma)-Tāpanī, Vāsudeva, Mudgala, Śāṇḍilya, Paiṅgala, Bhikṣu, Mahat-Śāriraka, (Yoga)-Śikhā, Turīyātīta, Sannyāsa, (Paramahaṃsa)-Parivrājaka, Akṣamālikā, Avyakta, Ekākṣara, (Anna)-Pūrṇā, Sūrya, Akṣi, Adhyātma, Kuṇḍikā, Sāvitrī, Ātman, Pāśupata, Parabrahman, Avadhūta, Tripuratāpanī, Devī, Tripurā, Kara, Bhāvanā, (Rudra)-Hṛdaya, (Yoga)-Kuṇḍalinī, Bhasma-(Jābāla) Rudrākṣa, Gaṇapati, Darśana, Tārasāra, Mahāvākya, Pañcabrahma, (Prāṇa)-Agnihotra, Gopāla-Tāpanī, Kṛṣṇa, Yājñavalkya, Varāha, Śāṭyāyanī, Hayagrīva, Dattātreya, Gāruḍa, Kali-(Santāraṇa), Jābāla, Saubhāgya, Sarasvatīrahasya, Bahvṛca, and Muktika. These 108 (Upaniṣads) are able to do away with the three *bhāvanās* [of doubt, vain thought, and false thought], conferring *jñāna* and *vairāgya*, and destroying the three *vāsanās*[1] [of book-lore, world and body].

"The twice-born—after learning the 108 Upaniṣads, together with the *śānti* as prescribed both before and after from the lips of a guru well-versed in the observances of Vedic knowledge and study—become liberated in life (*jīvanmukta*) till the destruction of their *prārabdha*; in course of time as the accumulated *karma* from past lives (*prārabdha*), is destroyed, they attain my disembodied salvation. Of this there is no doubt. O son of Vāyu, these 108 Upaniṣads, which are the essence of all the Upaniṣads and are capable of destroying all sins through their mere study, have been imparted by me to you as a disciple. This science of the 108 Upaniṣads taught by me, is an occult one and will free persons from bondage, whether they read them with or without knowledge. To gratify the desire of a supplicant, a kingdom may be given or wealth, but never shall the 108 Upaniṣads be imparted to an atheist, an ungrateful person, one intent on vicious actions, one having no devotion towards me, or one who loses his path in the cave of books. On no account shall they be given to one devoid of devotion. O Māruti, it is only after a thorough examination that they should be imparted to a disciple doing service [to a guru], to a well-disposed son, or to one devoted to me, following good observances, belonging to a good family and being of good intelligence. Whoever studies or hears the 108 Upaniṣads attains me. Of this there is no doubt. This is stated in the verse *(ṛk)* thus—Vidyā (Sarasvatī) went to a Brāhmaṇa [and addressed him] thus: 'Protect me. I am your treasure. Do not give me away to the envious, to one not treading the right path, or to the rogue. Then I shall be potent.' Impart this *ātmaniṣṭha-vīdyā* relating to Viṣṇu to one after examining him; to one who has proficiency in learning, is alert, intelligent, observant of the vow of celibacy and serving [the guru]."

Then Hanūmān asked Śrī-Rāmacandra to relate the *śānti* of each Upaniṣad according to the divisions of the Ṛgveda and others to which they belong. To which Śrī-Rāma replied: "Aitereya, Kauṣītaki, Nāda-(Bindu), Ātma-Bodha, Nirvāṇa, Mudgala,

1. For meaning of technical terms see Glossary.

Akṣamālikā, Tripurā, Saubhāgya and Bahvṛca—these ten Upaniṣads are of Ṛgveda and have the *śānti* beginning with '*vāṅme-manasi*', etc. Īśa, Bṛhadāraṇyaka, Jābāla, Haṃsa, (Parama)-Haṃsa, Subāla, Mantrikā, Nirālamba, Triśikhī-Brāhamaṇa, Maṇḍala-Brāhmaṇa, Advaya-Tāraka, Paiṅgala, Bhikṣu, Turīyātīta, Adhyātma Tārasāra, Yājñāvalkya, Śāṭyāyanī, and Muktika—these nineteen Upaniṣads are of the Śukla Yajurveda and have the *śānti* beginning with '*pūrṇamadaḥ*', etc.

"Kaṭha, Tittiri, Brahma, Kaivalya, Śvetāśvatara, Garbha, Nārāyaṇa, (Amṛta)-Bindu, (Amṛta)-Nāda, Kālāgnirudra, Kṣurikā, Sarvasāra, Śukarahasya, Tejo-(Bindu), Dhyāna-(Bindu), (Brahma)-Vidyā, Yoga-Tattva, Dakṣiṇā-(Mūrti), Skanda, Śāriraka, (Yoga)-Śikhā, Ekāśara, Akṣi, Avadhūta, Kara, (Rudra)-Hṛdaya, (Yoga)-Kuṇḍalinī, Pañcabrahma, (Prāṇa)-Agnihotra, Varāha, Kali-(Santāraṇa), and Sarasvatīrahasya—these thirty-two Upaniṣads are of the Kṛṣṇa Yajurveda and have the *śānti* beginning with '*sahanāvavatu*,' etc.

"Kena, Chāndogya, Āruṇi Maitrāyaṇī, Maitreyī, Vajra-sūcikā, (Yoga)-Cūḍā-(Maṇi), Vasudeva, Mahat-Sannyāsa, Avyakta, Kuṇḍikā, Sāvitrī, Rudrākṣa, Jābāla, Darśana, and Jābāli—these sixteen Upaniṣads are of the Sāmaveda and have the *śānti* beginning with '*āpyāyantu*,' etc.

"Praśna, Muṇḍaka, Māṇḍūkya, (Atharva)-Śiras, (Atharva)-Śikhā, (Bṛhat)-Jābāla, (Nṛsimha)-Tāpanī, (Nārada-Parivrājaka), Sītā, Śarabha, Mahā-Nārāyaṇa, (Rāma)-Rahasya, (Rāma)-Tāpanī, Śāṇḍilya, (Parama-Haṃsa)-Parivrājaka, (Anna)-Pūrṇā, Sūrya, Ātman, Pāśupata, Parabrahma, Tripura-Tapanī, Devī, Bhāvanā, Bhasma-(Jābāla), Gaṇapati, Mahāvākya, Gopāla-Tāpanī, Kṛṣṇa, Hayagrīva, Dattātreya and Gāruḍa—these thirty-one Upaniṣads of the Atharvaṇa-Veda have the *śānti* commencing with '*bhadram-karṇebhiḥ*,' etc.

"Persons desirous of emancipation and having developed the four means of salvation should, with presents in their hands, approach a guru full of faith, of good family, proficient in the Vedas, scripture-loving, of good qualities, straightforward, intent upon the welfare of all beings and an ocean of compassion; and after studying under him, according to the rules, the 108 Upaniṣads, he should ever be going through the process of studying, thinking and reflecting upon them. With the cessation of the three bodies through the destruction of accumulated *karma* from previous lives (*prārabdha*), they attain the state of plenum, bereft of any *upādhis* like the ether in the pot [after the pot is broken]. This is the embodied salvation, this is the final emancipation. Therefore, even those in Brahmaloka through the studying of Vedānta from the lips of Brahmā attain with him the final emancipation. Hence to all these is stated the final emancipation through the path of knowledge (*jñāna*) and not through action [*karma*], Sāṅkhya-Yoga, and other *upāsanās*. Thus is the Upaniṣad."

ADHYĀYA II

Again Māruti (Hanūmān) addressed Śrī-Rāmacandra thus: "What is *jīvanmukti*? What is *videhamukti*? What is the authority therein? What about its perfection? What is the object of such a perfection?"

[Śrī-Rāma replied:] "The dharma of a man's *citta* that has the characteristics of agency and enjoyment is fraught with pains and hence tends towards bondage. The control of the *citta* in life is liberation (*jīvanmukti*). *Videhamukti* follows when through the extinction of accumulated *karma* (*prārabdha*), the removal of the vehicles [of the bodies] takes place like the ether in the pot [after the pot is broken]. The authority on the points of *jīvanmukti* and *videhamukti* is the 108 Upaniṣads. Its object [of perfection] is the attaining of eternal bliss through the removal of the pains of agency, etc. This has to be achieved through human effort. Like progeny obtained through the *putrakāmeṣṭi* sacrifice, wealth in trade or heaven through the *jyotiṣṭoma* sacrifice, so liberation in life (*jīvanmukti*) is gained through *samādhi* arising through Vedāntic study, and accomplished through human efforts. It has to be won through the extinction of all *vāsanās*. Regarding it, there are verses thus: 'The efforts of man are stated to be of two kinds, those that transcend scriptures and those that are according to scriptures. Those that transcend scriptures tend to harm while those that are according to scriptures tend to reality.' To men, true *jñāna* does not arise through the *vāsanās* of the world, scripture, and body. *Vāsanā* is divided into two, the pure and the impure. If thou art led by the pure *vāsanās*, thou shalt thereby soon reach by degrees my seat. But should the old impure *vāsanās* land thee in danger, they should be overcome through efforts. This river of *vāsanās* towards objects, which flows in the pure and impure paths, should be diverted to the pure path through human efforts. The impure ones have to be transmuted into the pure. That which is diverted from the impure turns towards the pure. So also the reverse. This child, *citta*, has to be fondled through human efforts. O killer of enemies, it is only when through means of practice both *vāsanās* quite abandon thee, that thou wilt be able to realise the effects of [such] practice. Even in the case of doubt, the pure *vāsanās* alone should be practised.

"O son of Vāyu, there is nothing wrong in the increase of the pure *vāsanās*. The extinciton of *vāsanās*, *vijñāna* and the destruction of *manas* [as these three] when practised together for a long time are regarded, O great and intelligent one, as fruitful. So long as these are not equally practised again and again, so long the [supreme] seat is not attained even after the lapse of hundreds of years. Even should one of these [three] be practised for a long time, it will not yield its fruit like a mantra imperfectly done. Through the practice of these for a long time, the firm knots of the heart are cut, without doubt, like the breaking of the threads in a lotus-stalk rent in twain. The illusory *vāsanā* that has arisen through the practice of [many] hundreds of lives never perishes except through the practice of Yoga for a long time. Therefore, O Somya (disciple), after having put away to a distance the desire of enjoyment through discriminative human effort, resort to these three alone. The wise know that a mind associated with *vāsanā* tends to bondage, while a mind well freed from *vāsanā* is said to be an emancipated one. O Great Monkey, practise the state of a mind devoid of *vāsanā*. *Vāsanā* perishes through well-conducted deliberation and truth. Through the absorption of *vāsanā*, *manas* attains quiescence like a lamp [without oil]. He whose mind, devoid of destruction, is [centred] on me as of the nature of consciousness alone *(cinmātra)*, abandoning the *vāsanā*, is no other than myself of the nature of (being) *saccidānanda*. Whether *sāmadhi* and action are performed or not, one who has a supreme *citta* with a heart devoid of all desires is an emancipated person. He whose mind is freed from *vāsanā* is not subject to the fruits arising from the performance or non-performance of actions, or *samādhi* or *jñāna*. Except through the entire giving up of *vāsanā* and through the observance of silence *(mauna)* towards objects, the supreme seat is not attained. Though devoid of *vāsanās*, the eye and other organs are involuntarily prompted to their [respective] external objects through habit. Just as the eye without any desire sees without any effort the objects that fall on it, so also the undaunted man of intelligence enters into the affairs [of the world] without any desire. O Māruti, the sages know that as *vāsanā* which is manifested through the consciousness of objects, which is of the nature of the object itself and which is the cause of the origination and absorption of *citta*. This excessively fluctuating *citta* is the cause of birth, bondage and death, due to the identification of itself with objects practised firmly [for a long time]. Like the analogy of the seed and the tree, the vibration of vital breaths arises through *vāsanā* and [vice versa] the *vāsanā* through the former—these forming the seed of *citta*. To the tree of *citta*, there are two seeds: the vibration of *prāṇa* and *vāsanā*. Should either one perish, the other would perish soon. Through the actions of the world being done without attachment, through the abandoning of the [thought of the] reality of the universe and the conviction of the destructibility of the body, *vāsanā* does not arise. Through the complete giving up of *vāsanā*, *citta* becomes non-*citta*. When the mind does not think at all, being completely devoid of *vāsanā*, then dawns the state of mindlessness which confers the great peace. So long as you are without a mind of [true] discrimination and are not a knower of the supreme seat, so long should you follow whatever has been decided by the teacher and the authorities of the sacred books. When your sins are burnt up and you are a knower of the reality without any anxiety, then all the good *vāsanās* also should be given up.

"The destruction of *citta* is of two kinds, that with form and that without form. [The destruction of] that with form is of the liberated in life (*jīvanmukta*); [the destruction of], that without form being of the *videhamukta*. O son of Vāyu, listen to [the means of] the destruction of *citta*. That is said to be the destruction of *citta* when it, associated with all the attributes of friendship and others, becomes quiescent [without any resurrection]. Of this there is no doubt. Then the *manas* of one who is liberated in life (*jīvanmukta*) is free from fresh rebirth; to him, there is the destruction of *manas* without form. It is *manas* that is the root of the tree of the world (*saṃsāra*) with its thousands of shoots, branches, tender leaves and fruits. I think it to be *saṅkalpa* alone. In order that the tree of *saṃsāra* may wither soon, dry up its root through the quiescence of *saṅkalpa*. There is only one means to control one's mind. That is to destroy the mind as soon as it rises. That is the (great) dawn. In the case of the wise, the mind is destroyed: but in the case of the ignorant, it is indeed a fetter. So long as the mind is not destroyed through the firm contemplation of the one reality, so long are *vāsanās* prancing about in the heart like *vetāla* (goblin) in the night-time. The *vāsanās* of enjoyment of one who has destroyed the egoism of *citta* and controlled the organs, the enemies, decay like lotuses in mid-winter. Pressing one hand against the other, setting teeth against teeth, and forcing one limb against the other, he should first conquer his mind.

"It is not possible for one steeped in the sensory world to control the mind by sitting up again and again except through the approved means. As a vicious rutting elephant is not subject to control except through the goad, so in the matter of the control of the mind, the effective means are the attainment of spiritual knowledge, association with the wise, the entire abdication of all *vāsanās* and the control of *prāṇas*. While such are the [prescribed] means, should persons try to control the mind through violence, they are like those that search in darkness, having thrown aside the light [in their hands]. Those who endeavour to control the mind through force are but trying to bind a mad elephant with the filaments of a lotus-stalk.

"To the tree of the mind having the ever-growing branches of modifications, there are two seeds. One is the fluctuation of *prāṇa* and the other is the firmness of *vāsanā*. The [One] all-pervading consciousness is agitated by the fluctuation of *prāṇa*. The means of contemplation *(dhyāna)* by which [the one] *jñāna* is attained through the one-pointedness of the mind is now imparted to you. After duly resolving back the things originated [in the universe] with all their changes, meditate upon that which remains—namely, the consciousness alone *(cinmātra)*, which is also consciousness-bliss (*cidānanda*). The wise say that the interval experienced by yogins after the inspiration and before the [next] expiration is [the internal] cessation of breath (*kumbhaka*); while the interval of complete equilibrium after expiration and before the next inspiration is the external *kumbhaka*. Through the force of the practice of *dhyāna*, the current of the modification of *manas* devoid of self that is of Brāhmic nature is said to be *samprajñāta-samādhi*, while the mind with the utter quiescence of modifications that confers upon one supreme bliss, is said to be *asamprajñāta-samādhi* that is dear to yogins. This [state] that is devoid of light, *manas* and *buddhi*, and that is of the nature of consciousness *(citta)*, is styled by the sages *atadvyāvṛtt-samādhi* (a *samādhi* that does not care or require the aid of another). It is plenum above, below and in the middle, and is of the nature of Śiva. This noumenal *samādhi* (*vidhi mukha*) is itself sanctioned by scriptures or Brahmā.

"The clinging to objects without previous or subsequent deliberation through intense thought [or longing] is stated to be *vāsanā*. O Chief of Monkeys, whatever is meditated upon by a person with ardent impetuosity without any other *vāsanā*, that he soon becomes. A person that is entirely subject to *vāsanā* becomes of the nature of that. When he regards this [universe] as real, then he is subject to delusion. Because of strong *vāsanās*, he does not abandon the nature of the universe. This person of wrong vision sees everything under infatuation like one deluded. *Vāsanās* are of two kinds—the pure and the impure. The impure ones are the cause of rebirth, while the pure are the destroyers of rebirth. The impure are said by the wise to be of the nature of intense *ajñāna*, associated with the great *ahaṃkāra* and generative of rebirth. Of what avail is the chewing again and again of the many stories from the scriptures to one who has abandoned the seed of rebirth, having turned it into a burnt one? O Māruti, you should, with effort, seek the effulgence within. O Tiger of Monkeys, whoever, after having abandoned the visible and the invisible, is as the one alone is not a mere knower of Brahman but is Brahman itself. One who, having studied the four Vedas and the various books does not cognize the reality of Brahman, is like the ladle, ignorant of the taste of the dainty[food]. Therefore, what other advice of indifference can be imparted to a person who has not attained indifference to the impure *vāsanā* of delusion [or body]? This body is very impure while the one (ātman) that dwells in it is very pure. When the difference between the two are [thus] known, what then may be ordained as purification? The bondage of *vāsanā* is the [real] bondage, while the destruction of *vāsanā* is salvation. After wholly abandoning the *vāsanā*, give up even the desire for salvation. After first giving up the *vāsanā* of objects dependent upon the *vāsanā* of the mind, attract unto yourself the pure *vāsanās* associated with friendship *(maitri)* and others. Though engaged in the world with these pure *vāsanās*, give them up too and retire within the quiescent desires and become of the form of the longing after, *cit* alone. Then O Māruti! giving up that also associated as it is with *manas* and *buddhi*, may you become established in me in [the state of] *samādhi*. O son of Vāyu! always worship my reality that is destructive of pains, without sound, touch, form, decay, taste, destruction of smell and without name and clan (*gotra*). I am that non-dual one (Brahman) that is of the nature of the visible, like the sky, supreme, always shining, without birth, non-dual, without destruction, without attachment and all-pervading. I am the All and of the nature of salvation. One should ever meditate upon me thus: 'I am of the form of the visible (*jñāna*), the pure, of changeless nature and have really no objects in me. I am the ever-full Brahman, transverse and across, up and down.' Also meditate upon me thus: 'I am birthless, deathless, ageless, immortal, self-shining, all-pervading, destructionless, causeless, pure beyond the effect [of the universe] and ever gratified.' When one's body becomes a prey to time, he gives up the state of *jīvanmukti* as the wind attains the motionless state.

"The following is said in the *Ṛg*[*Veda*] also: Like the eye which is spread in the sky (seeing all things without any obstacle), so the wise ever see the supreme seat of Viṣṇu. The Brāhmaṇas that have ever the divine vision praise in diverse ways and illumine the supreme seat of Viṣṇu."

Oṃ tat sat is the Upaniṣad

2

Sarvasāra Upaniṣad of Kṛṣṇa Yajurveda

1. *What is Bondage (bandha).*

   Ātman (the self) falsely superimposing the body and others which are not-self upon himself, and identifying himself with them—this identification forms the bondage of the self.

2. *What is Emancipation (mokṣa)?*

   The freedom from that [identification] is emancipation.

3. *What is Ignorance (avidyā)?*

   That which causes this identification—that indeed is ignorance.

4. *What is Knowledge (vidyā)?*

   That which removes this identification is knowledge.

5. *What are the states of the waking (jāgrat), the dreaming (svapna), the dreamless sleep (suṣupti) and the fourth state (turīya)?*

Waking (*jāgrat*) is that [state] during which ātman enjoys the gross objects of senses as sound, etc. through the fourteen organs (the five organs of the senses, the five organs of action and four of the internal organs, viz. *manas*, *buddhi*, *citta*, *ahaṅkāra*) having the sun and the rest as their presiding deities.

Dreaming (*svapna*) is that [state] during which ātman experiences through the fourteen organs, sound and other objects which are the form of affinities (*vāsanās*) created for the time being, even in the absence of [the gross] sound and others.

Dreamless sleeping (*suṣupti*) is experienced by ātman when there is a cessation of the functions of the fourteen organs, and there is no special enjoying consciousness on account of the absence of these organs. The fourth state (*turīya*) is that state during which ātman is a witness to the existence of the above-mentioned three states, though it is in itself without [their] existence and non-existence and during which it is uninterrupted consciousness alone. And that consciousness (*caitanya*) is connected with the three states, which is without the three states, and which is pure.

6. *What are the sheaths (kośās)—Annamaya, Prāṇamaya, Manomaya, Vijñānamaya and Ānandamaya kośas?*

Annamaya kośa is the aggregate of the materials formed by food. When the ten vital airs (*vāyus*), *prāṇas* and others flow through the *annamaya kośa*, then it is called the *prāṇamaya kośa*. When ātman connected with the above two sheaths performs the functions of hearing, etc., through the fourteen organs of *manas* and others, then it is called *manomaya kośa*.

When in the (*antaḥkaraṇa*) internal organs connected with the above three sheaths, there arise the modfications of contemplation, meditation, etc. about the peculiarities of the sheaths, then it is called *vijñānamaya kośa*.

When the self-cause *jñāna* is in its self-bliss like the banyan tree in its seed, though associated with these four sheaths caused by *ajñāna*, then it is called *ānandamaya kośa*. Ātman which is associated with the vehicle (*upādhi*) of these sheaths is figuratively called *kośa*.

7. *What is meant by actor (kartṛ), the five groups (jīva pañcavarga), the lord of the field (kṣetrajña), witness (sākṣin), the latent guide (kūṭastha) and Antaryāmin?*

The actor *(kartṛ)* is the one who possesses the body and the internal organs through their respective desires proceeding from the idea of pleasure and pain. The idea of pleasure is that modification of the mind known as love. The idea of pain is that modification of the mind known as hate. The cause of pleasure and pain are sound, touch, form, taste and odour.

Jīva is that deluded one *(adhyāsin)* that thinks that this body, which is obtained through the effects of good and bad *karmas*, is one not so obtained.

Pañcavarga (the five groups) are (1) *Manas*, viz., *manas*, *buddhi*, *citta* and *ahaṃkāra* (creating uncertainty, certitude, flitting thought and egoism), (2) *Prāṇa*, i.e. *prāṇa*, *apāna*, *vyāna*, *samāna* and *udāna*, (3) *Sattva*, i.e. *sattva*, *rajas* and *tamas*. (4) the [five] elements: earth, water, fire, air and ether, and (5) dharma and its opposite *adharma*.

The original *avidyā* which has the characteristics of the above five groups, which does not perish without ātma-*jñāna*, which appears eternal through the presence of ātman and which is the vehicle for [the manifestation of] ātman, is the seed of the subtle body *(liṅga)*. It is also the heart-knot *(hṛdaya-granthi)*.

The consciousness *(caitanya)* which is reflected and shines in it is *kṣetrajña*.

The witness *(sākṣin)* is that conscious one that is aware of the appearance and disappearance [of the three states] of the knower, the knowledge and the known, who is himself without [or not affected by] this appearance and disappearance, and who is self-radiant.

He who is found without exception in the *buddhi* of all creatures from Brahmā down to ants, who dwells as witness to the *buddhi* of all creatures and is shining as ātman, is *kūṭastha*.

Antaryāmin is the ātman that shines as the ordainer, being within all bodies like the thread [on which] beads [are strung] and serving to know the cause of the several differences of *kūṭastha* and others associated with him.

8. *Who is Pratyagātman?*

He is of the nature of truth, wisdom, eternity and bliss. He has no vehicles of body. He is abstract wisdom itself, like a mass of pure gold that is devoid of the changes of bracelet, crown, etc. He is of the nature of mere consciousness. He is that which shines as *caitanya* and Brahman. When he is subject to the vehicle of *avidyā* and is the meaning of the word "*tvam*" (thou in *tattvamasi*), then he is *Pratyagātman*.

9. *Who is Paramātman?*

Paramātman is he who is associated with truth, wisdom, eternity, bliss, omniscience, etc., who is subject to the vehicle of *māyā* and who is the meaning of the word *tat* (or that in *tattvamasi*).

10. *What is Brahman?*

Brahman is that which is free from all vehicles, which is absolute consciousness, devoid of particularities, which is beingness *(sat)*, which is without a second, which is bliss and which is bereft of *māyā*. It is different from the characteristics of that expressed by the word *tvam* (thou) subject of vehicles *(upādhis)*, or the characteristics of that expressed by the word *tat* subject to *upādhis*. It is itself differenceless and is seen as the seat of everything. It is the pure, the noumenal, the true and the indestructible.

And what is the true (satya)?

It is the beingness *(sat)* which is the goal pointed out by the Vedas. It is that which cannot be said to be non-beingness *(asat)*. It is that which is not affected by the three periods of time. It is that which continues to exist during the three periods of time. It is that which is. It is one without a second. It has not the difference of similarity or dissimilarity; nor it is that which is the source of all ideas. It is that which does not perish even though space, time, matter, cause, etc. perish.

And what is wisdom (jñāna)?

It is self-illumination. It is that which illuminates all. It is that absolute consciousness which is without any obscuration. It is that consciousness which has no beginning or end, which is perpetual and which is the witness to all modifications and their opposites.

And what is the eternal (ananta)?

It is that which is without origin and destruction. It is that which is not subject to the six changes (viz. birth, growth, manhood, decay, old age and death). It is free from all *upādhis*. It is that consciousness which, being all full and without destruction, permeates the created universe composed of *avyakta* and others, like the earth in the modifications of clay, the gold in the modifications of gold, and the thread in the modifications of thread.

And what is bliss (ānanda)?

It is the seat of all sentient beings, like the ocean of the water, is eternal, pure, partless and non-dual and is the sole essence of the bliss of consciousness *(cidānanda)*.

11. *Of how many kinds are substances?*

There are three kinds, beingness *(sat)*, non-beingness *(asat)* and illusion *(mithyā)*. *Sat* alone is Brahman. *Asat* is that which is not. *Mithyā* is the illusory ascription to Brahman of the universe that is not. What is fit to be known is Brahman, the ātman alone. Brahma-*jñāna* is the rooting out of all—bodies and such like—that are not self, and the merging in Brahman, the *sat*. The universe of ether and others including *jīva* is non-self.

12. *What is māyā?*

The root of this non-self is *māyā*. She appears in Brahman like clouds, etc. in the sky. She has no beginning but has an end. She is subject to proof and non-proof. She neither is, nor is not; nor is she a combination of both (*sat* and *asat*). Her seat is indescribable. She has the varieties of difference as extolled by the wise. It is she that truly is not. Her nature is *ajñāna*. She appears as *mūlaprakṛti*, *guṇasāmya* (a state where the three *guṇas* are found in equilibrium), *avidyā* and other forms, transforming herself into the form of the universe. Thus does a knower of Brahman cognize her.

Oṃ tat sat is the Upaniṣad

3
Nirālamba Upaniṣad of Śukla Yajurveda

HARIḤ-OṂ. I shall relate in the form of a catechism whatever should be known for the removal of all miseries that befall these ignorant creatures (men).

What is Brahman? Who is Īśvara? Who is Jīva? What is Prakṛti? Who is Paramātman? Who is Brahmā? Who is Viṣṇu? Who is Rudra? Who is Indra? Who is Yama? Who is Sūrya? Who is Candra? Who are Devas? Who are Rākṣasas? Who are Piśācas? Who are Manuṣyas? Who are Women? Who are Paśus etc.? What is Sthāvara? Who are Brāhmaṇas and others? What is Jāti? What is Karma? What is Akarma? What is Jñāna? What is Ajñāna? What is Sukha? What is Duḥkha? What is Svarga? What is Naraka? What is Bandha? What is Mokṣa? Who is Upāsya? Who is Vidvat? Who is Mūḍha? What is Āsura? What is Tapas? What is Paramapada? What is Grāhya? What is Agrāhya? Who is a Sannyāsin? Thus are the questions.

1. *What is Brahman?*

It is the *caitanya* that appears, through the aspects of *karma* and *jñāna*, as this vast mundane egg composed of *mahat, ahaṃkāra* and the five elements, earth, water, fire, air and ether—that is secondless—that is devoid of all vehicles *(upādhis)*, that is full of the potencies (*śaktis*), that is without beginning and end, that is described as pure, beneficial, peaceful, and *guṇa*-less and that is indescribable.

2. *Who is Īśvara and what are his characteristics?*

Brahman itself, having through his *śakti* called *prakṛti* (matter), created the worlds and being latent in them, becomes the ruler of *buddhi* and *indriyas,* organs of sense and action as well as Brahmā (the creator) and others. Hence he is named Īśvara.

3. *Who is Jīva?*

Īśvara himself, subject to the false superimposition upon himself [of the idea] "I am the gross" through the [assumption of the] names and forms of Brahmā, Viṣṇu, Rudra, Indra and others is *jīva*. Though one, he appears as many *jīvas*, through the force of the different karmas originating the bodies.

4. *What is Material nature (Prakṛti)?*

It is nothing else but the potency (*śakti*) of Brahman which is of the nature of *buddhi* that is able to produce the many motley worlds by virtue of the mere presence of Brahman.

5. *What is Paramātman?*

The supreme ātman or soul. It is Brahman alone that is Paramātman as it (the former) is far superior to bodies and others.

6. *Who is the creator (Brahmā)?*
7. *Who is the preserver (Viṣṇu)?*
8. *Who is the destroyer(Rudra)?*
9. *Who is Indra?*
10. *Who is the god of death (Yama)?*
11. *Who is the sun (Sūrya)?*
12. *Who is the moon (Candra)?*
13. *Who are the gods (Devas)?*
14. *Who are the demons (Asuras)?*
15. *Who are the evil spirits (Piśācas)?*

16. *Who are the men (manuṣyas)?*
17. *Who are women?*
18. *What are beasts, (paśus)etc.?*
19. *What are the fixed ones (sthāvaras)?*
20. *Who are Brāhmaṇas and others?*

That Brahman is Brahmā, Viṣṇu, Rudra and Indra, Yama, Sūrya and Candra, Devas, Asuras, Piśācas, men, women, beasts, etc., *sthāvaras*, Brāhmaṇas and others. Here there is no manyness in the least degree: all this is verily Brahman.

21. *What is caste (jāti)*

It cannot refer to the skin, the blood, the flesh or the bone. There is no caste for ātman; caste is only conventional.

22. *What is Karma?*

Karma is that action alone which is performed by the organs and ascribed to ātman as "I do" (*viz.* agency being attributed to ātman).

23. *What is Inaction (akarma)?*

Inaction is the performance, without any desire for the fruits, of the daily and occasional rites, sacrifices, vows, austerities, gifts and other actions that are associated with the egoism of the actor and the enjoyer, and that are productive of bondage, rebirth, etc.

24. *What is Jñāna?*

It is the realisation by direct cognition of the fact that in this changing universe there is nothing but consciousness, that is of the form of the seer and the seen, pervading all things, that is the same in all and that is not subject to changes like pot, cloth, etc. This realisation is brought about by means of the subjugation of the body and the senses, the serving of a good guru, the hearing of the exposition of the Vedāntic doctrines and constant meditation thereon.

25. *What is Ajñāna?*

It is the illusory attribution, like the snake in the rope, of many souls (ātmans) through the diverse vehicles (*upādhis*) of the gods, beasts, men, the fixed ones, females, males, castes and orders of life, bondage and emancipation, etc. to Brahman that is secondless, all-permeating and of the nature of all.

26. *What is happiness (sukha)?*

It is a state of being of the nature of bliss, having cognized through experience the reality of *saccidānanda* (beingness, consciousness and bliss).

27. *What is sorrow (duḥkha)?*

It is the mere thinking *(saṅkalpa)* of the objects of mundane existence [or of non-self].

28. *What is heaven (svarga)?*

It is the association with truth *(sat)*.

29. *What is hell (naraka)?*

It is the association with that which brings about this mundane existence which is false *(asat)*.

30. *What is bondage (bandha)?*

Such *saṅkalpas* as "I was born," etc., arising from the affinities of beginningless *ajñāna* form bondage.

The thought obscuration (or mental ignorance) of the mundane existence of "mine" in such as father, mother, brother, wife, child, house, gardens, lands, etc. brings about bondage.

The thoughts of I-ness as actor, etc., are bondage.

The thought of the development in oneself of the eight higher psychical powers (*siddhis*) as *aṇimā* and others is bondage.

The thought of propitiating the gods, men, etc. is bondage.

The thought of going through the eight means of yoga practice *yama*, etc. is bondage.

The thought of performing the duties of one's own caste and order of life is bondage.

The thought that command, fear and doubt are the attributes of [or pertain to] ātman is bondage.

The thought of knowing the rules of performing sacrifices, vows, austerity and gift is bondage. Even the mere thought of desire for emancipation (*mokṣa*) is bondage. By the very act of thought, bondage is caused.

31. *What is liberation (mokṣa)?*

Mokṣa is the [state of] annihilation, through the discrimination of the eternal from the non-eternal, of all thoughts of bondage, like those of "mine" in objects of pleasure and pain, lands, etc. in this transitory mundane existence.

32. *Who is fit to be worshipped (upāsya)?*

That guru who enables the disciple to attain to Brahman, the consciousness that is in all bodies.

33. *Who is the disciple (śiṣya)?*

The disciple is that Brahman alone that remains after the consciousness of the universe has been lost [in him] through Brāhmic wisdom.

34. *Who is the learned (vidvat)?*

It is he who has cognized the true form (of reality) of his own consciousness that is latent in all.

35. *Who is the ignorant (mūḍha)?*

He who has egoistic conception of the body, caste, orders of life, actor, enjoyer and others.

36. *What is the demoniacal (āsura)?*

It is the austerity *(tapas)* practised by one inflicting trouble on the ātman within through *japa* (or inaudible muttering of mantras), abstinence from food, *agnihotra* (the performance of the worship of fire), etc. attended with cruel desire, hatred, pain, hypocrisy and the rest, for the purpose of acquiring the powers of Viṣṇu, Brahmā, Rudra, Indra and others.

37. *What is austerity (tapas)?*

Tapas is the act of burning—through the fire of direct cognition of the knowledge that Brahman is the truth and the universe a myth—the seed of the deep-rooted desire to attain the powers of Brahmā, etc.

38. *What is the supreme abode (paramapada)?*

It is the seat of the eternal and emancipated Brahman which is far superior to *prāṇas* (the vital airs), the organs of sense and action, the internal organs [of thought], the *guṇas* and others, which is of the nature of *saccidananda* and the witness to all.

39. *What is grāhya?*

Only the reality of absolute consciousness which is not conditioned by space, time or substance.

40. *What is agrāhya?*

The thought that this universe is truth—this universe which is different from one's self and which being subject to illusion (*māyā*) forms the object of [cognition of] *buddhi* and the organs.

41. *Who is the ascetic (sannyāsin)?*

A *sannyāsin* is an ascetic who having given up all the duties of castes and orders of life, good and bad actions, etc., being freed from [the conceptions of] "I" and "mine" and having taken his refuge in Brahman alone, roams at large practising *nirvikalpa samādhi* and being firmly convinced of "I am Brahman" through the realisation of the meaning of such sacred (Vedic) sentences as "Thou art That" "All this is verily Brahman" and "Here there is no differentiation from manyness in the least." He only is a *yogin*, an emancipated person. He only is fit to be adored. He only is a Paramahaṃsa. He only is an Avadhūta. He only is a Brāhmaṇa. Whoever studies the *Nirālamba-Upaniṣad* becomes, through the grace of the guru, pure like fire. He becomes pure like air. He does not return. He is not born again.

Oṃ tat sat is the Upaniṣad

4
Maitreya Upaniṣad of Sāmaveda

ADHYĀYA I

A king named Bṛhadratha, thinking this body to be impermanent and having acquired indifference [to objects], retired to the forest, leaving his eldest son to rule over [his] kingdom. With hands uplifted and eyes fixed on the sun, he performed a severe austerity *(tapas)*. At the end of a thousand days, the Lord Śākāyanya muni, a knower of ātman, who was like fire without smoke and who was as a scorching fire with his spiritual lustre *(tejas)* approached the king and addressed him: "Rise, rise and choose a boon." The king prostrated before him and said: "O Lord, I am not a knower of ātman *(ātmavid)*. Thou art a *tattvavid*, we hear. Please enlighthen me about *sattva,* the state of Brahman (*sat*)." [To which] The sage replied thus: "O thou that art born of the race of Ikṣvāku: To begin with, your question is difficult [to explain]. Do not question me. Ask for any other thing you desire." Thereupon the King touched the feet of Śākāyanya and recited the [following] verse:

"What is the use of these to me or any other? Oceans dry up. Mountains sink down. The positions of the Pole Star (Dhruva) and of trees change. Earth is drowned. The gods run away, leaving their [respective] places. [While such is the case], I am he in reality.

Therefore of what avail to me is the gratification of desires, since one who clings to the gratification of desires is found to return again and again to this *saṃsāra*? Thou art able to extricate me [from this *saṃsāra*]. I am drowned like a frog in a dry well. Thou art my refuge.

"O Lord! this body was the result of sexual intercourse. It is without wisdom; it is hell [itself]. It came out through the urinary orifice. It is linked together by bones. It is coated over with flesh. It is bound by skin. It is replete with faeces, urine, air, bile, phlegm, marrow, fat, serum and many other impurities. O Lord! to me in such a foul body [as this], thou art my refuge."

Thereupon Lord Śākāyanya was pleased and addressed the king thus: "O Mahārāja Bṛhadratha, the flag of the Ikṣvāku race, thou art an *ātmajñānin*. Thou art one that has done his duty. Thou art famous by the name of Marut." At which the King asked: "O Lord! in what way, can you describe ātman?" To which he replied thus: "Sound, touch, and others which seem to be wealth (*artha*) are in fact evil (*anartha*). The gross body *(bhūtatman)* clinging to these, never remembers the supreme abode. Through *tapas*, purity is acquired; through, purity (*sattva*) mind is acquired; and through mind, the higher self (*paramātman*) is reached. Through attaining ātman, one gets liberation. Just as fire without fuel is absorbed into its own womb, so thought (*citta*) through the destruction of its modification is absorbed into its own womb. To a mind that has attained quiescence and truth, and which is not affected by sense-objects, the events that occur to it through the bondage of *karma* are merely unreal. It is *citta* alone that is *saṃsāra*. It should be cleansed with effort. Whatever his *citta* [thinks], of that nature he becomes. This is an archaic mystery. With the purifying of *citta*, one makes both good and bad *karmas* perish. One whose mind is thus cleansed attains the indestructible bliss [through his own self]. Just as *citta* becomes united with an object that comes across it, so why should not one [be released] from bondage, when one is united with Brahman. One should meditate in the middle of the lotus of the heart, Parameśvara (the highest Lord) who is the witness to the play of *buddhi*, who is the object of supreme love, who is beyond the reach of mind and speech, who has no beginning or end, who is *sat* alone being of the nature of light only, who is beyond meditation, who can neither be given up nor grasped [by the mind], who is without equal or superior, who is the permanent, who is of unshaken depth, who is without light or darkness, who is all-pervading, changeless and vehicleless, and who is wisdom of the nature of salvation (*mokṣa*). I am he—that *paramātman* who is the eternal, the pure, the liberated, of the nature of wisdom, the true, the subtle, the all-pervading, the secondless, the ocean of bliss and one that is superior to the lower self *pratyagātman*, there is no doubt. How will calamity approach me who am depending upon my own bliss in my heart, who have put to shame the ghost of desires, who look upon this universe as [but] a jugglery and who am not associated with anything. The ignorant with their observance of the castes and orders of life obtain their fruits according to their *karmas*. Men who have given up all duties of castes, etc. rest content in the bliss of their own self. The distinctions of caste and orders of life have divisions among them, have beginning and end, and are very painful. Therefore having given up all identification with sons as well as with the body, one should dwell in that endless and most supreme bliss."

ADHYĀYA II

The Lord Maitreya went to [Mount] Kailāśa and having reached it asked Him [Śiva] thus: "O Lord! please initiate me into the mysteries of the highest *tattva*." To which Mahādeva replied: "The body is said to be a temple. The *jīva* in it is Śiva alone. Having given up all the cast-off offerings of *ajñāna*, one should worship him with *So'ham* (I am he). The cognition of everything as non-different from oneself is wisdom (*jñāna*). Abstracting the mind from sensual objects is meditation *(dhyāna)*. Purifying the mind of its impurities is bathing (*snāna*). The subjugation of the sense organs *(indriyas)* is purification *(śauca)*. One should drink the nectar of Brahman and beg food for maintaining the body. Having one [thought] alone, he should live in a solitary place without a second. The wise man should observe thus: then he obtains absolution.

"This body is subject to birth and death. It is of the nature of the secretion of the father and mother. It is impure, being the seat of happiness and misery. [Therefore] bathing is prescribed for touching it. It is bound by the *dhātus* (skin, blood, etc.), is liable to severe diseases, is a house of sins, is impermanent and is of changing appearance and size. [Therefore] bathing is prescribed for touching it. Foul matter is naturally oozing out always from the nine holes. It [the body] contains bad odour and foul excrement. [Therefore] bathing is prescribed for touching it. It is tainted with the child-birth impurity of the mother and is born with it. It is also tainted with death impurity. [Therefore] bathing is prescribed for touching it. [The conception of] "I and mine" is the odour arising from the besmeared dung and urine. The release from it is spoken of as the perfect purification. The [external] purification by means of water and earth is on account of the wordly. The destruction of the threefold affinities [of śāstras, world and body] generates the purity for cleansing *citta*. That is called the [real] purification which is done by means of the earth and water of wisdom (*jñāna*) and indifference (*vairāgya*) to objects.

"The conception of *Advaita* (non-dualism) should be taken in as the alms *(bhikṣā)*; [but] the conception of dualism *(dvaita)* should not be taken in. To a *sannyāsin bhikṣā* is ordained as dictated by the scriptures and the guru. After becoming a *sannyāsin*, a learned man should himself abandon his native place and live at a distance, like a thief released from prison. When a person gives up ego-sense *(ahaṃkāra)* the son, wealth, the brother, delusion, the house, and desire, the wife, there is no doubt that he is an emancipated person. Delusion, the mother is dead. Wisdom, the son is born. In this manner while two kinds of pollution have occurred, how shall we [the ascetics] obṣerve the conjunction rites (*sandhy*ās)? The luminous consciousness of the sun is ever shining in the resplendent space of the heart. He neither sets nor rises; while so, how shall we perform the *sandhyās*? Solitude (*ekānta*) is that state of one without second as determined by the words of a guru. Monasteries or forests are not solitudes. Emancipation is only for those who do not doubt. To those who doubt, there is no salvation even after many births. Therefore one should attain faith. [Mere] abandoning of the *karmas* or of the mantras uttered at the initiation of a *sannyāsin* will not constitute *sannyāsa*. The union of the lower self (*jīvātman*) and the higher self (*paramātman*) at the two twilight hours, morning and evening *(sandhis)* is termed *sannyāsa*. Whoever has a nausea for all desires and the rest as for vomited food and is devoid of all affection for the body, is qualified for *sannyāsa*. At the moment when indifference towards all objects arises in the mind, a learned person may take up *sannyāsa*. Otherwise, he is a fallen person. Whoever becomes a *sannyāsin* on account of wealth, food, clothes and fame, becomes fallen both as a *sannyāsin* and as a householder; [then] he is not worthy of salvation.

"The thought of [contemplation upon] *tattvas* is the transcendental one; that of the scriptures, the middling and that of mantras, the lowest. The delusion of pilgrimages is the lowest of the lowest. Like one, who, having seen in water, the reflection of fruits in the branches of trees, tastes and enjoys them, the ignorant without self-cognition, are in vain overjoyed with [as if they reached] Brahman. That ascetic is an emancipated person who does not abandon the internal alms-taking, namely the meditation upon the non-dual, generating *vairāgya* as well as faith, the wife, and wisdom, the son. Those men [termed] great through wealth, age, and knowledge, are only servants to those that are great through their wisdom as also to their disciples. Those whose minds are deluded by my *māyā*, however learned they may be, do not attain me, the all-full ātman and roam about like crows, simply for the purpose of filling up their belly, well burnt up [by hunger, etc.]. For one that longs after salvation, the worship of images made of stone, metals, gems or earth, is productive of rebirth and enjoyment. Therefore the ascetic should perform his own heart-worship alone, and relinquish external worship in order that he may not be born again. Then like a vessel full to its brim in an ocean, he is full within and full without. Like a vessel void in the ether, he is void within and void without. Do not become [or differentiate between] the ātman that knows or the ātman that is known. Do become of the form of that which remains, after having given up all thoughts. Relinquishing with their *vāsanās* the seer, the seen and the visual, worship ātman alone, the resplendent supreme presence. That is the real supreme state wherein all resolves (*saṅkalpas*) are at rest, which resembles the state of a stone, and which is neither waking nor sleeping."

ADHYĀYA III

"I am "I" (the self). I am also another (the non-self). I am Brahman. I am the source [of all things]. I am also the guru of all worlds. I am of all the worlds. I am he. I am myself alone. I am *siddha*. I am the pure. I am the supreme. I am. I am always he. I am the eternal. I am stainless. I am *vijñāna*. I am the excellent. I am Soma. I am the all. I am without honour or dishonour. I am without qualities *(guṇas)*. I am Śiva (the auspicious). I am neither dual nor non-dual. I am without the dualities [of heat or cold, etc.] I am he. I am neither existence nor non-existence. I am language. I am the shining one. I am the glory of void and non-void. I am the good and the bad. I am happiness. I am without grief. I am *caitanya*. I am equal [in all]. I am the like and the non-like. I am the eternal, the pure, and the ever felicitous. I am without all and without not all. I am *sāttavika*. I am always existing. I am without the number one. I am without the number two. I am without the difference of *sat* and *asat*. I am without *saṅkalpa*. I am without the difference of manyness. I am the form of immeasurable bliss. I am one that exists not. I am the one that is not another. I am without body, etc. I am with asylum. I am without asylum. I am without support. I am without bondage or emancipation. I am the pure Brahman. I am he. I am without *citta*, etc. I am the supreme and the supreme of the supreme. I am ever of the form of deliberation and yet am without deliberation. I am he. I am of the nature of the *akāra* [a] and *ukāra* [u] as also of *makāra* [m]. I am the earliest. The contemplator and contemplation I am without. I am one that cannot be contemplated upon. I am he. I have full form in all. I have the characteristics of *saccidānanda*. I am of the form of places of pilgrimage. I am the higher self and Śiva. I am neither the thing defined nor non-defined. I am the non-absorbed essence. I am not the measurer, the measure or the measured. I am Śiva. I am not the universe. I am the seer of all. I am without the eyes, etc. I am the full grown. I am the wise. I am the quiescent. I am the destroyer. I am without any sensual organs. I am the doer of all actions. I am one that is content with all Vedāntas [either books or ātmic wisdom]. I am the easily attainable. I have the name of one that is pleased as well as one that is not. I am the fruits of all silence.

I am always of the form of absolute consciousness. I am always beness (*sat*) and consciousness (*cit*). I am one that has not anything in the least. I am without the *hṛdaya-granthi*. I am the being in the middle of the lotus. I am without the six changes. I am without the six sheaths and without the six enemies. I am within the within. I am without place and time. I am of the form of bliss having the quarters as my garment. I am the emancipated one, without bondage. I am without the "no". I am of the form of the partless. I am the partless. I have *citta*, though released from the universe. I am without the universe. I am of the form of all light. I am the light in absolute consciousness. I am free from the three periods [of time past, present and future]. I am without desires. I am without body. I am one that has no body. I am qualityless. I am alone. I am without emancipation. I am without truth or untruth. I am always one that is not different from beingness *(sat)*. I have no place to travel. I have no going, etc. I am always of the same form. I am the quiescent. I am Puruṣottama (the Lord of souls). There is no doubt that he who has realised himself thus, is myself. Whoever hears [this] once becomes himself Brahman. Yes, he becomes himself Brahman."

Oṃ tat sat is the Upaniṣad

5
Kaivalya Upaniṣad
of
Kṛṣṇa Yajurveda

Hariḥ-Oṃ. Then Āśvalāyana went to Lord Brahmā and addressed him thus: "Please initiate me into divine wisdom *(brahmavidyā)*, the most excellent, which is ever enjoyed by the wise which is ever by mystic and by which the learned, after having soon freed themselves from all sins, attain *Puruṣa*, the supreme of the supreme."

To him grandfather [thus] replied: "Know [it] through faith *(sraddhā)*, devotion *(bhakti)*, meditation *(dhyāna)* and yoga. Persons attain salvation not through action, progeny or wealth but through renunciation alone. Ascetics of pure mind through the realisation of the meaning well-ascertained by *vedānta-vijñāna* and through *sannyāsa-yoga* [enter] into that which is above *svarga* and is in the cave of the heart. They all attain the supreme self (*paramātman*), in the deluded world and are finally emancipated.

"Being seated in a pleasant posture in an unfrequented place with a pure mind, and with his neck, head, and body erect, having given up the duties of the [four] orders of life, having subjugated all the organs [of the senses], having saluted his guru with devotion, having looked upon the heart [lotus] as being free from *rajoguṇa* and as pure, and having contemplated upon the heart-centre the Supreme Lord who is always with his consort Umā, who is pure and free from sorrow, who is unthinkable and invisible, who is of endless forms, who is of the nature of joy, who is very quiescent, who is of the form of emancipation, who is the source of illusion (*māyā*), who has no beginning, middle or end, who is One, who is all-pervading, who is consciousness and bliss, who is formless, who is wonderful, who is the lord of all, who has three eyes, who has a blue neck (Nīlakaṇṭha) and who is serenity [itself]—the sage attains the absolute self, the womb of all elements, the all-witness, and above *tamas*. He is Brahmā. He only is Śiva. He only is Indra. He only is the indestructible. He only is supreme. He only is self-shining. He only is *prāṇa*. He only is time. He only is *agni* (fire). He only is the moon. He only is all things that exist or will hereafter exist. He only is eternal. Having known him, one crosses death. There is no other path to salvation. He only attains the supreme Brahman who sees in himself all elements and himself in all elements. There is no other way. Having constituted his body, an *araṇi* (the lower attritional piece of wood) and *praṇava* (Oṃ), the upper *araṇi*, a wise man burns ignorance *(ajñāna)* by the churning of meditation.

"It is he (*paramātman*) who, deluded by *māyā*, assumes a body with the internal organs and is active in everything. It is only he who in the waking state is gratified with women, food, drink and other diverse enjoyments. In the dreaming state, the *jīva* enjoys pleasures and pains in the several worlds which are created by his *māyā*. In the dreamless sleeping state, when all are absorbed, he, replete with *tamas*, attains the state of happiness. Then, through the force of the *karmas* of previous births, that *jīva* again wakes up and goes to sleep. All the diversified objects [of the universe] emanate from the *jīva*, who sports in the three bodies [gross, subtle and causal]. The three bodies are finally absorbed in him who is the source of all, who is bliss, and who is absolute wisdom. From him, arise *prāṇa, manas,* all the organs of sense and action, *ākāśa*, *vāyu*, *agni,* water and the earth supporting all. Parabrahman, identical with all forms, is the supreme abode of this universe, subtlest of the subtle, eternal, is the individual Self.

You are only That. One who knows himself to be that Parabrahman that shines as the universe in the waking, dreaming, dreamless and other states, will be relieved from all bondage. I am that Sadāśiva, who is other than the enjoyer, the enjoyed, and the enjoyment in the three seats [or bodies], and who is witness and *cinmātra*. All emanate from me alone. All exist in me alone. All merge into me alone. I am that non-dual Brahman. I am the atom of atoms; so am I the biggest [of all]. I am this diversified universe. I am the oldest of all. I am Puruṣa. I am Īśa (the Lord). I am of the form of light *(jyotis)* and of the form of joy. I have neither hands nor feet. I have power unthinkable. I see without eyes. I hear without ears. I am omniscient. I have one kind of form only. None is able to know me fully. I am always of the form of consciousness. I am the one that should be known through all the Vedas. I am the guru who revealed the Vedānta. I have no sins or virtues. I have no destruction. I have no birth, body, organs of sense or action, or *buddhi*. To me there is no earth, water or fire. There is no air; there is no space. He who thinks Paramātman as being in the cave [of the heart], as having no form, as being secondless, as being the witness of all and as being neither *sat* nor *asat*, attains the pure form of Paramātman.

"Whoever recites this Upaniṣad belonging to Yajurveda, he becomes as pure as fire *(agni)*. He becomes purified from the sins of theft of gold. He becomes purified from the sins of drinking alcohol. He becomes purified from the sins of murder of a Brāhman. He becomes purified from the sins of ommission (of those that ought not to be done) and the sins of omission (of those that ought to be done). Therefore he becomes a follower of Brahman. Were one who has stepped beyond the duties of the four orders of life to recite [this Upaniṣad] always or even once, he acquires the wisdom that destroys the ocean of *saṃsāra*. Therefore, having known him, he attains the *kaivalya* state—Yes, he attains the *kaivalya* state."

Oṃ tat sat is the Upaniṣad

6
Amṛtabindu Upaniṣad of Kṛṣṇa Yajurveda

Oṃ. Mind *(manas)* is said to be of two kinds, the pure and the impure. That which is associated with the thought of desire is the impure, while that which is without desire is the pure. To men, their mind alone is the cause of bondage or emancipation. That mind which is attracted by objects of sense tends to bondage, while that which is not so attracted tends to emancipation. Now since to a mind without a desire for sensual objects there is stated to be salvation, the aspirant, after emancipation should render his mind ever free from all longing after material objects. When a mind freed from the desires for objects and controlled in the heart attains the reality of the true self (ātman), then it is in the supreme seat. Till that which arises in the heart perishes, till then it [*manas*] should be controlled. This only is [true] wisdom. This only is true meditation. Other ways are but long or tedious. It [Brahman] cannot be the object of contemplation. It is not one that cannot be contemplated upon. It is not capable of contemplation, [and yet] it should be contemplated upon. Then one attains Brahman that is devoid of division. Yoga should be associated with sound, accent (*svara*). Brahman, should be meditated upon without *svara*. By meditating without *svara* upon Brahman, that which is cannot become non-existent. Such a Brahman is part-less, devoid of fancy and quiescent (or free from the action of mind). Whoever cognizes "I" to be that Brahman attains certainly Brahman. A wise man having known that Brahman, that is without fancy, without end, without cause or example, beyond inference and without beginning, is emancipated. There is [for him then] no destruction, no creation, no person in bondage, no devotee, no aspirant for salvation, no emancipated person. This is the truth. Ātman that should be contemplated upon is One in [the three states], the waking, the dreaming and the dreamless sleep. There is no rebirth to him who goes beyond the three states. The one self is in all beings. Like the moon [reflected] in water, he appears as one and as many. While a pot is being carried [from one place to another], the ether that is within is not carried [along with it]. As the pot alone is carried, *jīva* [within the body] may be likened to the ether. Like the pot, the body has various kinds of forms. The body which perishes again and again is not conscious of its own destruction. But he, the *jīva,* knows [it] always. He who is enveloped by the *māyā* of sound, is never able to come to [or see] the sun (of Parabrahman) from the darkness (of ignorance). Should such darkness be cleared, then he alone sees the non-dual state. Parabrahman is *śabdākṣara*. What remains after the cessation of *śabda-vedas*, that is *akṣara* [indestructible], should be meditated upon, by a learned man who wishes to secure quiescence in himself.

Two *vidyās* are fit to be known, viz. *śabdabrahman* and Parabrahman. One who has completely mastered *śabdabrahman* attains Parabrahman. Having studied well the books, the learned should persevere studiously in the acquisition of knowledge and self-realisation. Then he should discard the whole of the books, as a person in quest of grain gives up the chaff. Though there are cows of different colours, yet their milk is of the same colour. Likewise milk is seen as *jñāna*, and cows are seen as forms in the universe. As ghee is latent in milk, so is self-realisation latent in every being. Through churning always with the churning-stick of *manas* and the string of *jñāna*, Parabrahman that is partless, calm and quiescent should be brought out like fire from the wood. I am that Brahman. That Vāsudeva who is the support of all beings, who lives in all and who protects all creatures, is myself. That Vāsudeva is myself.

Oṃ tat sat is the Upaniṣad

7
Ātmabodha Upaniṣad of Ṛgveda

Oṃ. Prostrations to Nārāyaṇa holding a conch, a discus, and a mace, by whom the yogin is released from the bondage of the cycle of rebirth through the utterance of him who is of the form of *praṇava*, the Oṃ, composed of the three letters, A, U, and M, who is the uniform bliss and who is the all-pervading the Brahmapuruṣa. Oṃ. Therefore the reciter of the mantra "*Oṃ namo Nārāyaṇāya*" reaches the Vaikuṇṭha world. It is the heart-lotus, viz. the city of Brahman. It is effulgent like lightning, shining like a lamp. It is Brahmaṇya (the presider over the city of Brahman) that is the son of Devakī. It is Brahmaṇya that is Madhusūdana (the slayer of Madhu). It is Brahmaṇya that is Puṇḍarikākṣa (lotus-eyed). It is Brahmaṇya, Viṣṇu that is Acyuta (the indestructible). He who meditates upon that sole Nārāyaṇa, latent in all beings, the causal Puruṣa, causeless, Parabrahman, the Oṃ, without pains and delusion and all-pervading—that person is never subject to pains. From the dual, he becomes the fearless non-dual. Whoever sees this [world] as manifold [with the differences of I, you, he, etc.], passes from death to death. In the centre of the heart-lotus is Brahman, which is the all, which has *prājñā* as its eye and which is established in *prajñāna* alone. To creatures, *prajñāna* is the eye and *prājñā* is the seat. It is *prajñāna* alone that is Brahman. A person who meditates [thus], leaves this world through *prajñāna*, the ātman and ascending attains all his desires in the supreme heaven *(svarga)*. Oh! I pray thee place me in that nectar-everflowing unfailing world where the light always shines and where one is revered. [There is no doubt] he attains nectar also. *Oṃ-namaḥ*.

I am without *māyā*. I am incomparable. I am solely of the nature of wisdom. I am without I-am-ness (*ahaṅkāra*). I am without the difference of the universe, *jīva* and Īśvara. I am the Supreme identical with individual ātman. I am with ordinances and prohibitions destroyed without remainder. I am with observances of life (*āśramas*) well given up. I am of the nature of the vast and all-full wisdom. I am one that is witness and without desire. I reside in my glory alone. I am without motion. I am without old age, without destruction, without the differences of my party or another. I have wisdom as the chief essence. I am the mere ocean of bliss called salvation. I am the subtle. I am changeless. I am ātman merely, bereft of the illusion of qualities. I am the seat devoid of the three *guṇas*. I am the cause of the many worlds in [my] womb. I am the supreme cosmic-consciousness (*kūṭastha-caitanya*). I am of the form of the light, free from motion. I am not one that can be known by inference. I alone am full. I am of the form of the stainless salvation. I am without limbs or birth. I am the essence which is *sat* itself. I am of the nature of the true wisdom without limit. I am the state of excellent joy. I am one that cannot be differentiated. I am the all-pervading and without stain. I am the limitless and endless *sattva* alone. I am fit to be known through Veda. I am the one fit to be worshipped. I am the heart of all the worlds. I am replete with supreme bliss. I am of the nature of joy, which is supreme bliss. I am pure, secondless, and eternal, I am devoid of beginning. I am free from the three bodies (gross, subtle and causal), I am of the nature of wisdom. I am the emancipated one. I have a wondrous form. I am free from impurity. I am the one latent [in all]. I am the equal ātman of eternal *vijñāna*. I am the refined supreme truth. I am of the nature of wisdom-bliss alone.

Though I cognize as the secondless ātman by means of discriminative wisdom and reason, yet is found the relation between bondage and salvation. Though to me the universe is gone, yet it shines as true always. Like the truth in the [illusory conception of a] snake in the rope, so the truth of Brahman alone is and is the substratum on which this universe plays. Therefore the universe is not. Just as sugar is found permeating all the sugar-juice (from which the sugar is extracted), so I am full in the three worlds in the form of the non-dual Brahman. Like the bubbles, waves, etc. in the ocean, so all beings, from Brahmā down to worm, are fashioned in me; just as the ocean does not long after the motion of the waves, so to me, there is no longing after sensual happiness, being myself of the form of [spiritual] bliss. Just as in a wealthy person the desire for poverty does not arise, so in me who am immersed in Brāhmic bliss, the desire for sensual happiness cannot arise. An intelligent person who sees both nectar and poison rejects poison; so having cognized ātman, I reject those that are not-ātman. The sun that illuminates the body within and without is not destroyed with the destruction of the body. To me there is no bondage; there is no salvation, there are no books, there is no guru; for these shine through *māyā* and I have crossed them and am secondless. Let vital airs (*prāṇas*) according to their laws be fluctuating. Let mind (*manas*) be blown about by desire. How can pains affect me who am by nature full of bliss? I have truly known ātman. My ignorance *(ajñāna)* has fled away. The egoism of agency has left me. There is nothing I should yet do. Brāhman's duties, family, gotra (clan), name, beauty, and class—all these belong to the gross body and not to me who am without any mark [of body]. Inertness, love, and joy—these attributes appertain to the causal body and not to me, who am eternal and of changeless nature. Just as an owl sees darkness only in the sun, so a fool sees only darkness in the self-shining supreme bliss. Should the clouds screen the eyesight, a fool thinks there is no sun; so an embodied person full of *ajñāna* thinks there is no Brahman. Just as nectar which is other than poison does not commingle with it, so I, who am different, from inert matter, do not mix with its stains. As the light of a lamp, however small, dispels immense darkness, so wisdom, however slight, makes *ajñāna*, however immense, perish.

Just as [the delusion of] the serpent does not exist in the rope in all the three periods of time (past, present, and future), so the universe from *ahaṅkāra* [down] to body does not exist in me who am the non-dual one. Being of the nature of consciousness alone, there is not inertness in me. Being of the nature of truth, there is not non-truth to me. Being of the nature of bliss, there is not sorrow in me. It is through *ajñāna* that the universe shines as truth.

Whoever recites this Ātmabodha-Upaniṣad for a *muhūrta* (48 minutes) is not born again—yes, is not born again.

Oṃ tat sat is the Upaniṣad

8

Skanda Upaniṣad of Kṛṣṇa Yajurveda

Oṃ O Mahādeva Lord of gods, I am indestructible through a small portion of thy grace. I am replete with awareness. I am Śiva (bliss). What is higher than it? Truth does not shine as such on account of the display of the internal organs (*antaḥkaraṇa*). Through the destruction of the *antaḥkaraṇa*, Hari abides as consciousness alone *(samvid)*. As I am also a form of *samvid*, I am without birth. What is higher than it? All inert things being other [than ātman] perish like dreams. That Acyuta (the indestructible or Viṣṇu), who is the seer of the conscious and the inert, is of the form of *jñāna*. He alone is Mahādeva. He alone is Mahāhari (Mahāviṣṇu). He alone is the light of all lights. He alone is Parameśvara. He alone is Parabrahman. That Brahman I am. Of this there is no doubt, *jīva* is Śiva. Śiva is *jīva*. That *jīva* is Śiva alone. Bound by husk, it is paddy; freed from husk, it is rice. In like manner *jīva* is bound [by *karma*]. If *karma*, perishes, he *(jīva)* is Sadāśiva. So long as he is bound by the bonds of *karma*, he is *jīva*. Freed from its bonds, he is Sadāśiva. Prostrations to Śiva who is of the form of Viṣṇu and Viṣṇu who is the form of Śiva. The heart of Viṣṇu is Śiva. The heart of Śiva is Viṣṇu. As I see no difference [between these two], therefore to me they are prosperity and life. There is no difference between Śiva and Keśava (Viṣṇu). The body is said to be the divine temple. The Śiva [in the body] is the god Sadāśiva (eternal bliss).

Having given up the cast-off offerings of ignorance, one should worship him with the thought, "I am He". To see oneself as not different from him is wisdom. To free the mind from sensual objects is meditation. The giving up of the stains of the mind is bathing (*snāna*). The subjugation of the senses is cleansing (*śauca*). The nectar of Brahman should be drunk. For the upkeep of the body, one should go [begging] for alms. He should dwell alone in a solitary place. He should be with the sole thought of the non-dual One. The wise person who conducts himself thus, attains salvation. Salutations to the supreme light. May prosperity and long life attend [me]. O Narasiṃha! O Lord of gods! Through thy grace, persons cognize the true nature of Brahman that is unthinkable, undifferentiated, endless and immutable, through the forms of the gods, Brahmā, Nārāyaṇa, and Śaṅkara.

Like the eye which sees without any obstacle the things spread in the sky, so the wise always see the supreme abode of Viṣṇu. Brāhmaṇas with divine eyes who are always spiritually awake, praise in diverse ways and illuminate the supreme abode of Viṣṇu. Thus is the teaching of the Vedas for salvation.

Oṃ tat sat is the Upaniṣad

9

Paiṅgala Upaniṣad of Śukla Yajurveda

ADHYĀYA I

Oṃ. Paiṅgala, having served under Yājñavalkya for twelve years, asked him to initiate him into the supreme mysteries of *kaivalya*. To which Yājñvalkya replied thus: "O gentle one, at first, this [universe] was be-ness *(sat)* only. It is spoken of as Brahman which is ever free [from the trammels of matter], which is changeless, which is truth, wisdom, and bliss and which is full, permanent, and one only without a second. In it, was like a mirage in the desert, silver in mother-of-pearl, a person in the pillar, or colour, etc. in the crystals, *mūlaprakṛti*, having in equal proportions the *guṇas*, red *(rajas)*, white *(sattva)*, and black *(tamas)*, and being beyond the power of speech. That which is reflected in it is the witness-consciousness *(sākṣī-caitanya)*. The *mūlaprakṛti* undergoes change with the preponderance of *sattva* and assumes the form of *āvaraṇa śakti* named *avyakta*. That which is reflected in it *(avyakta)* is Īśvara-*caitanya*. He (Īśvara) has *māyā* under his control, is omniscient, the original cause of creation, preservation and dissolution, and the seed of this universe. He caused the universe which was latent in him, to manifest itself through the bonds of *karma* of all creatures like a painted canvas unfurled. Again through the extinction of their *karmas*, he makes it disappear. In him alone is latent the universe, wrapped up like a painted cloth. Then from the supreme *āvaraṇa śakti*, dependent on or appertaining to Īśvara, arose, through the preponderance of *rajas*, *vikṣepa śakti* called *mahat*. That which is reflected in it is *hiraṇyagarbha-caitanya*. Presiding (as he does) over *mahat*, he as Hiraṇyagarbha has a body, both manifested and unmanifested. From *vikṣepa-śakti* of Hiraṇyagarbha arose, through the preponderance of *tamas*, the gross *śakti* called *ahaṅkāra*. That which is reflected in it is *Virāṭ-caitanya*. He (Virāṭ) presiding over it *(ahaṅkāra)* and possessing a manifested body becomes Viṣṇu, the chief Puruṣa and protector of all gross bodies. From that ātman arose *ākāśa*; from *ākāśa* arose *vāyu*, from *vāyu, agni*, from *agni, apa*, and from *apa, pṛthivī*. The five *tanmātras* or the rudimentary properties above are the *guṇas* (of the above five). That generating cause of the universe (Īśvara) wishing to create and having assumed *tamo-guṇa*, wanted to convert the elements which were subtle *tanmātras* into gross ones. In order to create the universe, he divided into two parts each of those divisible elements; and having divided each moiety into four parts, made a fivefold mixture, each element having moiety of its own original element and one-fourth of a moiety of each of the other elements, and thus evolved out of the fivefold classified gross elements, the many myriads of Brahmāṇḍas (Brahmā's egg or macrocosm), the fourteen worlds pertaining to each sphere, and the spherical gross bodies (microcosm) fit for the [respective] worlds. Having divided the *rajas*-essence of the five elements into four parts, he out of three such parts created [the five] *prāṇas* having fivefold function. Again out of the [remaining] fourth part, he created the organs of action (*karmendriyas*). Having divided their *sattva*-essence into four parts, he out of three such parts created the internal organs (*antaḥkaraṇa*) having fivefold function. Out of the [remaining] fourth part of *sattva*-essence, he created the organs of sense (*jñānendriyas*). Out of the collective totality of *sattva*-essence, he created the deities (*devatās*) ruling over the organs of sense and actions. Those *devatās* he created, he located in the spheres pertaining to them. Through his orders, they began to pervade the macrocosm. Through his orders, Virāṭ associated with *ahaṅkāra*, created all the gross things. Through his command, Hiraṇyagarbha protected the subtle elements. Without him they that were located in their spheres were unable to move or to do anything. Then he wished to infuse life *(cetanā)* into them. Having pierced the Brahmāṇḍa and head-fontanelle (*brahmarandhra*) in all the microcosmic beings he entered within. Though they were [at first] inert, they were then able to perform *karmas* like beings of intelligence. The omniscient Īśvara entered the microcosmic bodies with a particle of *māyā* and being deluded by that *māyā*, acquired the state of *jīva*. Identifying the three bodies with himself, he acquired the state of the actor and enjoyer. Associated with the attributes of the states of *jāgrat*, *svapna*, *suṣupti*, trance, and death and being immersed in sorrow, he is [whirled about and] deluded like a water-lift or a potter's wheel, as if subject to birth and death."

ADHYĀYA II

Paiṅgala again addressed Yājñavalkya thus: "How did Īśvara, who is the creator, preserver, and destroyer and the lord of all the worlds, acquire the state of *jīva*?" To which Yājñavalkya replied: "I shall tell in detail the nature of *jīva* and Īśvara, together with a description of the origin of the gross, subtle, and causal bodies. Hear attentively with one-pointed mind.

"Īśvara having taken a small portion of the quintuplicated great elements (*mahābhūtas*), made in regular order the gross bodies, both collective and segregate. The skull, the skin, the intestines, bone, flesh, and nails are of the essence of *pṛthivī*, blood, urine, saliva, sweat and others are of the essence of *āpas*. Hunger, thirst, heat, delusion, and copulation are of the essence of *agni*. Walking, lifting, breathing and others are of the essence of *vāyu*. Passion, anger, etc. are of the essence of *ākāśa*. The collection of these having touch and the rest is this gross body that is brought about by *karma*, that is the seat of egoism in youth and other states and that is the abode of many sins. Then he created *prāṇas* out of the collective three parts of *rajas*-essence of the fivefold divided elements. The modifications of *prāṇa* are: *prāṇa*, *apāna, vyāna, udāna*, and *samāna; nāga, kūrma, kṛkara, devadatta* and *dhanañjaya* are the auxiliary *prāṇas*. [Of the first five], the heart, anus, navel, throat and the whole body are respectively the seats. Then he created the *karmendriyas* out of the fourth part of the *rajo-guṇa*. Of *ākāśa* and the rest the mouth, legs, hands and the organs of secretion and excretion are the modifications. Talking, walking, lifting, excreting, and enjoying are their functions. Likewise out of the collective three parts of *sattva*-essence he created the internal organ (*antaḥkaraṇa*). *Antaḥkaraṇa*, manas, *buddhi*, *citta*, and *ahaṅkara* are the modifications. Resolve (*saṅkalpa*), certitude, memory, egoism, and enquiry (*anusandhāna*) are their functions. Throat, face, navel, heart, and the middle of the brow are their seats. Out of the [remaining] fourth part of *sattva*-essence, he created the organs of sense (*jñānendriyas*). Ear, skin, eyes, tongue, and nose are the modifications. Sound, touch, form, taste, and odour are their functions. The quarters *(diś)*, Vāyu, Arka, Varuṇa, Aśvini Devas, Indra, Upendra, Mṛtyu, Prajāpati, the Moon, Viṣṇu, the four-faced Brahmā and Śambhu (Śiva) are the presiding deities of the organs. There are the five sheaths *(kośas)*, viz. *annamaya, prāṇamaya, manomaya*, *vijñānamaya*, and *ānandamaya*. *Annamaya* sheath is that which is created and developed out of the essence of food, and is absorbed into the earth which is of the form of food. It alone is the gross body. The *prāṇa* with the organs of action (*karmendriyas*) is the *prāṇamaya* sheath. *Manas* with the organs of sense (*jñānendriyas*) is the *manomaya* sheath. *Buddhi* with the *jñānendriyas* is the *vijñānamaya* sheath. These three sheaths constitute the subtle body (*liṅgaśarīra*). [That which tends to] the ignorance of the reality [of the true self] is the *ānandamaya* sheath. This is the causal body. Moreover the five organs of sense, the five organs of action, the five *prāṇas* and others, the five *ākāśa* and other elements, the four internal organs, *avidyā*, passion, *karma*, and *tamas*—all these constitute this dwelling [of the body].

"Virāṭ, under the command of Īśvara having entered this microcosmic body and having *buddhi* as his vehicle, reaches the state of *viśva*. Then he goes by the several names of Vijñānātman, Cidābhāsa, Viśva, Vyāvahārika, the one presiding over the waking gross body and the one generated by *karma*. Sūtrātman, under the orders of Īśvara, having entered the microcosmic subtle body, and having *manas* as his vehicle, reaches the *taijasa* state. Then he goes by the names of *taijasa*, *prātibhāsika* and *svapnakalpita* (the one arising out of dream). Then under the command of Īśvara, he who is coupled with *avyakta*, the vehicle of *māyā* having entered the microcosmic *kāraṇa* body, reaches the state of *prajñā*. He goes then by the names of *prājña*, *avicchinna*, and *pāramārthika* and *suṣupti-abhimānin* (the presider over *suṣupti*). Such sacred sentences, as *tattvamasi* (That art thou) and others speak of the identity with the Brahman of the *pāramārthika-jīva* enveloped by *ajñāna*, which is but a small particle of *avyakta*; but not *vyāvahārika* and *prātibhāsika* (*jīvas*). It is only that *caitanya* which is reflected in *antaḥkaraṇa* that attains the three states. When it assumes the three states of *jāgrat*, *svapna*, and *suṣupti*, it is like a water-wave as if [experiencing] grief, birth and death. There are five *avasthās*—*jāgrat-avasthā* is that in which there is the perception of objects, of sound, etc., through the grace of the devatā presiding over each of them. In it, the *jīva*, being in the middle of the eyebrows and pervading the body from head to foot, becomes the agent of actions, such as doing, hearing and others. He becomes also the enjoyer of the fruits thereof; and such a person doing *karma* for the fruits thereof goes to other worlds and enjoys the same there. Like an emperor tired of worldly acts [in the waking state], he strives to find the path to retire into his abode within. The *svapna-avasthā* is that in which, when the senses are at rest, there is the manifestation of the knower and the known, along with the affinities of [things enjoyed in] the waking state. In this state *viśva* alone, its actions in the waking state having ceased, reaches the state to *taijasa*, who moves in the middle of the nerves (*nāḍīs*), illuminates by his lustre the multiplicity of this universe which is of the form of senses, and himself enjoys according to his wish. The *suṣupti-avasthā* is that in which the *citta* is the sole organ [at play]. Just as a bird, tired of roaming, flies to its nest with its stomach filled, so also the *jīva,* being tired of the actions of the world in the waking and dreaming states, enters the state of illusion and enjoys bliss. Then trance is attained which resembles death, and in which one with his collection of organs quails, as it were, through fear and ignorance, like one beaten unexpectedly by a hammer, club or any other weapon. Then death *avasthā* is that which is other than the *avasthās* of *jāgrat*, *svapna*, *suṣupti*, and trance, which produces fear in all *jīvas* from Brahmā down to small insects and which dissolves the gross body. The *jīva* that is surrounded by *avidyā* and the subtle elements, takes with it the organs of sense and action, their objects and *prāṇas* along with the kārmic actions and goes to another world, assuming another body. Through the ripening of the fruits of previous karmas, the *jīva* has no rest like an insect in a whirlpool. It is only after many births that the desire of emancipation arises in man through the ripening of good *karma*. Then having resorted to a good guru and served under him for a long time, one out of many attains *mokṣa*, freedom from bondage. Bondage is through non-inquiry and *mokṣa* through inquiry. Therefore there should always be inquiry [into the nature of the real self]. The reality should be ascertained through illusory attribution (*adhyāropa*) and withdrawal or recession of that idea (*apavāda*). Therefore there should be always inquiring into the universe, *jīva* and *paramātman*. Were the nature of *jīva* and the universe known, then there remains Brahman which is identical with *pratyagātman*."

ADHYĀYA III

Then Paiṅgala asked Yājñavalkya to offer an exposition on the sacred sentences of the Vedas (the *mahākāvy*as). To which Yājñavalkya replied: "One should scrutinise [the sacred sentences], *tattvamasi* (That art Thou), *tvaṃ tadasi* (Thou art That), *tvaṃ brahmāsi* (Thou art Brahman) and *ahaṃ brahmāsmi* (I am Brahman). The word '*tat*' denotes the cause of the universe that is variegated beyond perception, has the characteristics of omniscience, has *māyā* as his vehicle and has the attributes of being-consciousness-bliss. It is he that is the basis of the notion 'I' which has the differentiated knowledge produced by *antaḥkaraṇa*; and it is he that is denoted by the word '*tvam*' (Thou). That is the undifferentiated Brahman, which remains as the aim [or meaning] of the words *tat* and *tvam* after freeing itself from *māyā* and *avidyā* which are respectively the vehicles of *paramātman* and *jīvātmā*. The inquiry into the real significance of the sentences *tattvamasi* and *ahaṃ brahmāsmi* forms [what is called] hearing—the first stage of inquiry (*śravaṇa*). To inquire in solitude into the significance of *śravaṇa* is *manana*. The concentration of the mind with one-pointedness upon that which should be sought after by *śravaṇa* and *manana* is *nididhyāsana*. *Samādhi* is that state in which *citta* having given up [the conception of the difference of] the meditator and the meditation, becomes of the form of the meditated like a lamp in a place without wind. Then arise the modifications pertaining to self. Such [modifications] cannot be known; but they can only be inferred through memory [of the *samādhi* state]. The myriads of *karmas* committed in this beginningless cycle of rebirths are annihilated only through them. Through proficiency in practice, the current of nectar always rains down [from the crown of head] in diverse ways. Therefore those who know yoga call this *samādhi dharma-megha* (cloud). Through these [modifications of self], the collection of affinities is absorbed without any remainder whatever. When the accumulated good and bad *karmas* are wholly destroyed, these sentences (*tattvamasi* and *ahaṃ brahmāsmi*), like the myrobalan in the palm of the hand, bring him face to face with the ultimate reality, though it was before invisible. Then he becomes a *jīvanmukta*.

"Īśvara desired to involute the five-fold differentiated elements. Having drawn into their causal source Brahmā's egg and its effects of worlds and mixed together the subtle organs of sense and action and the four internal organs and dissolved all things composed of the elements into their cause, the five elements, he then caused *pṛthivī* to merge into water, water into *agni, agni* into *vāyu*, *vāyu* into *ākāśa, ākāśa* into *ahaṅkāra*, *ahaṅkāra* into *mahat*, *mahat* into *avyakta* and *avyakta* into *Puruṣa* in regular order. Virāṭ, Hiraṇyagarbha and Īśvara being freed from the vehicle of *māyā*, are absorbed into *paramātman*. This gross body composed of the five differentiated elements and obtained through accumulated *karma*, is merged into its subtle state of non-quintuplicated elements, through the extinction of [bad] *karma* and increase of good *karma*, then attains its causal state (*kāraṇa*) and [finally] is absorbed into its cause, namely *kūṭastha-pratyagātman*. *Viśva* and *taijasa* and *prājña*, their *upādhi* (of *avidyā*) having become extinct, are absorbed in *pratyagātman*. This sphere [of universe] being burnt up by the fire of *jñāna* is absorbed along with its cause into *paramātman*. Therefore a Brāhmaṇa should be careful and always meditate upon the identity of *tat* and *tvam*. Then ātman shines, like the sun freed from the [obscuration of the] clouds. One should meditate upon ātmā in the midst [of the body] like a lamp within a jar.

"Ātman, the *kūṭastha*, should be meditated upon as being of the size of a thumb, as being of the nature of the light (*jyotis*) without smoke, as being within, illuminating all and as being indestructible. That sage who meditates [upon the self always] until sleep or death comes upon him passes into the state of emancipation like the immovable state of the wind. Then there remains that One (Brahman) without sound, touch, free from destruction, without taste or odour, eternal, without beginning or end, which is beyond the *tattva* of *mahat* and which is permanent and without stain or disease."

ADHYĀYA IV

Then Paiṅgala addressed Yājñavalkya thus: "To the wise, what is their *karma*? And what is their state?" To which Yājñavalkya replied: "A lover of *mokṣa*, having humility and other possessions [or virtues], enables twenty-one generations to cross [to ātman]. One through his being a *brahmavid* alone, enables one hundred and one generations to cross. Know ātmā to be the rider and the body as the chariot. Know also *buddhi* as the charioteer and *manas* as the reins. The wise say the organs are the horses, the objects are the roads [through which the horses travel] and the hearts are the moving balloons. Great sages say that ātmā, when associated with the sense organs and *manas*, is the enjoyer. Therefore it is the actual Nārāyaṇa alone that is established in the heart. Till his accumulated *karma* (*prārabdha karma*) is worn out, he exists [in his body] as in the [cast-off] slough of a serpent [without any desire for the body]. An emancipated person having such a body roves about like a moon gladdening all with no settled place of abode. He gives up his body whether in a sacred place or in an outcaste's house [without any distinction whatever] and attains salvation. Such a body [when seen by a person] should be offered as a sacrifice to the quarters (*diś*) or should be buried [underground]. It is only to the wise, that renunciaton (*sannyāsa*) is ordained and not to others. In case of the death of an ascetic who is of the form [or has attained the nature] of Brahman, there is no pollution [to be observed]; neither the ceremonies of fire (as burning the body, *homa,* etc.); nor the balls of rice (*piṇḍas*), nor ceremonies of water, nor the periodical ceremonies (monthly and yearly). Just as food once cooked is not again cooked, so a body once burnt [by the fire of wisdom] should not be burnt [or exposed to fire] again. To one whose body was burnt by the fire of wisdom there is neither *śrāddha* [required to be performed], nor [funeral] ceremony. So long as there is the *upādhi* of non-wisdom in one, so long should he serve the guru. He should conduct himself towards his guru's wife and children as he does to his guru. If being of a pure mind, of the nature of immaculate *cit* and resigned and having the discrimination arising from the attainment of wisdom 'I am He' he should concentrate his heart on Paramātman and obtain firm peace in his body, then he becomes of the nature of light, void of manas and buddhi. Of what avail is milk to one content with nectar? Of what avail are the Vedas to him who has known his ātman thus? For a yogin content with the nectar of wisdom, there is nothing more to be done. If he has to do anything, then he is not a knower of *tattva*. Pratyagātman, though far [or difficult of attainment] is not far; though in the body, he is devoid of it [since] he is all-pervading. After having purified the heart and contemplated on the One without disease (viz. Brahman), the cognizing of 'I' as the supreme and the all is the highest bliss. Like water mixed with water, milk with milk, and ghee with ghee, so jīvātman and Paramātman are without difference. When the body is rendered bright through wisdom and the *buddhi* becomes of the partless One, then the wise man burns the bondage of *karma* through the fire of *brahmajñāna*. Then he becomes purified, of the nature of the non-dual named Parameśvara and the light like the stainless sky. Like water mixed with water, so *jīva* (ātmā) becomes freed from the bonds of matter. Ātman is, like *ākāśa*, of an invisible form. [Therefore] the inner ātmā is invisible like *vāyu*. Though he is within and without, he is the immovable ātmā. Through the torch of wisdom, the internal ātmā sees (or knows).

"A wise man, in whatever place or manner he dies, is absorbed in that place like the all-pervading *ākāśa*. It should be known that ātmā is absorbed as truly as the *ākāśa* in the pot (when broken). Then he attains the all-pervading wisdom-light that is without support. Though men should perform *tapas* standing on one leg for a period of 1,000 years, it will not, in the least, be equal to one-sixteenth part of *dhyāna-yoga*. One desirous of knowing what knowledge (*jñana*) and the object to be known (*jñeya*) are, will not be able to attain his desired end, even though he may study the *śāstras* for 1,000 years. That which is alone should be known as the indestructible. That which exists [in this world] is only impermanent. [Therefore] after having given up [the study of] the many *śāstras*, one should worship that which is truth (*satya*). The many *karmas*, purity (of mind and heart), the muttering of mantṛas (*japa*), sacrifice and pilgrimages—all these should be observed till the essence (*tattva*) is known. For noble souls to be always in [the conception of] 'I am Brahman' conduces to their salvation. There are two causes [that lead] to bondage and emancipation. They are 'mine' and 'not mine'. Through "mine" creatures are bound, whereas through "not mine", they are released from bondage. Then the mind attains the state of *unmani* above *manas*, viz. when it is destroyed, then there is never the conception of duality. When the *unmani* state occurs, then is the supreme seat [attained]. [After which] wherever the mind goes, there is the supreme seat (that is, the mind enjoys salvation wherever it is). That which is equal in all is Brahman alone. One may attain the power to strike the *ākāśa* with his fist; he may appease his hunger by eating husks [of grain], but never shall he attain emancipation who has not the self-cognition, 'I am Brahman'.

"Whoever recites this Upaniṣad becomes as immaculate as *agni*. He becomes as pure as Brahmā. He becomes as pure as *vāyu*. He becomes like one who has bathed in all the holy waters. He becomes like one who has studied all the Vedas. He becomes like one that has undergone all Vedic observances. He obtains the fruit of the recitation of Itihāsas, Purāṇas and Rudramantras a lakh of times. He becomes like one that has pronounced *praṇava* (Oṃ) ten thousand times. He purifies his ancestors ten degrees removed and his descendants ten degrees removed. He becomes purified of all those that sit with him for dinner. He becomes a great personage. He becomes purified from the sins of the murder of a Brāhman, the drinking of alcohol, theft of gold and sexual cohabitation with the guru's wife, and from the sins of associating with those that commit such sins.

"Like the eye pervading the *ākāśa* (seeing without effort everything above), a wise man sees [always] the supreme seat of Viṣṇu. The Brāhmaṇas who have always their spiritual eyes wide open praise and illuminate in diverse ways the supreme seat of Viṣṇu."

Oṃ tat sat is the Upaniṣad

10

Adhyātma Upaniṣad of Śukla Yajurveda

The One unborn (*aja*) is ever located in the cave [of the heart] within the body. The earth is his body; though he pervades the earth, it does not know him. The waters are his body; though he pervades the water, they do not know him. *Agni* is his body; though he pervades *agni*, it does not know him. *Vāyu* is his body; though he pervades *vāyu*, it does not know him. *Ākāśa* is his body; though he pervades *ākāśa*, it does not know him. *Manas* is his body; though he pervades *manas*, it does not know him. *Buddhi* is his body; though he pervades *buddhi*, it does not know him. *Ahaṃkāra* is his body; though he pervades *ahaṅkāra*, it does not know him. *Avyakta* is his body; though he pervades *avyakta*, it does not know him. *Akṣara* is his body; though he pervades *akṣara*, it does not know him. *Mṛtyu* is his body; though he pervades *mṛtyu*, it does not know him. He who is the inner soul of all creatures and the purifier of sins, is the one divine Lord Nārāyaṇa.

The wise should, through the practice of deep meditation of Brahman, leave off the [recurrent] conception of "I" and "mine" in the body and the senses which are other than self. Having known himself as *pratyagātman*, the witness of *buddhi* and its actions, one should ever think "I am That" (so'ham) and leave off the idea of self in all others. Shunning the pursuits of the world, the body and the śāstras, set about removing the false attribution of self. In the case of a yogin staying always in his own self, his mind perishes having known his self as the self of all, through inference, Vedas and self-experience. Never giving the slightest scope to sleep, worldly talk, sounds, etc., think of ātman, in yourself to be the supreme ātman. Shun like a *caṇḍāla* [the thought of] the body, which is generated out of the impurities of parents and is composed of excreta and flesh. Then you will become Brahman and be [in a] blessed [state]. O Sage, having dissolved *jīvātman* into *paramātman* with the thought of its being part-less, like the ether of a jar in the universal ether, be ever in a state of taciturnity. Having become that which is the seat of all ātmans and the self-resplendent, give up the macrocosm and microcosm like an impure vessel. Having merged into *cidātman*, which is ever blissful, the conception of "I" which is rooted in the body, and having removed the [conception of] separateness, becomes ever the alone (*kevala*). Having known "I am that Brahman" in which alone the universe appears like a city in a mirror, become one that has performed his duty, O sinless one. The ever-blissful and the self-effulgent One being freed from the grip of *ahaṅkāra* attains its own state, like the spotless moon becoming full [after an eclipse].

With the extinction of actions, there arises the extinction of [dualities]. From it arises the decay of *vāsanās*; and from the latter, arises *mokṣa*; and this is called *jīvanmukti*. Looking upon everything in all places and times as Brahman brings about the destruction of *vāsanās* through the force of *vāsanās* of *sāttvic* nature. Carelessness in by or meditation of Brahman (*brahmaniṣṭhā*) should not in the least be allowed [to creep in]. Knowers of Brahman style this carelessness, in Brāhmic science, as death [itself]. Just as the moss [momentarily] displaced [in a tank] resumes its original position in a minute, so *māyā* envelops even the wise, should they be careless [even for a moment]. He who attains the *kaivalya* state during life becomes a *kevala* even after the death of his body. Ever devoted to *samādhi*, become the changeless one, a *nirvikalpa*, O sinless one. The knot of the heart, full of *ajñāna*, is broken completely only when one sees his ātman as secondless through *nirvikalpa samādhi*.

Now, having strengthened the conception of ātman and well given up that of "I" in the body, one should be indifferent as he would be towards jars, cloth, etc. From Brahmā down to a pillar, all the *upādhis* are only unreal. Hence one should see [or cognize] his ātman as all-full and existing by itself [alone]. Brahmā is *svayam* (ātman); Viṣṇu is ātman; Rudra is ātman; Indra is ātman; all this universe is ātman and there is nothing but ātman. By expelling, [from the mind] without any remainder, all objects which are superimposed on one's ātman, one becomes himself *parabrahman*, the full, the secondless and the actionless. How can there be the heterogeneity of the universe of *saṅkalpa* and *vikalpa* in that one principle which is immutable, formless and homogeneous? When there is no difference between the seer, the seen and sight, there being the decayless and *cidātman*, full like the ocean at the end of a *kalpa* and effulgent, all darkness, the cause of false perception, merges in it. How can there be heterogeneity in that one supreme principle which is alike? How can there be heterogeneity in the highest *tattva* which is one? Who has observed any heterogeneity in the dreamless sleep (*suṣupti*), where there is happiness only? This *vikalpa* has its root in *citta* only. When *citta* is not, there is nothing. Therefore unite the *citta* with *paramātman* in its *pratyagātmic* state. If one knows ātman as unbroken bliss in itself, then he imbibes always the essence of bliss in his self, whether internally or externally.

The fruit of renunciation (*vairāgya*) is spiritual wisdom (*bodha*); the fruit of *bodha* is renunciation (*uparati*); peace (*śānti*) is attained out of the enjoyment of the bliss of one's ātman and this *śānti* is the fruit of *uparati*. If the latter in each of these is absent, the former is useless. The path of return (*nivṛtti*) leads to the highest contentment and [spiritual] bliss is said to be beyond all analogy. That which has *māyā* as its *upādhi* is the womb of the world; that true one which has the attribute of omniscience, etc. and has the variegated mystery is denoted by the word "*tat*" (that). That is called the other or inferior (*apara*) which shines through meditation upon the idea and the world *asmat* and the consciousness of which is developed by *antaḥkaraṇa*. By separating the *upādhis māyā* and *avidyā* from *parā* and *jīva* (cosmic and human souls respectively), one realises *parabrahman* which is partless and being-consciousness-bliss. Making the mind dwell upon such sentences [or ideas] as the above constitues hearing (*śravaṇa*). It becomes contemplation (*manana*) when such ideas are quieted [in one] through logical reasoning. When [their] meaning is confirmed through these [two processes], the concentration of the mind on it alone constitutes *nididhyāsana*. That is called *samādhi* in which the *citta*, rising above the conception of the contemplator and contemplation, merges gradually into the contemplated, like a light undisturbed by the wind. Even the mental states are not known at the time when one is within the scope of ātman. But they are only inferred from the recollection which takes place after *samādhi*. Through this *samādhi* are destroyed crores of *karmas* which have accumulated during cycles of births without beginning and pure dharma is developed. Knowers of yoga call this *samādhi dharma-megha* (cloud), inasmuch at it showers nectarine drops of *karma* in great quantities, when all the hosts of *vāsanās* are destroyed entirely through this and when the accumulated *karmas*, virtuous and sinful, are rooted out. Then that in which speech was hidden till now, appears no longer so, and shines as *sat*; and direct cognition reveals itself, like the myrobalan in the palm of the hand. *Vairāgya* begins from where the *vāsanās* cease to arise towards objects of enjoyment. The cessation of the rising of the idea of "I" is the highest limit of *buddhi*; *uparati* begins from where the mental states once destroyed do not again arise. That ascetic is said to possess *sthitaprajñā* who enjoys bliss always and whose mind is absorbed in Brahman that is formless and actionless. That state of mind is termed *prajñā* that realises the oneness of Brahman and ātman after deep inquiry, and that has the *vṛtti* of *nirvikalpa* and *cinmātra*. He who possesses this always is a *jīvanmukta*. He is a *jīvanmukta* who has neither the conception of "I" in the body and the senses, nor the conception of another [different from himself] in everything else. He is a *jīvanmukta* who sees through his *prajñā* no difference between his own ātman and Brahman as well as between Brahman and the universe. He is a *jīvanmukta* who preserves equanimity of mind, either when revered by the good or reviled by the vicious. One who has cognized the true nature of Brahman is not subject to rebirth as before. But were he so subjected, then he is not a true knower, the knowing of Brahman being external only. A man is subject to *prārabdha* so long as he is affected by pleasure, etc. The attainment of a result is always preceded by action; and nowhere is it without *karma*. Through the cognition "I am Brahman" are destroyed the *karmas* accumulated during hundreds of crores of previous births, like the actions in the dreaming state [that are destroyed] during the waking state.

An ascetic having known himself as associateless and indifferent like ether, is not at all affected by any of his *karmas* at any time. Just as the ether is not affected by the alcoholic smell through its contact with a pot, so ātman is not affected by the *guṇas* produced by its *upādhi*. The *prārabdha-karma* that has begun to act before the dawn of *jñāna* is not checked by it; and one should reap its fruit, as in the case of an arrow let loose at a target. An arrow that is discharged towards an object with the idea that it is a tiger, does not stop when it (the tiger) is found to be a cow; but it [even] pierces the mark through its speed, without stopping. When one realises his ātman is free from old age and death, then how will *prārabdha* affect him? *Prārabdha* accomplishes [its work] only when one considers his body as the true self. This conception of ātman as body is not at all a desirable one; so it should be given up along with *prārabdha*, since it is simply a delusion to attribute *prārabdha* to this body. How can there be reality to that which is superimposed upon another? How can there be birth to that which is not real? How can there be death to that which is not born? How can there be *prārabdha* to that which is unreal? The Veda speaks of *prārabdha* in an external sense only, to satisfy those foolish persons that doubt, saying: "If *jñāna* can destroy all the results of *ajñāna* [such as body, etc.], then whence is the existence of this body to such a one?" but not to inculcate to the wise, the existence of the body.

Ātman is all-full, beginningless, endless, immeasurable, unchangeable, replete with *sat, cit*, and *ānanda*, decayless, the one essence, the eternal, the differentiated, the plenum, the endless, having its face everywhere, the one that can neither be given up nor taken up, the one that can neither be supported nor be made to support, the *guṇa*-less, the actionless, the subtle, the changeless, the stainless, the indescribable, the true nature of one's ātman, above the reach of speech and mind, the one full of beingness, the self-existent, the immaculate, the enlightened and the incomparable; such is Brahman, one only without a second. There are not in the least many. He who knows his ātman himself through his own cognition, as the one who is not restricted by any, is a *siddha* (one who has accomplished his object), who has identified his ātman with the one changeless ātman. Whither is this world gone, then? How did it appear? Where is it absorbed? It was seen by me just now, but now it is gone. What a great miracle! What is fit to be taken in? And what to be rejected? What is other [than self]? And what is different [from it]? In this mighty ocean of Brahman full of the nectar of undivided bliss, I do not see, hear, or know anything. I remain in my ātman only and in my own nature of *sat*, *ānandarūpa*. I am an *asaṅga* (or the associateless). I am without any attributes. I am Hari the Lord taking away sin. I am the quiescent, the endless, the all-full and the ancient. I am neither the agent nor the enjoyer. I am the changeless and the decayless. I am of the nature of pure enlightenment. I am the one and the perpetual bliss.

This science was imparted to Apāntarātman who gave it to Brahmā. Brahmā gave it to Ghora-Aṅgiras. Ghora-Aṅgiras gave it to Raikva, who gave it to Rāma. And Rāma gave it to all beings. This is the teaching of *nirvāṇa*; and this is the teaching of the Vedas.

Yes, this is the teaching of the Vedas.

Oṃ tat sat is the Upaniṣad

11
Subāla Upaniṣad of Śukla Yajurveda

KHAṆḌA I

Then he (Raikva) asked: "What was at first?" To which the Lord replied:

"There was neither be-ness (*sat*) nor not-be-ness (*asat*) nor a commingling of both.(*sat-asat*). From it darkness (*tamas*) was evolved. From *tamas* came *bhūtādi*; from *bhūtādi* came *ākāśa*, from *ākāśa*, *vāyu*; from *vāyu*, *agni* from *agni, ap*; and from *ap*, *pṛthivī*. Then it became an egg. After remaining so for one [divine] year, it split into two and became the earth below, the sky above and in the midst, the infinite *puruṣa* of a divine form of myriads of heads, eyes, feet and hands. Prior to the elements (*bhūta*), he had created death *(mṛtyu)*. With his broken axe (*khaṇḍa-paraśu*), he [divided eternal time into its parts], i.e. in the syllables, [*bhūḥ bhuvaḥ svaḥ*], the three heads and the three feet. To him, Brahmā spoke. He entered Brahmā himself and evolved mentally the seven sons and these created the seven mind- born sons as well as the seven progenitors (*prajāpatis*). Brāhmaṇas were born from his mouth, Kṣatriyas from his hands, Vaiśyas from his thighs and from the feet were born the Śudraṣ. The moon was born from his mind (*manas*), the sun from his eyes, *vāyu* from [his] ears and *prāṇas* from [his] heart. Thus all things were born."

KHAṆḌA II

"From *apāna* came *niṣādas, yakṣas, rākṣasas*, and *gandharvas*. From [his] bones, arose the mountains. From his hairs arose the herbs and the trees. From his forehead, Rudra was born through his anger. The breath of this great being became the Ṛgveda, Yajurveda, Sāmaveda, Atharvaveda, Śikṣā (the science of the proper pronunciation and articulation of sounds), Kalpa (the science of methodology), Vyākaraṇa (grammar), Nirukta (glossarial explanation of obsolete and other terms in Vedas), Chandas (prosody or Vedic metre), Jyotiṣa (astronomy), Nyāya (logic), Mīmāṃsā (including rituals and Vedānta), Dharmaśāstras (commentaries, glosses and all beings). This ātman (the self of Puruṣa) is *hiraṇyajyotis* (or golden or effulgent light) into which all the universe is absorbed. He divided himself into two moieties; out of one moiety, the woman was created; and out of the other, man. Having become a *deva*, he created the *devas*. Having become a *ṛṣi*, he created the *ṛṣis*; also he created *yakṣas, rākṣasas, gandharvas*, wild and domestic beasts and others such as cows, bulls, mares and horses, she-asses and asses and the supporter *(viśvambhara)* and the earth *(viśvambharā)*. Becoming fire *(vaiśvānara)* at the end [of creation], he burnt up all objects. Then [in dissolution], *pṛthivī* was absorbed in *āp, āp* in *agni, agni* in *vāyu, vāyu* in *ākaśa, ākāśa* in *indriyas* (organs), *indriyas* into *tanmātras* (rudimentary properties), *tanmātras* into *bhūtādi, bhūtādi* into *mahat, mahat* into *avyakta, avyakta* into *akṣara* (the indestructible), *akṣara* into *tamas* (darkness). And *tamas* becomes one with the supreme Lord. And then there is neither *sat* nor *asat*, nor *sat-asat*. This is the teaching of *nirvāṇa* and this is the teaching of the Vedas. Yes, This is the teaching of the Vedas."

KHAṆḌA III

"At first, there was *asat*, unborn, non-existent, unsupported, soundless, touchless, formless, tasteless, odourless, and decayless.

The undaunted man never grieves, as he knows self to be great, all-pervading and unborn. The ātman is *prāṇa*-less, mouthless, earless, tongueless, *manas*-less, *tejas*-less, eyeless, nameless, *gotra*-less (or clanless), headless, handless, feetless, non-unctuous, bloodless, non-measurable, neither long nor short, neither gross nor atomic, neither great nor small, endless, indescribable, non-returnable, non-luminous, not hidden, having neither inside nor outside, neither eating anything nor being eaten by others. Someone [out of many] attains to this [ātman] by the six means of truth (*satya*), charity (*dāna*), religious austerities (*tapas*), non-injury to any creature, celibacy and complete indifference to wordly objects; and there are no other means. Whoever feels happy with the thought 'I know That', that learned person's *prāṇa* will never get out of his body at the moment of death, but will become absorbed in Brahman; and being absorbed in Brahman, he attains the state of Brahman itself as he who knows this."

KHAṆḌA IV

"In the middle of the heart is a red fleshy mass in which is the *dahara*-lotus. Like the lotus, it opens into many [petals]. There are ten openings in the heart. The [different kinds of] *prāṇas* are located there. Whenever he [ātman] is united with *prāṇa*, he sees cities with rivers and other variegated things; when united with *vyāna*, he sees *devas* and *ṛṣis*; when united with *apāna*, he sees *yakṣas, rākṣasas* and *gandharvas*; when united with *udāna*, he perceives the celestial world, devas, Skanda (Kārtikeya) and Jayanta (Indra's son); when united with *samāna*, he sees the celestial world and the treasures [of Kubera]; when united with *rambhā* [a *nāḍī* hereafter given out], he sees whatever is seen or not seen, heard or not heard, eaten or not eaten, *asat* or *sat* and all else.

"There are ten *nāḍīs*; each of these are subdivided into seventy-one. And these become 72,000 branch *nāḍīs*. When ātman sleeps therein, it produces sound; but when ātman sleeps in the second sheath (*kośa*) then it sees this world and the higher as also knows all the sounds. This is spoken of as deep sleep rest (*samprasāda*). Then prāṇa protects the body. The *nāḍīs* are full of blood, of the colours green, blue, yellow, red, and white. Now this *dahara*-lotus has many petals like a lily. Like hair divided into 1,000 parts are the *nāḍīs,* called *hita*. The divine ātman sleeps in the *ākāśa* of the heart, in the supreme *kośa* (or *ānandamaya* sheath); sleeping there, it has no desires, no dreams, no deva-worlds, no sacrifice or sacrificer, no mother or father, no relative, no kinsman, no thief, or no Brāhman-slayer. Its body is resplendent effulgence *(tejas)* and of the nature of nectar [or the immortal]. It is as if in sport, a water-lotus. When he returns again to the waking state by the same way [he quit or went in before to the heart], he is *samrāḍ*. Thus says he."

KHAṆḌA V

"Those which join one place [or centre] with another are the *nāḍīs* which bind them. The eye is *adhyātman* (pertaining to the body); the visible objects are *ādhibhūta* (pertaining to the elements) and the sun is *adhidaivata* (spiritual). The *nāḍīs* form their bond (or connect them). He who moves in the eye, in the visible, in the sun, in the *nāḍīs*, in *prāṇa*, in *vijñāna*, in *ānanda*, in the *ākāśa* of the heart, and within all else—that is ātman. It is that which should be worshipped. It is without old age, death, fear, sorrow, or end.

"The ear is *adhyātma*, the audible *adhibhūta* and *diś* (the quarters) is *adhidaivata*. The *nāḍīs* bind them. He who moves in the ear, in the audible, in the quarters, in the *nāḍīs*, in *prāṇa*, in *vijñāna*, in *ānanda*, in the *ākāśa* of the heart, and within all else—that is ātman. It is that which should be worshipped. It is without old age, death, fear, sorrow or end.

"The nose is *adhyātma*, the odoriferous *adhibhūta* and the earth is *adhidaivata*. The *nāḍīs* bind them. He who moves in the nose, the odoriferous, the earth, the *nāḍīs*, *prāṇa*, *vijñāna, ānanda*, the *ākāśa* of the heart, and within all else—that is ātman. It is that which should be worshipped. It is without old age, death, fear, sorrow or end.

"The tongue is *adhyātma*: the tastable *adhibhūta* and Varuṇa is *adhidaivata*. The *nāḍīs* bind them. He who moves in the tongue, the tastable, Varuṇa, the *nāḍīs*, *prāṇa*, *vijñāna, ānanda*, the *ākāśa* of the heart, and within all else—that is ātman. It is that which should be worshipped. It is without old age, death, fëar, sorrow or end.

"The skin is *adhyātma*, the tangiferous *adhibhūta* and *vāyu* is *adhidaivata*. The *nāḍīs* bind them. He who moves in the skin, the tangiferous, *vāyu*, the *nāḍīs*, *prāṇa*, *vijñāna*, *ānanda*, the *ākāśa* of the heart, and within all else—that is ātman. It is that which should be worshipped. It is without old age, death, fear, sorrow or end.

Speech (*vāc*) is *adhyātma*, that which is acted upon by *vāc* is *adhibhūta*, and *agni* is *adhidaivata*. The *nāḍīs* bind them. He who moves in *vāc*, that which is acted upon by *vāc*, *agni*, the *nāḍīs*, *prāṇa*, *vijñāna*, the *ākaśa* of the heart and within all else—that is ātman. It is that which should be worshipped. It is without old age, death, fear, sorrow or end.

"The hand is *adhyātma*, that which can be handled is *adhibhūta* and Indra is *adhidaivata*. The *nāḍīs* bind them. He who moves in the hand, that which can be handled by it, Indra, the *nāḍīs, prāṇa*, *vijñāna, ānanda*, the *ākāśa* of the heart, and within all else—that is ātman. It is that which should be worshipped. It is without old age, death, fear, sorrow, or end.

"The feet is *adhyātma*, that which is walked upon is *adhibhūta*, and Viṣṇu (or Upendra) is *adhidaivata*. The *nāḍīs* bind them. He who moves in the feet, that which is walked upon, Viṣṇu, the *nāḍīs, prāṇa, vijñāna, ānanda*, the *ākāśa* of the heart, and within all else—that is ātman. It is that which should be worshipped. It is without old age, death, fear sorrow or end.

"The anus is *adhyātma*, the excreta is *adhibhūta*, and *mṛtyu* is *adhidaivata*. The *nāḍīs* bind them. He who moves in the anus, the excreta, *mṛtyu*, the *nāḍīs*, *prāṇa*, *vijñāna*, *ānanda* the *ākāśa* of the heart and within all else—that is ātman. It is that which should be worshipped. It is without old age, death, fear, sorrow or end.

"The genitals is *adhyātma*, the secretion is *adhibhūta* and Prajāpati is *adhidaivata*. The *nāḍīs* bind them. He who moves in the genitals, the secretion, Prajāpati, the *nāḍīs, prāṇa*, *vijñāna*, *ānanda*, the *ākāśa* of the heart and within all else—that is ātman. It is that which should be worshipped. It is without old age, death, fear, sorrow or end.

"*Manas* is *adhyātma*, the mindscape is *adhibhūta* and the moon is *adhidaivata*. The *nāḍīs* bind them. He who moves in the *manas*, the mindscape, the moon, the *nāḍīs, prāṇa, vijñāna, ānanda*, the *ākāśa* of the heart and within all else—that is ātman. It is that which should be worshipped. It is without old age, death, fear, sorrow or end.

"*Buddhi* is *adhyātma*, the certainly knowable is *adhibhūta* and Brahmā is *adhidaivata*. The *nāḍīs* bind them. He who moves in *buddhi*, the certainly knowable, Brahmā, the *nāḍīs*, *prāṇa, vijñāna, ānanda*, the *ākāśa* of the heart and within all else—that is ātman. It is that which should be worshipped. It is without old age, death, fear, sorrow or end.

"*Ahaṅkāra* is *adhyātma*, that which is acted upon by *ahaṅkāra* is *adhibhūta* and Rudra is *adhidaivata*. The *nāḍīs* bind them. He who moves in *ahaṅkāra*, that which is acted upon by *ahaṅkāra*, Rudra, the *nāḍīs, prāṇa, vijñāna, ānanda*, the *ākāśa* of the heart and within all else—that is ātman. It is that which should be worshipped. It is without old age, death, fear sorrow or end.

"*Citta* is *adhyātma*, that which is acted upon by *citta* [producing fluctuation of thought] is *adhibhūta* and *kṣetrajña* is *adhidaivata*. The *nāḍīs* bind them. He who moves in *citta*, that which is acted upon by the *citta, kṣetrajña*, the *nāḍīs, prāṇa, vijñāna, ānanda*, the *ākaśa* of the heart, and within all else—that is ātman. It is that which should be worshipped. It is without old age, death, fear sorrow or end.

"He is the knower of all, the Lord of all, the ruler of all, the one latent in all, the one worshipped for the happiness of all, but himself not worshipping [or seeking] any happiness, the one worshipped by all the Vedas and other books and to which all this is food, but who does not become the food of another; moreover, the one who, as the eye, is the ordainer of all, the one who as *annamaya* is *bhūtātman,* the one who as *prāṇamaya* is *indriyātman*, the one as *manomaya* is *saṅkalpātman*, the one who as *vijñānamaya* is *kālātman,* the one who as *ānandamaya* is *layātman*, is one and not dual. How can it be said to be mortal? How can it be said that there is not immortality in it? It is neither internal-*prajñā* nor external-*prajñā*; it is neither known nor is it to know anything. Thus is the exposition of *nirvāṇa*; and thus is the exposition of the Vedas; yes, thus is the exposition of the Vedas."

KHAṆḌA VI

"At first there was not anything in the least. These creatures were born through no root, no support but the divine god, the one Nārāyaṇa. The eye and the visible are Nārāyaṇa; the ear and the audible are Nārāyaṇa; the tongue and the tastable are Nārāyaṇa; the nose and the smellable are Nārāyaṇa; the skin and the tangible are Nārāyaṇa; *manas* and that which is acted upon by it are Nārāyaṇa; *buddhi* and that which is acted upon by it are Nārāyaṇa; *ahaṅkāra* and that which is acted upon by it are Nārāyaṇa; *citta* and that which is acted upon by it are Nārāyaṇa; *vāc* and that which is spoken are Nārāyaṇa; the hand and that which is lifted are Nārāyaṇa; the leg and that which is walked upon are Nārāyaṇa; the anus and the excreted are Nārāyaṇa; the genitals and the enjoyment of pleasure are Nārāyaṇa. The originator and the ordainer, as also the agent and the causer of changes are the divine god Nārāyaṇa only. Ādityas, Rudras, Maruts, Vasus, Aśvins, the Ṛk, Yajus and Sāma, mantras, Agni, clarified butter and oblation—all these are Nārāyaṇa. The origin and the combination are the divine god Nārāyaṇa only. Mother, father, brother, residence, asylum, friends and dependents are Nārāyaṇa only. The divine *nāḍīs* known as *virajā, sudarśanā, jitā, saumyā, moghā, kumārā, amṛtā, satyā, sumadhyamā, nāsīrā, śiśirā, surā, sūryā*, and *bhāsvatī* (viz. fourteen *nāḍīs* in all), that which thunders, sings and rains, viz. Varuṇa, Aryaman (sun), Chandramas (moon), Kalā (part), Kavi (Śukra), the creator Brahmā and Prajāpati, Indra, Kāla (time) of days, half-days, *kalpa*, the upper, and the directions—all these are Nārāyaṇa. That which was and will be is this Puruṣa only. Like the eye [which sees without any obstacle] the thing spread in the sky, the wise ever see this supreme seat of Viṣṇu. Brāhmaṇas who are ever spiritually awake, praise in diverse ways and illuminate the supreme abode of Viṣṇu. Thus is the exposition to the attaining of *nirvāṇa*; thus is the teaching of the Vedas; yes, thus is the teaching of the Vedas."

KHAṆḌA VII

"Within the body, is the one eternal unborn (*aja*), located in the cave [of the heart]. Earth is his body. Though he moves in the earth, earth does not know him. Waters are his body. Though he moves in the waters, waters do not know him. *Tejas* is his body. Though he moves in *tejas*, *tejas* does not know him. *Vāyu* is his body. Though he moves in *vāyu*, *vāyu* dose not know him. *Manas* is his body. Though he moves in *manas*, *manas* does not not know him. *Buddhi* is his body. Though he moves in *buddhi*, *buddhi* does not know him. *Ahaṅkāra* is his body. Though he moves in *ahaṅkāra, ahaṅkāra* does not know him. *Citta* is his body. Though he moves in *citta, citta* does not know him. *Avyakta* is his body. Though he moves in *avyakta*, *avyakta* does not know him. *Akṣara* is his body. Though he moves in *akṣara, akṣara* does not know him. *Mṛtyu* (death) is his body. Though he moves in *mṛtyu*, *mṛtyu* does not know him. Such one is the self within all creatures, the remover of all sins and the divine god, the one Nārāyaṇa.

This knowledge was imparted [by Nārāyaṇa] to Apāntaratama who in turn imparted it to Brahmā. Brahmā imparted it to Ghora-Aṅgiras. He imparted it to Raikva, who in turn imparted it to Rāma. Rāma imparted it to all creatures. This is the teaching of *nirvāṇa*; this is the teaching of the Vedas; yes, this is the teaching of the Vedas."

KHAṆḌA VIII

"The ātman of all which is immaculate, is located within the cave in the body. Ātman, which lives in the midst of the body filled with fat, flesh and phlegm, in a seat very closely shut up with shining many-coloured walls resembling a Gandharva city and with the [subtle] essence going out of it [to other parts of the body], which seat may be likened to a plantain flower and is ever agitated like a water-bubble—this Ātman is of an unthinkable form, the divine god, associateless and pure, has *tejas* as its body, is of all forms, the Lord of all, the unthinkable and the body-less, placed within the cave, immortal, shining and bliss itself. He is a wise person who cognizes ātman thus, and not one who does not do so."

KHAṆḌA IX

Once Raikva questioned the Lord thus: "O Lord, in whom does everything merge?" He replied thus: "That which disappears in the eye becomes the eye only; that which disappears in the visible becomes the visible only; that which disappears in the sun becomes the sun only; that which disappears in *virāṭ* becomes *virāṭ* only; that which disappears in *prāṇa* becomes *prāṇa* only; that which disappears in *vijñāna* becomes *vijñāna* only; that which disappears in *ānanda* becomes *ānandaturya* only; that which disappears in *turya* becomes *turya* only—all these attain that which is deathless, fearless, sorrowless, endless and seedless."

Then he continued: "That which disappears in the ear becomes the ear itself; that which disappears in the audible becomes the audible only; that which disappears in space becomes space only; that which disappears in discus becomes the discus only: that which disappears in *apāna* becomes *apāna* only; that which disappears in *turya* becomes *turya* only—[all these] attain that which is deathless, fearless, sorrowless, endless and seedless."

Then he continued: "That which disappears in the nose becomes the nose only; that which disappears in the odoriferous becomes odoriferous only; that which disappears in earth becomes earth only; that which disappears in victory becomes victory only; that which disappears in *vyāna* becomes *vyāna* only; that which disappears in bliss becomes bliss only; that which disappears in *turya* becomes *turya* only—[all these] attain that which is deathless, fearless, sorrowless, endless and seedless."

Then he continued: "That which disappears in the mouth becomes the mouth only; that which disappears in the tasted becomes the tasted only; that which disappears in Varuṇa becomes Varuṇa only; that which disappears in *soumya* (Moon or Mercury) becomes *soumya* only; that which disappears in *udāna* becomes *udāna* only; that which disappears in *vijñāna* becomes *vijñāna* only; that which disappears in bliss becomes bliss only; that which disappears in *turya* becomes *turya* only—[all these] attain that which is deathless, fearless, sorrowless, endless and seedless."

Then he continued: "That which disappears in the skin becomes the skin only; that which disappears in touch becomes touch only; that which disappears in *vāyu* becomes *vāyu* only; that which disappears in cloud becomes cloud only; that which disappears in *samāna* becomes *samāna* only; that which disappears in *vijñāna* becomes *vijñāna* only; that which disappears in bliss becomes bliss only; that which disappears in *turya* becomes *turya* only—[all these] attain that which is deathless, fearless, sorrowless, endless and seedless."

Then he continued: "That which disappears in *vāc* becomes *vāc* only; that which disappears in speech becomes speech only; that which disappears in *agni* becomes *agni* only; that which disappears in *kumārā* becomes *kumārā* only; that which disappears in hostility becomes hostility itself; that which disapears in *vijñāna* becomes *vijñāna* only; that which disappears in bliss becomes bliss only; that which disappears in *turya* becomes *turya* only—[all these] attain that which is deathless, fearless, sorrowless, endless and seedless."

Then he continued: "That which disappears in the hand becomes the hand only; that which disappears in that which is lifted by the hand becomes that which is lifted by the hand; that which disappears in Indra becomes Indra only; that which disappears in the nectar becomes the nectar only; that which disappears in *mukhya* becomes *mukhya* only; that which disappears in *vijñāna* becomes *vijñāna* only; that which disappears in bliss becomes bliss only; that which disappears in *turya* becomes *turya* only—[all these] attain that which is deathless, fearless, sorrowless, endless and seedless."

Then he continued: "That which disappears in the leg becomes the leg only; that which disappears in that which is walked upon becomes that which is walked upon; that which disappears in Viṣṇu becomes Viṣṇu only; that which disappears in *satya* becomes *satya* only; that which disappears in the suppression of the breath and voice becomes the suppression of the breath and voice; that which disappears in *vijñāna* becomes *vijñāna* only; that which disappears in *turya* becomes *turya* only—[all these] attain that which is deathless, fearless, sorrowless, endless and seedless."

Then he continued: "That which disappears in the anus becomes the anus only; that which disappears in that which is excreted becomes that which is excreted; that which disappears in *mṛtyu* becomes *mṛtyu* only; that which disappears in spirituous liquor becomes spirituous liquor only; that which disappears in hurricane becomes hurricane only; that which disappears in *vijñāna* becomes *vijñāna* only; that which disappears in *turya* becomes *turya* only—[all these] attain that which is deathless, fearless, sorrowless, endless and seedless."

Then he continued: "That which disappears in the genitals becomes the genitals only; that which disappears in that which is enjoyed becomes that which is enjoyed; that which disappears in that which is Prajāpati becomes Prajāpati only; that which disappears in *nāsīrā* becomes *nāsīrā* only; that which disappears in *kumāra* becomes *kumāra* only; that which disappears in *vijñāna* becomes *vijñāna* only; that which disappears in *ānanda* becomes *ānanda* only; that which disappears in the fourth state *turya* becomes *turya* only—[all these] attain that which is deathless, fearless, sorrowless, endless and seedless."

Then he continued: "That which disappears in *manas* becomes *manas* itself; that which disappears in the thinkable becomes the thinkable itself; that which disappears in the moon becomes the moon itself; that which disappears in *śiśu* becomes *śiśu* itself; that which disappears in *śyena ānanda* becomes *śyena* itself; that which disappears in *vijñāna* becomes *vijñāna* itself; that which disappears in bliss becomes *ānanda* bliss itself; that which disappears in *turya* becomes *turya* itself—[all these] attain that which is deathless, fearless, sorrowless, endless and seedless.'

Then he continued: "That which disappears in *buddhi* becomes *buddhi* itself; that which disappears in the certainty of the known becomes the certainty of the known itself; that which disappears in Brahmā becomes Brahmā himself; that which disappears in Kṛṣṇa becomes Kṛṣṇa himself; that which disappears in Sūrya becomes Sūrya himself; that which disappears in *vijñāna* becomes *vijñāna* itself; that which disappears in *ānanda* becomes *ānanda* itself; that which disappears in *turya* becomes *turya* itself—[all these] attain that whch is deathless, fearless, sorrowless, endless and seedless."

Then he continued: "That which disappears in *ahaṃkāra* becomes *ahaṅkāra* itself; that which disappears in that which is acted upon by ego becomes that itself; that which disappears in Rudra becomes Rudra himself; that which disappears in *asura* becomes *asura* itself; that which disappears in *śveta* becomes *śveta* itself; that which disappears in *vijñāna* becomes *vijñāna* itself; that which disappears in *ānanda* becomes *ānanda* itself; that which disappears in *turya* becomes *turya* itself—[all these] attain that which is deathless, fearless, sorrowless, endless and seedless."

Then he continued: "That which disappears in *citta* becomes *citta* itself; that which disappears in that which is acted upon by *citta* becomes that itself; that which disappears in *kśetrajña* becomes *kśetrajña* itself; that which disappears in *bhāsvatī* becomes *bhāsvatī* itself; that which disappears in *nāga* becomes *nāga* itself; that which disappears in *vijñāna* becomes *vijñāna* itself; that which disappears in *ānanda* becomes *ānanda* itself; that which disappears in *turya* becomes *turya* itself—[all these] attain that which is deathless, fearless, sorrowless endless and seedless.

"He who knows this as seedless in this manner becomes himself seedless. He is neither born, nor dies, nor is deluded, nor split, nor burnt, nor cut; he does not feel angry and hence he is said to be the self capable of burning all. Such a self is neither attained by a hundred sayings, nor by [the reading of] many scriptures, nor by mere intelligence, nor by hearing from others, nor by understanding, nor by Vedas, nor by scriptures, nor by severe *tapas*, nor *sāṅkhya*, nor yoga, nor observances of the orders of the life, nor by any other means [than the following]. Devoted Brāhmaṇas who repeat the Vedas according to rules and who worship him with praise attain him. He who is quiescent, self-controlled, indifferent to wordly objects and resigned, having centred his mind on ātman sees ātman and becomes one with the ātman of all, as also he who knows this."

KHAṆḌA X

Then Raikva asked Him: "O Lord, where do all things rest? He replied: "In the worlds of *rasātala* or nether worlds."

"In what are these [*rasātala* worlds] woven warp and woof?"

He replied: "In the worlds of *bhūḥ*."

"In what are these [worlds of *bhūḥ*] woven warp and woof?"

He replied: "In the world of *bhuvaḥ*."

"In what are these [*bhuvaḥ* worlds] woven warp and woof?"

"In the worlds of *suvaḥ*."

"In what are these [*suvaḥ* worlds] woven warp and woof?"

"In the worlds of *mahaḥ*."

"In what are these [*mahaḥ* worlds] woven warp and woof?"

"In the *janaloka.*"

"In what are these [*jana* worlds] woven warp and woof?" "In the *tapoloka.*"

"In what are these [*tapoloka*] woven warp and woof?"

"In the *satyaloka.*"

"In what are these [*satyaloka*] woven warp and woof?"

"In the *prajāpatiloka.*"

"In what are these [*prajāpatiloka*] woven warp and woof?"

" In the *brahmaloka.*"

"In what are these [*brahmaloka*] woven warp and woof?"

"In the *sarvaloka.*"

"In what are these [*sarvaloka*] woven warp and woof?"

"In ātman—which is Brahman, like beads [in a rosary] warp-wise and woof-wise."

Then he said: "All these rest in self and he who knows this, becomes self itself. Thus is the expositon of *nirvāṇa.* Thus is the exposition of the Vedas; yes, thus is the exposition of the Vedas."

KHAṆḌA XI

Again Raikva asked Him: "O Lord! what is the seat of self which is replete with *vijñāna*? And how does it leave the body and pervade the universe?"

To this he replied: "There is a mass of red flesh in the middle of the heart. In it, there is a lotus called *dahara.* It buds forth in many petals like a waterlily. In the middle of it is an ocean (*samudra*). In its midst is a bird (*koka*). In it there are four *nāḍīs.* They are *ramā, aramā, icchā* and *punarbhava.* Of these, *ramā* leads a man of virtue to a happy world. *Aramā* leads one of sins into the world of sins. [Passing] through *icchā* [*nāḍī*], one gets whatever he remembers. Through *punarbhava*, he splits open the sheaths; after splitting open the sheaths, he splits open the skull of the head; then he splits open the elements earth and water; then fire; then air; then space. Then he splits open *manas*; then *bhūtādi*; then *mahat*; then *avyakta*; then *akṣara*; then he splits open *mṛtyu* and *mṛtyu* becomes one with the supreme god. Beyond this, there is neither *sat* nor *asat*, nor *sat-asat*. Thus is the exposition of *nirvāṇa*; and thus is the exposition of the Vedas; yes, thus is the exposition of the Vedas."

KHAṆḌA XII

"Food *(anna)* came from Nārāyaṇa. It was first cooked in Brahmaloka in the *Mahā-saṃvartaka* fire. Again it was cooked in the sun; again it was cooked in *kravyādi* (lit. the fire that burns raw flesh, etc.); again it was cooked in *jvālakīla* (the flaming *kīla*); then it became pure and not stale. One should eat whatever has fallen to his lot and without begging; one should never beg any [food]."

KHAṆḌA XIII

"The wise man should conduct himself like a lad, with the nature of a child, without company, blameless, silent and wise and without exercising any authority. This description of *kaivalya* is stated by Prajāpati. Having found with certitude the supreme seat, one should dwell under a tree with torn clothes, unaccompanied, single and engaged in *samādhi*. He should be longing after the attaining of self and having attained this object, he is desireless, his desires have decayed. He fears none, though he finds the cause of death in such as elephants, lions, gadflies, mosquitoes, ichneuma, serpents, *yakṣas, rākṣasas*, and *gandharvas*. He will stand like a tree. Though cut down, he will neither get angry nor tremble. He will remain like a lotus. Though pierced, he will neither get angry nor tremble. He will stand like space; though struck, he will neither get angry nor tremble. He will stand by truth (*satya*), since ātman is *satya*.

"Earth is the heart [or centre] of all odours; water is the heart of all taste; fire is the heart of all forms; air is the heart of all touch; space is the heart of all sounds; *avyakta* is the heart of *gītās* (or sounds); *mṛtyu* is the heart of all *sattvas*; and *mṛtyu* becomes one with the supreme. And beyond him, there is neither *sat* nor *asat*, nor *sat-asat*. Thus is the exposition of *nirvāṇa*; thus is the exposition of the Vedas; yes, thus is the exposition of the Vedas."

KHAṆḌA XIV

"Earth is the food, and water is the eater; water is the food and fire is the eater; fire is the food and air is the eater; air is the food and space is the eater; space is the food and the organs are the eaters; *indriyas* are the food and *manas* is the eater; *manas* is the food and *buddhi* is the eater; buddhi is the food and *avyakta* is the eater; *avyakta* is the food and *akṣara* is the eater; *akṣara* is the food, and *mṛtyu* is the eater; and *mṛtyu* becomes one with the supreme. Beyond him, there is neither *sat* nor *asat*, nor *sat-asat*. Thus is the exposition of *nirvāṇa* and thus is the exposition of the Vedas; yes, thus is the exposition of the Vedas."

KHAṆḌA XV

Again Raikva asked: "O Lord, when this dense mass of consciousness (*vijñāna-ghana*) goes out [of the body or the universe], what does it burn and how?"

To which he replied: "When it goes away, it burns *prāṇa, apāna, vyāna, udāna, samāna, vairambha, mukhya, antaryāma, prabhañjana, kumāra, śyena, kṛṣaṇa, śveta*, and *nāga*. Then it burns earth, water, fire, air and space. Then it burns the waking, the dreaming, the dreamless sleep and the fourth state as well as the *mahalokas* and worlds higher; then it burns the *lokāloka* [the highest world forming a limit to the other worlds]. Then it burns *dharma* and *adharma*. Then it burns that which is beyond, is sunless, limitless and worldless. Then it burns *mahat*, it burns *avyakta*; it burns *akṣara*; it burns *mṛtyu*; and *mṛtyu* becomes one with the great Lord. Beyond him, there is neither *sat* nor *asat*, nor *sat-asat*. Thus is the expositon of *nirvāṇa* and thus is the exposition of the Vedas; yes, thus is the exposition of the Vedas."

KHAṆḌA XVI

"This Subāla-Bīja-Brahma-Upaniṣad should neither be given out nor taught to one who has not controlled his passions, who has no sons, who has not gone to a guru and having become his disciple has not resided with him for a year and whose family and conduct are not known. These doctrines should be taught to him who has supreme devotion to the Lord and as much to his guru. Then these truths shine in his great soul. Thus is the exposition of *nirvāṇa*; thus is the exposition of the Vedas; yes, thus is the exposition of the Vedas."

Oṃ tat sat is the Upaniṣad

12
Tejobindu Upaniṣad of Kṛṣṇa Yajurveda

CHAPTER I

Supreme meditation *(param dhyāna)* should be upon the resplendent point *(tejobindu)*, which is the ātman of the universe, seated in the heart, of the size of an atom, which pertains to Śiva, which is quiescent, gross and subtle, as also above these qualities. That alone should be the *dhyāna* of the sages as well as of men, full of pains, difficult to meditate on, difficult to perceive, the emancipated one, decayless and which is difficult to attain. One whose food is moderate, whose anger has been controlled, who has given up all love for society, subdued his passions, overcome all pairs [of heat and cold etc.], given up his egoism, who does not bless anyone nor take anything from others and also who goes where they naturally ought not to go and naturally would not go where they like to go—such persons also obtain three[levels of consciousness]. Haṃsa is said to have three seats. Therefore know it is the greatest of mysteries, without sleep and without support. It is very subtle, of the form of *soma*, and is the supreme seat of Viṣṇu. That seat has three faces, three *guṇas* and three *dhātus* and is formless, motionless, changeless, sizeless and supportless. That seat is without *upādhi* and is above the reach of speech and mind. It is self-nature (*svabhāva*) reachable only by *bhāva*. The indestructible seat is associateless, without bliss, beyond mind, difficult to perceive, emancipated and changeless. It should be meditated upon as the liberated, the eternal, the permanent and the indestructible. It is Brahman, is *adhyātma* (or the deity presiding as ātman) and is the highest seat of Viṣṇu. It is inconceivable, of the nature of *cidātman* and above the *ākāśa*, is void and non-void, and beyond the void and is abiding in the heart. There is [in it] neither meditation nor meditator, nor the meditated, nor the non-meditated. It is not the universe. It is the highest space; it is neither supreme nor above the supreme. It is inconceivable, unknowable, non-truth and not the highest. It is realised by the sages, but the gods do not know the supreme one. Avarice, delusion, fear, pride, passion, anger, sin, heat, cold, hunger, thirst, thought and fancy— [all these do not exist in it]. [In it] there is no pride of [belonging to] the Brāhmaṇa caste, there is no fear, no happiness, no pains neither fame nor disgrace. That which is without these states is the supreme Brahman.

Forbearance (*yama*), religious observance (*niyama*), renunciation (*tyāga*), silence (*mauna*) according to time and place, posture (*āsana*), *mūlabandha*, seeing all bodies as equal, the position of the eye, control of breath (*prāṇa-samyamana*), subjugation of the senses (*pratyāhāra*), *dhāraṇā*, *ātma-dhyāna* and *samādhi*—these are spoken of as the parts [of yoga] in order. That is called *yama* in which one controls all his organs [of sense and actions] through the *vijñāna* that all is Brahman; this should be practised often and often. *Niyama*, in which there is the supreme bliss enjoyed through the flowing [or inclination] of the mind towards things of the same spiritual kind (viz. Brahman) and the abandoning of things differing from one another is practised by the sages as a rule. In renunciation (*tyāga*), one abandons the manifestation [or objects] of the universe through the cognition of ātman that is *sat* and *cit*. This is practised by the great and is the giver of immediate salvation. Silence (*mauna*), in which, without reaching That, speech returns along with mind, is fit to be attained by the yogins and should be ever worshipped by the ignorant [even]. How is it possible to speak of "That" from which speech returns? How should it be described as the universe as there is no word to describe it? It is "That" which is [really] called silence, and which is naturally understood [as such]. There is silence in children, but with words [latent]; whereas the knowers of Brahman have silence but without words. "That" should be known as "the lonely seat" in which there is no one in the beginning, middle or end, and through which all this [universe] is fully pervaded. The illusion of Brahmā and all other beings takes place within one twinkling [of his eye]. "That" should be known as posture (*āsana*), in which one has with ease and without fatigue, uninterrupted meditation of Brahman; that is described by the word time (*kāla*), that is endless bliss and that is secondless. Everything else is the destroyer of bliss. "That" is called *siddha*-posture in which the psychical personages (*siddhas*) have succeded in realising the endless One as the support of the universe containing all the elements etc. "That" is called the *mūlabandha*, which is the root of all worlds and through which the root *citta* is bound. It should be always practised by the rājayogins.

One after having known the equality of the parts of (*aṅgas*) yoga point to one and the same Brahman, should be absorbed in that equal [or uniform] Brahman; if not, there is not that equality [attained]. Then like a dry tree, there is straightness [or uniformity throughout]. Making one's vision full of spiritual wisdom, one should look upon the world as full of Brahman. That vision is very noble. It is [generally] aimed at the tip of the nose; but it should be directed towards that seat [of Brahman] wherein the cessation of the seer, the seen, and sight will take place and not towards the tip of the nose. That is called the control of breath (*prāṇāyāma*), in which there is the control of the modifications [of mind] through the cognition of Brahman in all the states of *citta*, and others. The checking of [the conception of the reality of] the universe, is said to be expiration. The holding on to this conception without agitation is cessation of breath. Such is the practice of the enlightened. The ignorant close their nose. That should be known as *pratyāhāra*, through which one sees ātman [even] in the objects of sense and pleases *citta* through *manas*. It should be practised often and often. Through seeing Brahman wherever the mind goes, the *dhāraṇā* of the mind is obtained. *Dhāraṇā* is thought of highly by the wise. By *dhāraṇā* is meant that state where one indulges in the good thought, "I am Brahman alone," and is without any support. This *dhyāna* is the giver of supreme bliss. Being first in a state of changelessness, and then thoroughly forgetting [even] that state owing to the cognition of the [true] nature of Brahman—this is called *samādhi*. This kind of bliss should be practised by a wise person till his cognition itself is united in a moment with the state of *pratyagātman*. Then this king of yogins becomes a *siddha*, and is without any aid [outside himself]. Then he will attain a state, inexpressible and unthinkable.

When *samādhi* is practised, the following obstacles arise with great force—absence of right inquiry, laziness, inclination to enjoyment, sweat, and absent-mindedness. All these obstacles should be overcome by inquiring into Brahman. Through worldly thoughts *(bhāvavṛttis)*, one gets into them. Through void thoughts (*śūnyavṛttis*), one gets into them. But through the *vṛttis* of Brahman, one gets fullness. Therefore one should develop fullness through this means [of Brahman]. He who abandons this *vṛtti* of Brahman, which is very purifying and supreme—that man lives in vain like a beast. But he who understands this *vṛtti* and having understood it makes advances in it, becomes a good and blessed person, deserving to be worshipped by the three worlds. Those who are greatly developed through the ripening [of their past *karmas*] attain the state of Brahman; others are simply reciters of words. Those who are clever in arguments about Brahman but are without the action pertaining to Brahman, and who are greatly attached to the world—those certainly are born again and again through their *ajñāna*; [the former] never remain, even for half a moment—without the *vṛtti* of Brahman, like Brahmā and others, Sanaka, Śuka and others. When a cause is subject to changes, it [as an effect] must also have its cause. When the cause ceases to exist in truth, the effect perishes through right discrimination. Then that substance which is beyond the scope of words, remains pure. After that, *vṛtti jñāna* arises in the purified mind; through meditation with transcendental energy, there arises a firm certitude.

After reducing the visible into the invisible state, one should see everything as Brahman. The wise should ever stay in bliss with their understanding full of the essence of *cit*. Thus ends the first chapter of Tejobindu.

CHAPTER II

Then the Kumāra asked Śiva: "Please explain to me the nature of *cinmātra*, that is the partless non-dual essence." The great Śiva replied: "The partless non-dual essence is the visible. It is the world, it is the existence, it is the self, it is mantra, it is action, it is spiritual wisdom, it is water. It is the earth, it is *ākāśa*, it is the books, it is the three Vedas, it is the Brahman, it is the religious vow, it is *jīva*, it is the unborn, it is Brahmā, it is Viṣṇu, it is Rudra; it is I, it is ātman, it is the guru. It is the aim, it is sacrifice, it is the body, it is *manas*, it is *citta*, it is happiness, it is *vidyā*; it is the undifferentiated, it is the eternal, it is the supreme, it is everything. O six-faced one, different from it there is nothing. None, none but that; that is I. It is gross, it is subtle, it is knowable, it is thou; it is the mysterious; it is the knower; it is existence, it is mother, it is father, it is brother, it is husband, it is *sūtra* (ātman), it is Virāṭ. It is the body, it is the head, it is the internal, it is the external, it is full, it is nectar, it is clan *(gotra)*, it is the house (*gṛha*), it is the preservable, it is the moon, it is the stars, it is the sun, it is the holy seat. It is forgiveness, it is patience, it is the *guṇas*, it is the witness. It is a friend, it is a relative, it is an ally, it is the king, town, kingdom and subjects. It is Oṃ, recitation *(japa)*, meditation, the seat, the one worthy to be taken [in], the heart, the Light, heaven and self.

"All the partless non-dual essence should be regarded as *cinmātra*. *Cinmātra* alone is the absolute consciousness; and this partless non-dual essence alone is the [real] essence. All having consciousness alone except those having changes, are *cinmātra*. All this is *cinmātra*. He is *cinmaya*; the state of ātman is known as *cinmātra* and the partless non-dual essence. The whole world is *cinmātra*. Your state and my state are *cinmātra*. Space, earth, water, air, fire, Brahmā, Viṣṇu, Śiva and all else that exist or do not, are *cinmātra*. That which is the partless non-dual essence is *cinmātra*. All the past, present and future are *cinmātra*. Substance and time are *cinmātra*. Knowledge and the knowable are *cinmātras*. The knower is *cinmātra*, everything is *cinmātra*. Every speech is *cinmātra*. Whatever else is *cinmātra*. *Asat* and *sat* are *cinmātra*. The beginning and end is *cinmātra*; that which is in the beginning and end is *cinmātra*. The guru and the disciple are *cinmātra*. If the seer and the seen are *cinmātra*, then they are always *cinmaya*. All things wondrous are *cinmātra*. The [gross] body is *cinmātra*, as also the subtle and causal bodies. There is nothing beyond *cinmātra*. I and thou are *cinmātra*. Form and non-form are *cinmātra*. Virtue and vice are *cinmātra*. The body is a symbol of *cinmātra*. *Saṅkalpa*, knowing, mantra and others, the gods invoked in mantras, the gods presiding over the eight quarters, the phenomenal and the supreme Brahman are nothing but *cinmātra*. There is nothing without *cinmātra*. *Māyā* is nothing without *cinmātra*. Worship is nothing without *cinmātra*. Meditation, truth, sheaths and others, the [eight] *vasus*, silence, non-silence and indifference to objects—are nothing without *cinmātra*. Everything is from *cinmātra*. Whatever is seen and however seen—it is *cinmātra* so far. Whatever exists and however distant, is *cinmātra*. Whatever elements exist, whatever is perceived and whatever is Vedānta—all these are *cinmātra*. Without *cinmātra*, there is no motion, no emancipation and no goal aimed at. Everything is *cinmātra*. Brahman, that is the partless non-dual essence is known to be nothing but *cinmātra*. Thou O Lord, art the partless, non-dual essence [stated] in the books, in me, in thee, and in the ruler. He who thus perceives "I" as pervading everywhere will at once be emancipated through this spiritual wisdom. He is his own guru with this profound spiritual wisdom." Thus ends the second chapter of Tejobindu.

CHAPTER III

The Kumāra addressed his father [again]: "Please explain to me the realisation of true self." To which the great Śiva said: "I am the nature of the Parabrahman. I am the supreme bliss. I am solely of the nature of divine wisdom. I am the sole supreme, the sole quiescence, the sole *cinmaya,* the sole unconditioned, the sole permanent and the sole *sattva.* I am the 'I' that has given up 'I'. I am one that is without anything. I am full of the void of consciousness (*cidākāśa*). I am the sole fourth one. I am the sole one above the fourth [state of *turya*]. I am the nature of [pure] consciousness. I am ever of the nature of the bliss-consciousness. I am of the nature of the non-dual. I am ever a pure nature, solely of the nature of divine wisdom, of the nature of bliss, without fancies, desires or diseases of the nature of bliss, without changes or differentiations and of the nature of the eternal one essence and *cinmātra.* My real nature is indescribable, of endless bliss, the bliss above *sat* and *cit* and the interior of the interior. I am beyond reach of manas and speech. I am of the nature of ātmic-bliss, true bliss and one who sports with [my] ātman. I am ātman and Sadāśiva. My nature is spiritual effulgence. I am the essence of the light. I am without beginning, middle or end. I am like the sky. I am solely unconditioned and pure. I am the being-consciousness and bliss, that is eternal, enlightened and pure. I am ever of the nature of the eternal *śeṣa* (the remainder as time). I am beyond all. My nature is beyond form. My form is supreme space. My nature is of the bliss of earth. I am ever without speech. My nature is that support of all. I am ever replete with consciousness, without the attachment of body, without thought, without the modifications of *citta*, the sole essence of *cidātman*, beyond the visibility of all and of the form of vision. My nature is ever full. I am ever fully contented, the all, and Brahman, and the very consciousness; I am 'I'. My nature is of the earth. I am the great ātman and the supreme of the supreme; I appear sometimes as different from myself; sometimes as possessing a body, sometimes as a pupil and sometimes as the basis of the worlds. I am beyond the three periods of time, am worshipped by the Vedas, am determined by the sciences and am fixed in the *citta.* There is nothing left out by me, neither the earth nor any other objects here. Know that here is nothing which is out of myself. I am Brahmā, a *siddha,* the eternally pure, non-dual one, Brahman, without old age or death. I shine by myself; I am my own ātman my own goal, enjoy myself, play in myself, have my own spiritual effulgence, am my own greatness and am used to play in my own ātman, look on my own ātman and am in myself happily seated. I have my own ātman as the residue, stay in my own consciousness and play happily in the kingdom of my own self. Sitting on the real throne of my own ātman, I think of nothing else but my own true essence. I am *cidrūpa* alone, Brahman alone, being-consciousness and bliss, the secondless, the one replete with bliss and the sole Brahman and ever without anything, have the bliss of my own ātman, the unconditioned bliss, and am always ātman-*ākāśa*. I alone am in the heart like the consciousness-sun. I am content in my own self, formless, decayless without the number one, have the nature of an unconditioned and emancipated one and I am subtler than space; I am without the existence of beginning or end, of the nature of the all-illuminating, the bliss greater than the great, of the sole nature of *sat*, of the nature of pure liberation, of the nature of truth and bliss, full of spiritual wisdom and bliss, of the nature of wisdom alone, and of the nature of *sat-cit-ānanda*. All this is Brahman alone. There is none other than Brahman and that is 'I'.

"I am Brahman that is essence and bliss and the ancient. The word 'thou' and the word 'that' are not different from me. I am of the nature of consciousness. I am alone the great Śiva. I am beyond the nature of existence. I am of the nature of bliss. As there is nothing that can witness me, I am without the state of witness. Being purely of the nature of Brahman, I am the eternal Ātman. I alone am the Ādiśeṣa, the primeval Śeṣa. I alone am the Śeṣa (the remainder representing time). I am without name and form, of the nature of bliss, of the nature of all beings unperceivable by the senses, and of the nature of all beings; I have neither bondage nor salvation. I am of the form of eternal bliss. I am the primeval consciousness alone, the partless and non-dual essence, beyond reach of speech and mind, of the nature of bliss everywhere, of the nature of fullness everywhere, of the nature of earthly bliss, of the nature of contentment everywhere, the supreme nectarine essence and the one and secondless *sat*, (viz. Brahman). Of this there is no doubt. I am of the nature of all-void. I am the one that is given out by the Vedas. I am of the nature of the emancipated and emancipation, of *nirvāṇic*-bliss, of truth and wisdom, of *sat* alone and bliss, of the one beyond the fourth, of the one without fancy and ever of the nature of the unborn. I am without passion or faults. I am the pure, the enlightened, the eternal, the all-pervading and of the nature of the significance of Oṃ, of the spotless and of *cit*. I am neither existing nor non-existing. I am not of the nature of anything. I am of the nature of the actionless. I am without parts. I have no semblance, no manas, no sense, no *buddhi*, no change, none of the three bodies, neither the waking, dreaming, nor dreamless sleep states. I am neither of the nature of the three pains nor of the three desires. I have neither *śravaṇa* nor *manana* in *cidātma* in order to attain salvation. There is nothing like me or unlike me. There is nothing within me. I have none of the three bodies.

"The nature of *manas* is unreal, the nature of *buddhi* is unreal, the nature of *aham* (the 'I') is unreal; but I am the unconditioned, the permanent and the unborn. The three bodies are unreal, the three periods of time are unreal, the three *guṇas* are unreal, but I am of the nature of the real and the pure. That which is heard is unreal, all the Vedas are unreal, the śāstras are unreal, but I am the real and of the nature of consciousness, the *cit*. The *mūrt*is [Bramhā, Viṣṇu, and Rudra having limitation] are unreal, all creation is unreal, all the *tattvas* are unreal, but know that I am the great Śadāśiva. The master and the disciple are unreal, the manṭras of the guru are unreal, that which is seen is unreal, but know me to be the real. Whatever is thought of is unreal, whatever is lawful is unreal, whatever is beneficial is unreal, but know me to be the real. Know the ego to be unreal, know the enjoyments to be unreal, know things seen and heard as unreal as also the one woven warp-wise and woof-wise, viz. this universe; cause and non-cause are unreal, things lost or obtained are unreal. Pains and happiness are unreal, all and non-all are unreal, gain and loss are unreal, victory and defeat are unreal. All the sound, all the touch, all the forms, all the taste, all the smell, and all *ajñāna* are unreal. Everything is always unreal—the mundane existence is unreal—all the *guṇas* are unreal. I alone am of the nature of *sat*.

"One should cognize his own self alone. One should always practise the mantra of his self. The mantra (*aham-bramhāsmi*) 'I am Brahman' removes all the sins of sight, destroys all other mantras, destroys all the sins of body and birth, the noose of Yama, the pains of duality, the thought of difference, the pains of thought, the disease of *buddhi*, the bondage of *citta*, all diseases, all griefs and passions instantaneously, the power of anger, the modifications of *citta*, *saṅkalpa*, crores of sins, all actions and the *ajñāna* of ātman. The mantra 'I am Brahman' gives indescribable bliss, gives the state of undecaying and kills the demon of non-self. The thunderbolt 'I am Brahman' clears all the hill of not-self. The wheel 'I am Brahman' destroys the *asuras* of not-self. The mantra 'I am Brahman' gives spiritual wisdom and bliss. There are seven crores of great mantras and there are *vratas,* vows of hundred crores of births. Having given up all other mantras, one should ever practise this mantra. He obtains at once salvation and there is even a particle of doubt about it. Thus ends the third chapter of the Tejobindu-Upaniṣad."

CHAPTER IV

The Kumāra asked the great Lord: "Please explain to me the nature of embodied salvation *(jīvanmukti)* and disembodied salvations *(videhamukti)*." To which the great Śiva replied: "I am *cidātman*. I am *para-ātman*. I am the greater than the greatest. One who ever dwells in the true self is called a *jīvanmukta*. He who realises: 'I am beyond the three bodies, I am the pure consciousness and I am Brahman,' is said to be a *jīvanmukta*. He is said to be a *jīvanmukta*, who is aware: 'I am of the nature of the blissful and of the supreme bliss and I have neither body nor any other thing except the certitude "I am Brahman" only'. He is said to be a *jīvanmukta* who has not at all got the 'I' in himself but who stays in absolute consciousness alone, whose interior is consciousness alone, identical with consciousness, whose self is of the nature of the all-full, who is rooted in all, who is devoted to bliss, who is undifferentiated, who is all-full of the nature of consciousness, whose self is of the nature of pure consciousness, who has given up all affinities [for sense-objects], who has unconditioned bliss, whose self is tranquil, who has got no other thought [than itself], and who is devoid of the thought of the existence of anything. He is said to be a *jīvanmukta* who realises: 'I have no *citta*, no *buddhi*, no *ahaṅkāra*, no sense, no body at any time, no *prāṇas*, no *māyā*, no passion and no anger, I am the great, I have nothing of these objects or of the world and I have no sin, no characteristics, no eye, no manas, no ear, no nose, no tongue, no hand, no waking, no dreaming or causal state in the least or the fourth state.' He is said to be a *jīvanmukta*, who realises: 'All this is not mine, I have no time, no space, no object, no thought, no bathing (*snāna*), no junction-period ceremonies at dawn and twilight (*sandhyās*), no deity, no place, no sacred places, no worship, no spiritual wisdom, no seat, no relative, no birth, no speech, no wealth, no virtue, no vice, no duty, no auspiciousness, no *jīva,* not even the three worlds, no salvation, no duality, no Vedas, no prescribed rules, no proximity, no distance, no knowledge, no secrecy, no guru, no disciple, no diminution, no excess, no Brahmā, no Viṣṇu, no Rudra, no moon, no earth, no water, no air, no space, no fire, no clan, no [object aimed at], no mundane existence, no meditator, no object of meditation, no *manas*, no cold, no heat, no thirst, no hunger, no friend, no foe, no illusion, no victory, no past, present or future, no quarters, nothing to be said or heard in the least, nothing to be attained, nothing to be contemplated, enjoyed or remembered, no enjoyment, no desire, no yoga, no absorption, no garrulity, no quietude, no bondage, no love, no joy, no instant joy, no hugeness, no smallness, neither length nor shortness, neither increase nor decrease, neither *adhyāropa* (illusory attribution) nor *apavāda* (withdrawal of that conception) no oneness, no manyness, no blindness, no dullness, no skill, no flesh, no blood, no lymph, no skin, no marrow, no bone, none of the seven *dhātus*, no whiteness, no redness, no blueness, no heat, no gain, neither importance nor non-importance, no delusion, no perseverance, no mystery, no race, nothing to be abandoned or received, nothing to be laughed at, no policy, no religious vow, no fault, no bewailments, no happiness, neither knower nor knowledge nor the knowable, no self, nothing belonging to you or to me, neither you nor I and neither old age nor youth nor manhood; but I am certainly Brahman. I am certainly Brahman. I am *cit*, I am *cit*. He is said to be a *jīvanmukta* who cognizes: 'I am Brahman alone, I am *cit* alone, I am the supreme.' No doubt need be entertained about this; 'I am *haṃsa* itself, I remain of my own will, I can see myself through myself, I reign happy in the kingdom of self and enjoy in myself the bliss of my own true self.' He is *jīvanmukta* who is himself, the foremost and the one undaunted person who is himself the lord and rests in his own self.

"He is a *videhamukta* who has become Brahman, whose self has attained quiescence, who is of the nature of Brāhmic bliss, who is happy, who is of a pure nature, and who is a great sage. He is a *videhamukta* who remains in *cinmātra* alone without [even] thinking thus: 'I am all ātman, the ātman that is equal [or the same] in all, the pure, without one, the non-dual, the all, the self only, the birthless and the deathless—I am myself, the undecaying ātman that is the object aimed at, the sporting, the silent, the blissful, the beloved and the bondless salvation—I am Brahman alone—I am *cit* alone'. He is a *videhamukta* who having abandoned the thought: 'I alone am the Brahman' is filled with bliss. He is a *videhamukta* who having given up the certainty of the existence or non-existence of all objects, is the pure consciousness-bliss, who having abandoned [the thought]: 'I am Brahman' [or] 'I am not Brahman' does not mingle his ātman with anything, anywhere or at any time, who is ever silent with the silence of *satya*, who does nothing, who has gone beyond *guṇas*, whose self has become the all, the great, and the purifier of the elements, who does not cognize the change of time, matter, place himself or other differences, who does not see [the difference of] 'I', 'thou', 'this' or 'that', who being of the nature of times is yet without it, whose self is void, subtle and universal, but yet without [them], whose ātman is divine and yet without gods, whose ātman is measurable and yet without measure, whose ātman is without inertness and within everyone, who is devoid of any *saṅkalpa*, who thinks always: 'I am *cinmātra*, I am simply Paramātman, I am only of the nature of spiritual wisdom, I am only of the nature of *sat*, I am afraid of nothing in this world,' and who is without the conception of gods, Vedas and sciences, 'All this is consciousness,' etc., and regards all as void. He is a *videhamukta* who has realised himself to be *caitanya* alone, who is remaining at ease in the pleasure-garden of his own ātman whose ātman is of an illimitable nature, who is without conception of the small and the great and who is the fourth of the fourth state and the supreme bliss. He is a *videhamukta* whose ātman is nameless and formless, who is the great spiritual wisdom of the nature of bliss and of the nature of the state beyond *turya*, who is neither auspicious nor inauspicious, who has yoga as his ātman, whose ātman is associated with yoga, who is free from bondage or freedom, without *guṇa* or non-*guṇa*, without space, time, etc., without the witnessable and the witness, without the small or the great and without the cognition of the universe or even the cognition of the nature of Brahman, but who finds his spiritual effulgence in his own nature, who finds bliss in himself, whose bliss is beyond the scope of words and mind and whose thought is beyond the beyond. He is said to be a *videhamukta* who has gone beyond [or mastered quite] the modifications of *citta*, who illumines such modification and whose self is without any modifications at all. In that case, he is neither embodied nor disembodied. If such a thought is entertained [even] for a moment, then he is surrounded [in thought] by all. He is a *videhamukta* whose external ātman invisible to others is the supreme bliss aiming at the highest Vedānta, who drinks of the nectar of Brahman, who has the nectar of Brahman as medicine, who is devoted to the juice of the nectar of Brahman, who is immersed in that juice, who has the beneficent worship of the Brāhmic bliss, who is not satiated with the juice of the nectar of Brahman, who realises Brāhmic bliss, who cognizes the Śiva bliss in Brāhmic bliss, who has the effulgence of the essence of Brāhmic bliss, who has become one with it, who lives in the household of Brāhmic bliss, has mounted the vehicle of Brāhmic bliss, who has an imponderable *cit* being one with it, who is supporting [all], being full of it, who associates with me having it, who stays in ātman having that bliss and who thinks: 'All this is of the nature of self, there is nothing else beside ātman, all is ātman, I am ātman, the great self, the supreme ātman and ātman of the form of bliss.' He who thinks: 'My nature is full, I am the great ātman, I am the all-contented and the permanent ātman. I am the ātman pervading the heart of all, which is not stained by anything, but which has no ātman; I am the ātman whose nature is changeless, I am the quiescent self; and I am the many ātman.' He who does not think 'this is *jīvātman* and that is Paramātman, whose ātman is of the nature of the emancipated and the non-emancipated, but without emancipation or bondage, whose ātman is of the nature of the dual and the non-dual one, but without duality and non-duality; whose ātman is of the nature of the all and the non-all, but without them; whose ātman is of the nature of the happiness arising from objects obtained and enjoyed, but without it; and who is devoid of any *saṅkalpa*—such a man is a *videhamukta*. He whose ātman is partless, stainless, enlightened, Puruṣa, without bliss, etc., of the nature of nectar, of the nature of the three periods of time, but without them; whose ātman is entire and non-measurable, being subject to proof though without proof; whose ātman is the eternal and the witness, but without eternality and witness; whose ātman is one without the second, who is the self-luminous one without a second, whose ātman cannot be measured by *vidyā* and *avidyā* and is without them; whose ātman is conditional, who is without this or the higher worlds, is without the six virtues beginning with *śama*, without the qualification of the aspirant after salvation, is without gross, subtle, causal, and the fourth bodies and without the *anna, prāṇa*, *manas*, and *vijñāna* sheaths; whose ātman is of the nature of bliss-sheath, but without five sheaths; whose ātman is of the nature of *nirvikalpa*, is devoid of *saṅkalpa*, without the characteristics of the visible or the audible and of the nature of void, owing to unceasing samādhi, who is without beginning, middle or end; who is devoid of the word *prajñāna*, without the idea 'I am Brahman', devoid [of the thought] of 'thou art', without the thought 'this is ātman', devoid of that which is described by Oṃ, who is above the reach of any speech or the three states and is the indestructible and the *cidātman* whose ātman is not the one which can be known by ātman, which has neither light nor darkness, such a personage is a *videhamukta*. Look only upon self; know it as your own. Enjoy your self yourself and stay in peace. O six-faced one, be content in your own true self, be wandering in your own self, and be enjoying your own self. Then you will attain *videhamukti*."

CHAPTER V

The sage named Nidāgha addressed the venerable Ṛbhu: "O Lord please explain to me the discrimination of self from non-self." The sage replied thus:

"The furthest limit of all speech (*vāk*) is Brahman; the furthest limit to all thoughts is the guru. That which is of the nature of all causes and effects but yet without them, that which is without *saṅkalpa*, of the nature of all bliss and the auspicious, that which is the great one of the nature of bliss, that which illuminates all luminaries and that which is full of the bliss of spiritual sound (*nāda*), without any enjoyment and contemplation and beyond *nādas* and *kalās*—that is ātman, that is the 'I', the indestructible. Being devoid of all the difference of ātman and non-ātman, of heterogeneity and homogeneity and of quiescence and non-quiescence—that is the one light *(jyotis)* at the end of *nāda*. Being remote from the conception of *mahāvākyārtha* (i.e. the meaning of *mahāvākyas*) as well of 'I am Brahman', being devoid of or without the conception of the word and the meaning and being devoid of the conception of the destructible and indestructible—that is the one *(jyotis)* at the end of *nāda*. Being without the conception 'I am the partless non-dual essence' or 'I am the blissful', and being of the nature of the one beyond all—that is the one *jyotis* at the end of *nāda*. He who is devoid of *saccidānanda*—he is alone ātman, the eternal. He who is undefinable and unreachable by the words of the Vedas, who has neither externals, nor internals and whose symbol is either the universe or Brahman—he is undoubtedly ātman. He who has no body, nor is a *jīva* made up of the elements and their compounds, who has neither form nor name, neither the enjoyable nor the enjoyer, neither *sat* nor *asat*, neither preservation nor regeneration, neither *guṇa* nor non-*guṇa*—that is undoubtedly my ātman. He who has neither the described nor description, neither *śravaṇa* nor *manana*, neither guru nor disciple, neither the world of the gods nor the gods nor demons, neither duty nor non-duty, neither the immaculate nor non-immaculate, neither time nor non-time, neither certainty nor doubt, neither mantra nor non-mantra, neither science nor non-science, neither the seer nor the seen which is subtle, nor the nectar of time—that is ātman. Rest assured that non-*ātman* is a misnomer. There is no *manas* as non-ātman. There is no world as non-ātman. Owing to the absence of all *saṅkalpas* and to the giving up of all actions, Brahman alone remains, and there is no non-ātman. Being devoid of the three bodies, the three periods of time, the three qualities of *jīva*, the three pains and the three worlds, and following the saying 'All is Brahman,' know that there is nothing to be known through the absence of *citta*; there is no old age through the absence of body; no motion through the absence of legs; no action through the absence of hands; no death through the absence of creatures; no happiness through the absence of *buddhi*; no virtue, no purity, no fear, no repetition of mantras, no guru nor disciple. There is no second in the absence of one. Where there is not the second, there is not the first. Where there is truth alone, there is no non-truth possible; where there is non-truth alone there is no truth possible. If you regard a thing auspicious as inauspicious, then auspiciousness is desired [as separate] from inauspiciousness. If you regard fear as non-fear, then fear will arise out of non-fear. If bondage should become emancipation, then in the absence of bondage will be no emancipation. If birth should imply death, then in the absence of birth, there is no death. If 'thou' should imply 'I', then in the absence of 'thou' there is no 'I'. If 'this' should be 'that', 'this' does not exist in the absence of 'that.' If being should imply non-being, then non-being will imply being. If an effect implies a cause, then in the absence of effect, there is no cause. If duality implies non-duality, then in the absence of duality, there is no non-duality. If there should be the seen, then there is the seer; in the absence of the seen, there is no seer. In the absence of the interior, there is no exterior. If there should be fullness, then non-fullness is possible. Therefore [all] this exists nowhere. Neither you nor I, nor this nor these exist. There exists no [object of] comparison in the true one. There is no simile in the unborn. There is [in it] no mind to think. I am the supreme Brahman. This world is Brahman only. Thou and I are Brahman only. I am *cinmātra* simply, and there is no non-ātman. Rest assured of it. This universe is not [really at all]. It was nowhere produced and stays nowhere. Some say that *citta* is the universe. Not at all. It exists not. Neither the universe nor *citta* nor *ahaṃkāra* nor *jīva* exists. Neither the creation of *māyā* itself exists. Fear does not [really] exist. Actor, action, hearing thinking, the two *samādhis*, the measurer, the measure, *ajñāna*, *aviveka*—none of these exists [truly] anywhere. Therefore the four moving considerations [viz.the subject (Brahman), object, relationship and the qualified person] and the three kinds of relationship exist not. There is no Gaṅgā, no Gayā, no bridge (*setu*), no elements or anything else, no earth, water, fire, air, and space anywhere, no gods, no guardians of the four quarters, no Vedas, no guru, no distance, no proximity, no time, no middle, no non-duality, no truth, no untruth, no bondage, no emancipation, no *sat*, no *asat*, no happiness, etc., no class, no motion, no caste, and no worldly business. All is Brahman only and nothing else—all is Brahman only and nothing else. There exists then nothing as that 'consciousness alone is'; there is [then] no saying such as '*cit* is I'. The statement 'I am Brahman' does not exist [then]; nor does exist [then] the statement: 'I am the eternally pure'. Whatever is uttered by the mouth, whatever is thought by *manas*, whatever is determined by *buddhi*, whatever is cognized by *citta*—all these do not exist. There is no yogin or yoga then. All are and are not. Neither day nor night, neither bathing nor contemplating, neither delusion nor non-delusion—all these do not exist then. Know that is no non-ātman.

"The Vedas, science, Purāṇas, effect and cause, Īśvara and the world and the elements and mankind—all these are unreal. There is no doubt of it. Bondage, salvation, happiness, relatives, meditation, *citta*, the gods, the demons, the secondary and the primary, the high and the low—all these are unreal. There is no doubt of it. Whatever is uttered by the mouth, whatever is willed by *saṅkalpa*, whatever is thought by manas—all these are unreal. Whatever is determined by buddhi, whatever is cognized by *citta*, whatever is discussed by the religious books, whatever is seen by the eye and heard by the ears, and whatever exists as *sat*, as also the ear, the eye, and the limbs—all these are unreal. Whatever is described as such and such, whatever is thought as so-and-so, all the existing thoughts such as 'thou art I', 'that is this', and 'He is I', and whatever happens in mokṣa, as also all *saṅkalpa*, delusion, illusory attribution, mysteries and all the diversities of enjoyment and sin—all these do not exist. So is also non-ātman. Mine and thine, my and thy, for me and for thee, by me and by thee—all these are unreal. [The statement] that Viṣṇu is the preserver, Brahmā is the creator, Rudra is the destroyer—know that these undoubtedly are false. Bathing, utterings of mantras, religious austerities (*tapas*), sacrifice (*homa*), study of the Vedas, worship of the devas, mantra, tantra, association with the good, the unfolding of the faults of *guṇas*, the working of the internal organ, the result of *avidyā* and the many crores of mundane eggs—all these are unreal. Whatever is spoken of as true according to the verdict of all teachers, whatever is seen in this world and whatever exists—all these are unreal. Whatever is uttered by words, whatever is ascertained, spoken, enjoyed, given or done by anyone, whatever action is done, good or bad, whatever is done as truth—know all these to be ureal. Thou alone art the transcendental ātman and the supreme guru of the form, of space, which is devoid of fitness [for it] and of the nature of all creatures. Thou art Brahman; thou art time; and thou art Brahman, that is ever and imponderable. Thou art everywhere, of all forms, and full of consciousness. Thou art the truth. Thou art one that has mastered the *siddhis*, and thou art the ancient, the emancipated, emancipation, the nectar of bliss, the god, the quiescent, the diseaseless, Brahman the full, and greater than the great. Thou art impartial, *saṭ* and the ancient knowledge, recognised by the words 'truth, etc'. Thou art devoid of all parts. Thou art the ever-existing—thou appear as Brahmā, Rudra, Indra, etc.—thou art above the illusion of the universe—shining in all elements—thou art without *saṅkalpa* in all—thou art known by means of the underlying meaning of all scriptures; thou art ever content; thou art without motion, etc. In all things, thou art without any characteristics; in all things thou art contemplated by Viṣṇu and other gods at all times; thou art the nature of *cit*, abiding *cinmātrā* in ātman itself, void of everything and without *guṇas*, blissful, the great, the one without a second, the state of *sat*, and *asat*, the knower, the known, the seer, the nature of being-consciousness-bliss, the lord of gods, the all-pervading, the deathless, the moving, the motionless, the all and the non-all, with quiescence and non-quiescence, *sat* alone, *sat* commonly [found in all], of the form of *nitya-siddha* (the eternally powerful one), and yet devoid of all *siddhis*. There is not an atom which thou do not permeate yet thou art without it. Thou art devoid of existence and non-existence as also the aim and object aimed at. Thou art changeless, decayless, beyond all *nādas*, without *kāla* or *kāṣṭha* (divisions of time) and without Brahmā, Viṣṇu and Śiva. Thou perceive into the nature of each and art beyond their nature. Thou art immersed in the bliss of self. Thou art the monarch of the kingdom of self and yet without the conception of self. Thou art of the nature of fullness and incompleteness. There is nothing that thou seest which is not in thyself. Thou dost not stir out of thy nature. Thou actest according to the nature of each. Thou art nothing but the nature of each. Have no doubt 'Thou art I'.

"This universe and everything in it, whether the seer or the seen, resembles the horns of a hare [or are illusory]. Earth, water, fire, air, space, *manas*, *buddhi*, *ahaṃkāra*, light, the worlds and the sphere of the universe, destruction, birth, truth, virtue, vice, gain, desires, passion, anger, greed, the object of meditation, wisdom, guru, disciple, limitation, the beginning and end, auspiciousness, the past, present, and future, the aim and the object of aim, mental restraint, inquiry, contentment, enjoyer, enjoyment, etc., the eight parts of yoga, *yama*, etc., the going and coming [of life], the beginning, middle and end, that which can be taken and rejected, Hari, Śiva, the organs, manas, the three states, the twenty-four *tattvas*, the four means, one of the same class or different classes, earth, and other worlds, all the castes and orders of life with the rules laid down for each, mantras and tantras, science and nescience, all the Vedas, the inert and the non-inert, bondage and salvation, spiritual wisdom and non-wisdom, the enlightened and the non-enlightened, duality and non-duality, the conclusion of all Vedāntas and śāstras, the theory of the existence of all souls and that of One only, whatever is thought by *citta*, whatever is willed by *saṅkalpa*, whatever is determined by *buddhi*, whatever one hears and sees, whatever the guru instructs, whatever is sensed by all the organs, whatever is discussed in Mīmāṃsā, whatever is ascertained by philosophy (Nyāya) and by the great ones who have reached the other side of the Vedas, the saying 'Śiva destroys the world, Viṣṇu protects it, and Brahmā creates it', whatever is found in the Purāṇas, whatever is ascertained by the Vedas and is the signification of all the Vedas—all these resemble the horns of a hare. The conception 'I am the body' is spoken of as the internal organ; the conception 'I am the body' is spoken of as the great mundane existence; the conception 'I am the body' constitutes the whole universe. The conception 'I am the body' is spoken of as the knot of the heart, as non-wisdom, as the state of *asat*, as nescience, as the dual, as the true *jīva* and as with parts, is certainly the great sin and is the disease generated by the fault of thirst after desires. That which is *saṅkalpa*, the three pains, passion, anger, bondage, all the miseries, all the faults and the various forms of time—know these to be the result of *manas*. *Manas* alone is the whole world, the ever-deluding, the mundane existence, the three worlds, the great sorrows, the old age and others, death and the great sin, the *saṅkalpa*, the *jīva*, the *citta*, the *ahaṅkāra*, the bondage, the internal organ and earth, water, fire, air and space. Sound, touch, form, taste, and odour, the five sheaths, the waking, the dreaming, and dreamless sleep states, the guardians of the eight quarters, Vasus, Rudras, Ādityas, the seen, the inert, the pairs and non-wisdom—all these are the products of manas. Rest assured that there is no reality in all that is *saṅkalpa*. The whole world, the guru, disciple, etc., do not exist, do not exist. Thus ends the fifth chapter of this Upaniṣad."

CHAPTER VI

Ṛbhu continued again: "Know everything as *saccinmaya*, full of being and consciousness. It pervades everything. *Saccidānanda* is non-dual, decayless, alone and other than all. It is 'I'. It alone is space and 'thou'. It is I. Untinged with *manas*, *buddhi*, *ahaṃkāra*, *citta*, or the collection of these—neither 'thou' nor I, nor anything else nor everything. Brahman alone is. Sentence, words, Vedas, letters, beginning, middle or end, truth, law, pleasure, pain, existence, *māyā, prakṛti*, body, face, nose, tongue, palate, teeth, lip, forehead, expiration and inspiration, sweat, bone, blood, urine, distance, proximity, limb, belly, crown, the movement of hands and feet, śāstras, command, the knower, the known, and the knowledge, the waking, dreaming and dreamless sleep and the fourth state—all these do not belong to me. Everthing is pure consciousness interwoven. No attributes pertaining to body, elements and spirit, no root, no vision, no *taijasa*, no *prājña*, no *virāṭ*, no *sūtrātman*, no Īśvara, and no going or coming, neither gain nor loss, neither the acceptable nor the rejectable, nor the censurable, neither the pure nor the impure, neither the stout nor the lean, no sorrow, time, space, speech, all fear, duality, tree, grass or mountain, no meditation, no *siddhi* of yoga, no Brāhmaṇa, Kṣatriya or Vaiśya, no bird or beast, or limb, no greed, delusion, pride, malice, passion, anger or others, no woman, Śudra, castes or others, nothing that is eatable or enjoyable, no increase or decrease, no belief in the Vedas, no speech, no worldliness or unworldliness, no transaction, no folly, no measure or measured, no enjoyment or enjoyed, no friends, son, etc. father, mother or sister, no birth or death, no growth, body or 'I', no emptiness or fullness, no internal organs or mundane existence, no night, no day, no Brahmā, Viṣṇu or Śiva, no week, fortnight, month or year, no unsteadiness, no Brahmaloka, Vaikuṇṭha, Kailāśa and others, no *svarga*, Indra, Agniloka, Agni, Yamaloka, Yama, Vāyuloka, guardians of the world, three worlds—*bhūḥ, bhuvaḥ, svaḥ, pātāla* or surface of earth, no science, nescience, *māyā, prakṛti*, inertness, permanency, transience, destruction, movement, running, object of meditation, bathing, mantra or object, no adorable object, anointment or sipping with water, no flower, fruit, sandal, lustration of lamp before god, praise, prostrations or circumambulation, no entreaty, conception of separateness even oblation of food, offered food, sacrifice, actions, abuse, praise, *gāyatrī* and twilight (*sandhi*), no mental state, calamity, evil desire, bad soul, low caste person, unbearableness, unspeakableness, hunter (*kirāta*), demon (*kaiṭava*), partiality, partisanship, ornament, chief, or pride, no manyness, no oneness, durability, triad, tetrad, greatness, smallness, fullness or delusion, Banares, *tapas*, clan, family, *sūtra*, greatness, poverty, girl, old woman or widow, no pollution, birth, introvision or illusion, no sacred sentences, identity, or the *siddhis, aṇimā*, etc.

"Everything being consciousness alone, there is no fault in anything. Everything being of the nature of *sat* alone is being-consciousness-bliss only. Brahman alone is everything and there is nothing else. 'That' is 'I', 'That' is 'I'. 'That' alone is 'I'. 'That' alone is 'I'. 'That' alone is 'I'. The eternal Brahman alone is 'I'. I am Brahman alone without being subject to mundane existence. I am Brahman alone without any manas, any buddhi, organs or body. I am Brahman alone and not perceivable. I am Brahman alone and not *jīva*. I am Brahman alone and not liable to change. I am Brahman alone and not inert. I am Brahman alone and have no death. I am Brahman alone and greater than the great. This is Brahman. Great is Brahman. Truth is Brahman. It is all-pervading. Time is Brahman. Kāla is Brahman. Bliss is Brahman. It is self-shining. One is Brahman. Two is Brahman. Delusion is Brahman. Sama and others are Brahman. Badness is Brahman. Goodness is Brahman. It is of the form of restraint, quiescence, the all-pervading and the all-powerful. The world (*loka*) is Brahman. Guru is Brahman. Disciple is Brahman. It is Sadāśiva. [That which] is before is Brahman. [That which will be] hereafter is Brahman. Purity is Brahman. Auspiciousness and inauspiciousness are Brahman. *Jīva* always is Brahman. I am being-consciousness and bliss. All are of the nature of Brahman. Brahman is itself. Of this there is no doubt. There is nothing out of itself. The letter Oṃ of the form of consciousness is Brahman alone. Everything is itself. I alone am the whole universe and the highest seat, have crossed the *guṇas* and am greater than the great, the supreme Brahman, guru of gurus, the support of all and the bliss of bliss. There is no universe besides the self. The universe is of the nature of self. There is no place without self. There is not even grass different from Brahman. There is no husk different from Brahman. The whole universe is of the nature of ātman. All this is of the nature of Brahman. *Asat* is not of the nature of Brahman. There is not a seat different from Brahman; there is not a guru different from Brahman; there is not a body different from Brahman. There is nothing different from Brahman like I-ness or you-ness. Whatever is seen in this world, whatever is spoken of by the people, whatever is enjoyed everywhere—all these are *asat* (unreal) only. The differences arising from the actor, action, qualities, likes, taste and gender—all these arise from *asat* and are [but] pleasurable. The differences arising from time, objects, actions, success or defeat and whatever else—all these are simply *asat*. The internal organ is *asat*. The organs are *asat*. All the prāṇas, the collections of all these, the five sheaths, the five deities, the six changes, the six enemies, the six seasons, and the six tastes, are non-real. I am being-consciousness and bliss. The universe is rootless. I am ātman alone, *cit* and *ānanda*. The scenes of mundane existence are not different. I am the Truth of the nature of bliss and of the nature of the imponderable *cit*. All this is of the nature of *jñāna*.

"I am the secondless, having knowledge and bliss. I am of the nature of an illuminator of all things. I am of the nature of all non-being. I alone shine always. Therefore how can I with such a nature become unreal? That which is called 'thou' is the great Brahman of the nature of the bliss of consciousness and of the nature of *cit* having void of consciousness and *cit* alone as the great bliss. Ātman alone is 'I'. *Asat* is not 'I'. I am *kūṭastha*, the great guru and being-consciousness and bliss alone. I am this born universe. No time, no universe, no *māyā*, no *prakṛti* [in me]. I alone am Hari, I alone am Sadāśiva. I am of the nature of pure consciousness. I am the enjoyer of pure essence. I am the only essence of the all-latent and the all-witness. I am the supreme ātman, the supreme light, the supreme wealth, the supreme goal, the essence of all Vedāntas, the subject discussed in all the śāstras, the nature of yogic bliss, the ocean of the supreme bliss, the effulgence of all wisdom, of the nature of supreme wisdom, the effulgence of the fourth state and the non-fourth, but devoid of them, the indestructible *cit*, truth, Vāsudeva, the birthless, and the deathless Brahmā, the void of consciousness, the unconditioned, the stainless, the immaculate, the emancipated, the utterly emancipated, the soulless, the formless and of the nature of the non-created universe.

"The universe which is assumed as truth and non-truth does not really exist. Brahman is of the nature of eternal bliss and is even by itself. It is endless, decayless, quiescent and of one nature only. If anything is other than myself, then it is as unreal as the mirage in an oasis. If one should be afraid of the son of a barren woman, or if a powerful elephant be killed by means of the horns of a hare, then the world [really is]. If one [person] can quench his thirst by drinking the waters of the mirage or if one should be killed by the horns of a man, then the universe really is. The universe exists always in the true Gandhāra city [merely unreal]. When the blueness of the sky really exists in it, then the universe really is. When the silver in mother-of-pearl can be used in making an ornament, when a man is bitten by [the conception of] a snake in a rope, when the flaming fire is quenched by means of a golden arrow, when milky food is obtained in the [barren] forest of Vindhya [mountains], when cooking can take place by means of the fuel of [wet] plantain trees, when a female [baby] just born begins to cook, when curds resume the state of milk, or when the milk [milked] goes back through the teats of a cow, then will the universe really be. When the dust of the earth shall be produced in the ocean, when the maddened elephant is tied by means of the hair of a tortoise, when [mountain] Meru is shaken by the thread in the stalk of a lotus, when the ocean is bound by its rows of tides, when the fire flames downwards, when flame shall become [really] cold, when the lotus shall grow out of flaming fire, when Indranīla (sapphire) arises in the great mountains, when Meru comes and sits in the lotus-eye, when a mountain can become the offspring of a black bee, when Meru shall shake, when a lion is killed by a gnat, when the three worlds can be found in the space of the hollow of an atom, when the fire which burns a straw shall last for a long time, when the objects seen in a dream shall come in the waking state, when the current of a river shall stand still, when the delivery of a barren woman shall be fruitful, when the crow shall walk like a swan, when the mule shall fight with a lion, when a great ass shall walk like an elephant, when the full moon shall become a sun, when Rāhu shall abandon the sun and the moon, when a good crop shall arise out of the waste [burnt] seeds, when the poor shall enjoy the happiness of the rich, when the lions shall be conquered by the bravery of dogs, when the heart of *jñānins* is known by fools, when the ocean is drunk by the dogs without any remainder, when the pure sky *(ākāśa)* shall fall upon men, when heaven shall fall on the earth, when the flower in the sky shall emit fragrance, when a forest appearing in pure sky, shall move, and when reflection shall arise in a glass simply [without mercury or anything else], then the world really is. There is no universe in the womb of the unborn Brahman—there is no universe in the womb of ātman. Duality and non-duality, which are but the result of differentiation, are really not. All this is the result of *māyā*. Therefore, there should be *brahma-bhāvanā*. If misery should arise from the conception of 'I am the body', then it is certain 'I am Brahman.' The knot of the heart is the wheel of Brahman, which cuts asunder the knot of existence. When doubt arises in one, he should have faith in Brahman. That non-dual Brahman, which is eternal and of the form of unconditioned bliss, is the guard of real self against the not-self. Through instances like the above is established the nature of Brahman. Brahman alone is the all-abode. Abandon the name even of the universe. Knowing for certain 'I am Brahman', give up the 'I'. Everything disappears as the flower from the hands of a sleeping person. There is neither body nor *karma*. Everything is Brahman alone. There are neither objects, nor actions, nor the four states. Everything which has the three characteristics of *vijñāna* is Brahman alone. Abandoning all action, contemplate 'I am Brahman. I am Brahman of the nature of *cit*. I am of the nature of being-consciousness and bliss.'

"This great science of Śaṅkara should never be explained to any ordinary person, to an atheist or to a faithless, ill-behaved or evil-minded person. It should be, after due examination, given to the high-souled ones whose minds are purified with devotion to their gurus. It should be taught for a year and a half. Leaving off thoroughly and entirely the practice recommended by the [other] Upaniṣads, one should study the Tejobindu-Upaniṣad always with delight. By once studying it, he becomes one with Brahman. Thus ends the sixth chapter."

Oṃ tat sat is the Upaniṣad

13
Brahma Upaniṣad of Kṛṣṇa Yajurveda

Oṃ. Śaunaka Mahāśāla questioned the holy sage Pippalāda of the Aṅgiras *gotra* thus: "In this beautiful Brahmapura of body, the fit residence of divine beings, how are [the deities of] *vāc*, etc., located? How do they function? To whom belongs this power? He to whom this power belongs, what is he?"

Pippalāda, then having deeply considered, imparted to him the divine wisdom *(brahma-vidyā)*, that most excellent of all things. "It is *prāṇa* (i.e.), ātmā that exercises this power. It is life of all gods. It is their death and [their] life. Brahman that shines pure, partless, resplendent and all-pervading in this divine *brahmapura* [of body], rules [all]. The *jīva* [identifying himself with] the senses, rules them like a spider. The spider throws, from a single thread out of his body a whole web and draws it into himself by that same thread; so *prāṇa*, whenever it goes, draws after it the objects of its creation. During *suṣupti*, [the *prāṇa*] goes to its seat (Brahman) through the *nāḍis* of which is the god, like an eagle that making air as the means of communication, reaches his abode. They say, as Devadatta, though beaten [during dreamless-sleeps] by a stick, etc., does not move, so also the actor does not suffer or enjoy for the merits or demerits of religious actions. Just as a child obtains happiness without desiring for it [in play], so also Devadatta obtains happiness in *suṣupti.* He certainly knows [being] supreme light and the person desiring light, enjoys bliss in the contemplation of light. Then he comes back to the dream-plane by the same way, like a caterpillar. Remaining on a blade of grass, the caterpiller first puts forward its foot on another blade in front, conveys its body to it, and having got a firm hold of it, then only leaves the former and not before. So this is the *jāgrat*-state. As this (Devadatta) bears at the same time eight skulls, so this *jāgrat*, the source of gods and Vedas, clings to a man like the breasts in a woman. During the waking-state, merit and demerit are postulated of this power; he is capable of great expansion and is the inner mover. He is bird *(khaga)*, crab *(karkaṭa)*, lotus *(puṣkara)*, space *(prāṇa)*, is both inner and outer, above and below, he is ātman and Brahman. This deity causes to know. He who knows thus obtains Brahman, the supreme, the support of all things and the knower of the field *(kṣetrajña)*. He obtains Brahman, the supreme, support of all things, and the *kṣetrajña.*

"The Puruṣa has four seats—navel, heart, neck, and head. There Brahman with the four feet specially shines. Those feet are waking *(jāgrat),* dreaming *(svapna)*, dreamless-sleep *(suṣupti)* and the fourth-state *(turya)*. In *jāgrat* he is Brahmā, in *svapna* Viṣṇu, in *suṣupti* Rudra, and in *turya* the supreme *akṣara*. He is Āditya, Viṣṇu, Īśvara, Puruṣa, *prāṇa*, *jīva*, *agni*, the resplendent. The Parabrahman shines in the midst of these. He is without manas, ears, hands, feet, and light. There, the worlds are no worlds, devas no devas, Vedas no Vedas, sacrifices no sacrifices, mother no mother, father no father, daughter-in-law no daughter-in-law, *caṇḍāla* no *caṇḍāla, paulkasa* no *paulkasa*, *śramaṇa* no *śramaṇa,* hermits no hermits; so only Brahman shines as different. In the space in the heart *(hṛdayākāśa)* is the *cidākāśa*. That is Brahman. It is extremely subtle. The *hṛdayākāśa* can be known. This moves in it. In Brahman, everything is strung. Those who thus know the Lord know everything. In him the gods, the worlds, the ancestors *(pitṛs)* and the sages do not rule. He who has awakened knows everything. All the gods are in the heart; in the heart are all the *prāṇas*: in the heart are *prāṇa, jyotis* and that three-plied holy thread. In the heart *prāṇa* is. This mantra is recited whenever the holy thread is worn:

> *Put on the holy thread (yajñopavīta), the supreme, the holy, which came into existence along with Prajāpati, which gives long life and which is very excellent; let this give you strength and tejas.*

The wise man having shaved his head completely, should throw away the external thread. He should wear, as the holy thread, the supreme and indestructible Brahman. It is called *sūtra*, because *sūcanāt* indicates that the ātman is in the heart. *Sūtra* means the supreme abode. He who knows that *sūtra* is a Brāhmaṇa (*vipra*), he has crossed the ocean of the Vedas. On that thread (*sūtra*), everything is strung, like the beads on the thread. The yogin, well versed in yoga and having a clear perception of truth, should wear the thread. Practising the noble yoga, the wise man should abandon the external thread. He who wears the *sūtra* as Brahman, he is an intelligent being. By wearing the *sūtra*, he is not polluted. They whose *sūtra* is within, whose *yajñopavīta* is *jñāna*—they only know the *sūtra*, and they only wear the *yajñopavīta* in this world. Those whose tuft of hair is *jñāna*, who are firmly grounded in *jñāna* and whose *yajñopavīta* is *jñāna*, consider *jñāna* only as supreme. *Jñāna* is holy and excellent. He whose tuft of hair *(śikhā)* is *jñāna* like the *śikhi* flame of Agni—he, the wise one, only wears a true *śikhā*; others wear a mere tuft of hair. Those Brāhmaṇas and others who perform the ceremonies prescribed in the Vedas—they wear this thread only as a symbol of their ceremonies. Those who know the Vedas say that he only is a true Brāhmaṇa who wears the *śikhā* of *jñāna* and whose *yajñopavīta* is the same [*jñāna*]. This *yajñopavīta*. *Yajña* means Viṣṇu or sacrifice and *upavīta* is that which surrounds; hence that which surrounds Viṣṇu is supreme and is the supreme refuge. He who wears that really knows—he only wears the *sūtra*, he is *yajña* (Viṣṇu) and he only knows *yajña* (Viṣṇu). One God hidden in all things, pervades all things and is the inner life of all things. He awards the fruits of *karma*, he lives in all things, he sees all things without any extraneous help, he is the soul of all, there is nothing like him and he is without any *guṇas*. He is the great wise one. He is the one doer among the many actionless objects. He is always making one thing appear as manifold. Those wise men who see him in *buddhi*, they only obtain eternal peace. Having made ātman as the [upper] *araṇi* (attritional piece of wood) and *praṇava* the lower *araṇi*, by constant practice of *dhyāna* one should see the concealed deity. As the oil in the sesamum seed, as the ghee in the curds, as the water in the rivers and as the fire in the *araṇi*, so they who practise truth and austerities see him in the *buddhi*. As the spider throws out and draws into itself the threads, so the *jīva* goes and returns during the *jāgrat* and the *svapna* states. The heart is in the form of a closed lotus-flower, with its head hanging down; it has a hole in the top. Know it to be the great abode of all. Know that during *jāgrat,* the *jīva* dwells in the eye and during *svapna* in the throat; during *suṣupti*, it is in the heart and during *turya* in the head. [Because *buddhi* unites] the *pratyagātma* with the Paramātmā, the worship of union *(sandhyā)* arose. So we should perform rites *(sandhyā-vandanā)*. The *sandhyā-vandana* performed by *dhyāna* requires no water. It gives no trouble to the body or the speech. That which unites all things is the *sandhyā* of the one-staffed *(sannyāsins)*. Knowing that from which speech and mind turn back without being able to obtain it and that which is the bliss of *jīva*, the wise one is freed. The secret of *brahmavidyā* is to reveal the real nature of the ātman that is all-pervading, that is like ghee in the milk, that is the source of *ātma-vidya* and *tapas* and to show that everything is in essence one.

Oṃ tat sat is the Upaniṣad

14
Vajrasūci Upaniṣad of Sāmaveda

I now proceed to declare the *vajrasūci* (the diamond needle) the weapon that is the destroyer of ignorance—which condemns the ignorant and praises the man of divine vision. There are four castes—the Brāhmaṇa, the Kṣatriya, the Vaiśya, and the Śūdra. Even the Smṛtis declare in accordance with the words of the Vedas that the Brāhmaṇa alone is the most important of them.

It remains to be examined. What is meant by Brāhmaṇa? Is it a *jīva*? Is it a body? Is it a class? Is it *jñāna*? Is it *karma*? Or is it a doer of dharma?

To begin with: is *jīva* the Brāhmaṇa? No. Since the *jīva* is the same in the many past and future bodies [of all persons] and since the *jīva* is the same in all of the many bodies obtained through the force of *karma*, therefore *jīva* is not the Brāhmaṇa.

Then is the body the Brāhmaṇa? No. since the body, as it is made up of the five elements, is the same for all people down to *caṇḍālas*, etc., since old age and death, dharma and *adharma* are found to be common to them all, since there is no absolute distinction that the Brāhmaṇas are white-coloured, the Kṣatriyas red, the Vaiśyas yellow and the Śūdras dark and since in burning the corpse of his father, the stain of the murder of the Brāhmaṇa will accrue to the son, therefore the body is not the Brāhmaṇa.

Then is a class the Brāhmaṇa? No. Since many great sages have sprung from other castes and orders of creation—Ṛṣyaṣṛṅga was born of deer; Kauśika, of *kuśa* grass; Jāmbuka of a jackal; Vālmīki is *valmīka* (an ant-hill); Vyāsa of a fisherman's daughter; Gautama, of the posteriors of a hare; Vasiṣṭha of Ūrvaśī and Agastya of a water-pot; thus have we heard. Of these, many sages outside the caste even have stood first among the teachers of divine wisdom; therefore a class is not the Brāhmaṇa.

Is *jñāna* the Brāhmaṇa? No. Since there were many Kṣatriyas and others well versed in the cognition of divine truth, therefore *jñāna* is not the Brāhmaṇa.

Then is *karma* the Brāhmaṇa? No. Since the *prārabdha*, *sañcita*, and *āgāmi karmas* are the same for all beings, and since all people perform their actions as impelled by *karma*, therefore *karma* is not the Brāhmaṇa.

Then is a doer of virtuous actions (dharma) the Brāhmaṇa? No. Since there are many Kṣatriyas, etc., who are givers of gold, therefore a doer of virtuous actions is not the Brāhmaṇa.

Who indeed then is Brāhmaṇa? Whoever he may be, he who has directly realised his ātman and who is directly cognizant, like the myrobalan in his palm, of his ātman that is without a second, that is devoid of class and actions, that is free from the faults of the six stains [viz. hunger, thirst, grief, confusion, old age and death]and the six changes, that is of the nature of truth, knowledge, bliss, and eternity, that is without any change in itself, that is the substratum of all the *kalpas*, that exists penetrating all things, that pervades everything within and without as space, that is of the nature of undivided bliss, that cannot be reasoned about and that is known only by direct cognition. He, who by the reason of having obtained his wishes, is devoid of the faults of thirst after worldly objects and passions, who is the possessor of the qualifications beginning with the six virtues: *śama*, *dama*, *uparati*, *titikṣā*, *samādhāna* and *śraddhā*, who is free from emotion, malice, thirst after worldly objects desire, delusion, etc., whose mind is untouched by pride, egoism etc., who possesses all these qualities and means—he only is the Brāhmaṇa.

Such is the opinion of the Vedas, the Smṛtis, the Itihāsa and the Purāṇas. Otherwise one cannot obtain the status of a Brāhmaṇa. One should meditate on his ātman as being-consciousness and bliss and the non-dual Brahman. Yes, one should meditate on his ātman as the being-conciousness and bliss [of] Brahman.

Oṃ tat sat is the Upaniṣad

15
Śārīraka Upaniṣad of Kṛṣṇa Yajurveda

Oṃ. The body is a compound of earth (*pṛthivī*) and other primordial elements, as water, fire or air and space. [In the body], that which is hard is [of the essence of] earth; that which is liquid is [of the essence of] water; that which is hot is [of the essence of] fire; that which moves about is [of the essence of] air; that which is perforated is [of the essence of] space. The ear is of the essence of space, the skin of the essence of air, the eye of the essence of fire, the tongue of the essence of water and the nose of the essence of earth; sound, touch, form, taste and odour being respectively the objects of perception for these organs. These arose respectively out of the primordial elements, beginning with earth. The mouth, the hands, the legs, the organs of excretion and the organs of generation are the organs of action. Their functions are respectively talking, lifting, walking, excretion, and enjoyment. *Antaḥkaraṇa* (or the internal organ) is of four kinds—*manas*, *buddhi*, *ahaṅkāra*, and *citta*. Their functions are respectively *saṅkalpa-vikalpa*, (resolve and doubt), determination, egoism, and memory. The seat of *manas* is the end of the throat, that of *buddhi* the face, that of *ahaṅkāra* the heart, and that of *citta* the navel. The bone, skin, *nāḍīs*, nerves, hair and flesh are of the essence of earth. Urine, phlegm, blood and sperm (*śukla*) and sweat are of the essence of water. Hunger, thirst, sloth, delusion and [desire of] copulation are of the essence of fire. Walking, scratching, opening and closing the gross eyes, etc., are of the essence of air. Desire, anger, avarice, delusion and fear are of the essence of space. Sound, touch, form, taste and odour are the properties of earth: sound, touch, form, and taste are the properties of water: sound, touch and form, are the properties of fire: sound and touch are the properties of air: sound alone is the property of space. There are three qualities: *sāttvika, rājasa,* and *tāmasa.* Non-killing, veracity, not stealing, continence, non-covetousness, refraining from anger, serving the guru, purity [in mind and body], contentment, right conduct, abstinence from self-praise, freedom from pompousness, firm conviction in the existence of God and not causing any injury to others—all these are to be known as *sāttvika-guṇas* chiefly. I am the actor, I am the enjoyer, I am the speaker and I am the egoistic—such are said by knowers of Brahman to be *rājasa-guṇas*. Sleep, sloth, delusion, desire, copulation and theft are said by expounders of the Vedas to be *tāmasa-guṇas*. Those having *sattva-guṇa* [go] up [viz. to higher spheres]—those having *tāmasa-guṇa* [go] down [viz. to hell, etc.]. Perfect [or divine] knowledge is of *sāttvika-guṇa*; knowledge of dharma is of *rājasa-guṇa*, and mental darkness is of *tāmasa*. The waking state *(jāgrat)*, dreaming state *(svapna)*, the state of dreamless sleep *(suṣupti)* and the state beyond these three *(turya)* are the four states. *Jāgrata* is [the state] having [the play of] the fourteen organs: the organs of sense [five], the organs of action [five], and the four internal organs. *Svapna* is [the state] associated with the four internal organs. *Suṣupti* is [the state] where the *citta* is the only organ. *Turya* is that state having *jīva* alone. Regarding *jīvātman* and Paramātman [enjoying the three states] of a person with opened eyes, with closed eyes and with eyes in an intermediate state with neither, *jīva* is said to be the *kṣetrajña* (the lord of the body). The organs of sense [five], the organs of action [five], *prāṇas* [five], *manas*, and *buddhi*—all these seventeen are said to constitute the *sūkṣma* or *liṅga* [viz. subtle] body. *Manas, buddhi, ahaṅkāra,* space, air, fire, water, and earth—these are the eight *prakṛtis* (or matter): ear, skin, eye, tongue, nose, the fifth, the organs of excretion, the organs of secretion, hands, legs, speech the tenth, sound, form, touch, taste and odour are the fifteen modifications [of the above eight *prakṛtis*]. Therefore the *tattvas* are twenty-three. The twenty-fourth is *avyakta* (the undifferentiated matter) or *pradhāna*. Puruṣa is other than [or superior to] this.

Oṃ tat sat is the Upaniṣad

16
Garbha Upaniṣad of Kṛṣṇa Yajurveda

Oṃ. The body is composed of the five [elements]; it exists in the five [objects of senses, etc.]; it has six supports: it is associated with the six *guṇas*; it has seven essential substances (*dhātus*) and three *malas* (impurities); it has three wombs (*yonis*) and is formed of four kinds of food.

Why is the body said to be composed of five? Because there are five elements in this body, viz. *pṛthivī, ap, agni, vāyu,* and *ākāśa*. In this body of five elements, what is the *pṛthivī* element? what *ap*? what *agni*? what *vāyu*? and what *ākāśa*? *Pṛthivī* is said to be that which is hard; *ap* is said to be that which is liquid; *agni* is said to be that which is hot; *vāyu* is that which moves; *ākāśa* is that which is full of empty hollows (*suśira*). Of these, *pṛthivī* is seen in supporting [objects], *āpas* in cohesion, *tejas* (or *agni*) in making forms visible, *vāyu* in moving, *ākāśa*, chiefly in *avakāśa* [viz. giving space]. Then what are the five objects of sense, etc.? The ear exists in sound, the skin in touch, the eye in forms, the tongue in taste and the nose in odour. [Then] the mouth [exists] in speech, the hand in lifting, the feet in walking, the anus in excreting, and the genitals in enjoying. [Then] through *buddhi*, one knows and determines; through *manas*, he thinks and fancies; through *citta*, he recollects; through *ahaṅkāra*, he feels the idea of 'I'. Thus these perform their respective functions.

Whence the six supports? There are six kinds of tastes (*rasas*)—sweet, sour, saltish, bitter, astringent, and pungent. There are six changes of state [viz.] the body exists, is born, grows, matures, decays, and dies. And there are also six vortices *(cakras)* depending on the *dhāmāni* [viz.] *mūlādhāra*, *svādhiṣṭhāna*, *maṇipūraka*, *anāhata*, *viśuddhi*, and *ājñā*. Also the *guṇas* are six—*kāma* (passion) and others *śama* (mental restraint) and others; there being properly—association [with the former] and devotion [to the latter]. Then there are seven kinds of sounds [viz.] *ṣaḍja* (sa), *ṛṣabha* (ri), *gāndhāra* (ga), *madhyama* (ma), *pañcama* (pa), *dhaivata* (dha), and *niṣāda* (ni), which are stated to be seven agreeable and disagreeable ones; and there are seven kinds of *dhātus* having seven colours, [viz.], white *(śukla)*, red *(rakta)*, dark-blue or indigo *(kṛṣṇa)*, blue *(dhūmra)*, yellow *(pīta)*, orange-red *(kapila)* and yellowish white *(pāṇḍara)*. In whomsoever these substances arise and increase, the essence *(rasa)* is the cause of the one following and so on [as stated below]. [These] *rasas* are six in number; from the *rasas* arises blood: from blood, flesh; from flesh, fat; from fat, bones; from bones, marrow; and from marrow, the male seminal fluid (*śukra*). From the union of *śukra* and the female vital energy *(śoṇita)*, occurs conception in the womb *(garbha)*. Being stationed in the heart, it [the energy] is led. In the heart of persons, [there is] an internal *agni*; in the seat of *agni*, there is bile; in the seat of bile, there is wind; in the seat of wind, is heart *(hṛdaya)*.

Through union of [male and female] the season (*ṛtu*) fit for conception, it [the embryo formed in the womb] is like water in the first night; in seven nights, it is like a bubble; at the end of half a month, it becomes a ball. At the end of a month, it is hardened; in two months, the head is formed; in three months, the region about the feet; and in the fourth month, the region about the stomach and the loins and also the ankle is formed; in the fifth month, the back (or spinal) bone; in the sixth, the nose, eyes and ears; in the seventh, it becomes united with *jīva* (ātman); in the eighth month, it becomes full [of all organs]; in the ninth, it becomes fatty. *Śukra* belongs to men and *śoṇita* to women. Each [by itself] is neutral [or is powerless]. [But in their combination] a son is born when the father's seed preponderates. A daughter is born when the mother's seed preponderates. Should both be equal, a eunuch is born. Since females have more of passion, on account of their deriving more pleasure [than males from sexual union], a greater number of females are born. Action corresponds to the mental state [of the actor]. Hence the child [born] takes after [the thought of] the parents. From parents with minds full of anxieties [at the time of union] are born the blind, the lame, the hunchback, the dwarf, and the limbless. [From impregnation] during the eclipses of the sun and the moon, children are born with defective limbs. Increase or decrease, similarities or dissimilarites of bodies arise [in children] through the influence of time, place, action, substance (*dravya*), and enjoyment. From a well-conducted intercourse [or union], the child being born with the form the father possesses his qualities, just as the image in a glass reflects truly the original. When *śukla* bursts into two through the interaction [or blowing against one another] of the *vāyu* of both *śukla* and *śoṇita*, then twins [of the same sex] are born. In the same manner when the *retas* the seminal fluids, [*viz. śukla* and *śoṇita*] of both the parents burst into two, then mixed progeny [male and female] is the result. Among mankind five embryos only can be formed at a pregnancy in the womb. A womb with one embryo is common. There are some with two. Those with three are only to be found [as rarely] as one in a thousand. Where there is a frequent pouring [of seminal fluid into the womb], a greater number of limbs is produced [in the child]. When the pouring [within the womb] is only once then the child becomes dried up [or contracts]. By pouring [within] more than once, couples are [sometimes] born.

Then, [*viz.* in the ninth month], this [the body] made of the five elements and able to sense odour, taste etc., through *tejas* (spiritual fire), etc., which is also made up of the five elements—this cognizes the indestructible Omkāra through its deep wisdom and contemplation. It cognizes as the one letter (Oṃ). Then there arise in the body the eight *prakṛtis* and the sixteen changes *(vikāras)*. Through the food and drink of the mother transmitted through her *nāḍīs*, the child obtains *prāṇa*. In the ninth month, it is full of all attributes.

It then remembers its previous births, finds out what has been done and what has not been done and discriminates between actions, right and wrong. [Then it thinks thus:] "Many thousands of wombs have been seen by me, many kinds of food have been tasted [by me] and many breasts have been suckled [by me]. All parts of the world have been my place of birth, as also my burning-ground in the past. In eighty-four lakhs of wombs, have I been born. I have been often born and have often died. I have been subject to the cycle of re-births very often. I have had birth and death, again birth and death, and again birth [and so on]. There is much suffering whilst living in the womb. Delusion and sorrow attend every birth. In youth are sorrow, grief, dependence on others, ignorance, the non-performance of what is beneficial, laziness and the performance of what is unfavourable. In adult age, [the sources of sorrow, are] attachments to sensual objects and the groaning under the three kinds of pain [those that arise from the body, the elements and the gods]. In old age anxiety, disease, fear of death, desires, love of self, passion, anger and non-independence—all these produce very great suffering. This birth is the seed of sorrow and being of the form of sorrow is unbearable. I have not attained the dharma of the means of overcoming the cycle of re-birth (viz. *nivṛtti*), nor have I acquired the means of yoga and *jñāna*. Alas! I am sunk in the ocean of sorrow and find no remedy for it. Fie on *ajñāna*! Fie on *ajñāna*! Fie on the troubles caused by passion and anger; fie on the fetters of the mundane existence *(saṃsāra)*. I shall attain wisdom from a guru. If I get myself freed from the womb, then I shall practise *Sāṅkhya-yoga* which is the cause of the extinction of all evil and the bestower of the fruit of emancipation. If I get myself freed from the womb, I shall seek refuge in Maheśvara [the great Lord] who is the cause of the extinction of all evil and bestower of the [four] ends of life [viz. passion (*kāma*), acquisition of wealth (*artha*), performance of duty (dharma) and salvation (*mokṣa*)]. If I get myself freed from the womb, then I shall seek refuge in the Lord of the world who is the *cidātman* of all *śaktis* and the cause of all causes. If I get myself freed from the womb, then I shall seek refuge in that supreme Lord Bhargaḥ (Śiva or Light) who is Paśupati, Rudra, Mahādeva and the guru of the world. If I get myself freed from the bondage of the womb, I shall perform great penances. If I get myself freed from the passage of the womb, I shall worship Viṣṇu in my heart who is the bestower of nectar, who is bliss, who is Nārāyaṇa and who never decays. I am now confined in my mother's womb; and were I freed from its bonds, I would please the divine Vāsudeva without diverting my mind from him. I am burnt through actions, good and bad, committed by me alone before for the sake of others, while those who enjoyed the fruits thereof have disappeared. Through non-belief, I formerly gave up all fear [of sin] and committed sins. I now reap their fruits. I shall become a believer hereafter.

Thus does the *jīva* (ātman) within the [womb] contemplate again and again the many kinds of miseries [it had undergone] and remembering always the miseries of the cycle of re-births, becomes disgusted [with the material enjoyments of the world], often fainting in the inmost centre [viz. heart] of all creatures at [the idea of] his *avidyā*, desire, and *karma*. Then this being, [who had entered many wombs in the previous births], comes to the mouth of the womb wishing to obtain release. Here being pressed by the neck of the uterus (*yantra*), it suffers much trouble. Moreover it is much affected by delivery (*prasūti vāyu*). As soon as it is born, it comes in contact with the *vaiṣṇavī vāyu* and ceases to remember anything of the past; it also ceases to see far and to be the cognizer of the real. Coming into contact with the earth, it becomes fierce-eyed and debased. The evil of the eye after it is rubbed with [or cleaned by] water vanishes; and with it, vanishes memory of birth and death, good and bad actions and their affinities. Then how does he understand *vāyu*, bile, and phlegm (*śleṣman*)? When they are in their proper state, they produce health: with their disturbance, diseases are generated. It should be known that one becomes capable of knowing through a proper quantity of bile; through having a little more he comes to know more. When the bile is changed [otherwise], he becomes changed and acts like a mad man. And that bile is *agni*. *Agni* influenced by *karma* is kindled by *vāyu*, the source [or seat] of virtue and vice, as fuel is kindled within by fire and from without by the wind.

And of how many kinds is that *agni*? It has three bodies, three seeds or progeny *(retas)*, three cities *(puras)*, three *dhātus* and three kinds of *agni* threefold. Of these three, *vaiśvānara* is bodiless. And that *agni* becomes [or is subdivided into] wisdom-fire *(jñānāgni)*, eye-fire *(darśanāgni)*, and digestive fire *(koṣṭhāgni)*. Of these *jñānāgni* pertains to the mind; *darśanāgni* pertains to the senses; and *koṣṭhāgni* pertains to *dahara* and daily cooks [or digests] equally whatever is eaten, drunk, licked or sucked through *prāṇa* and *apāna*. *Darśanāgni* is [in] the eye itself and is the cause of *vijñāna* and enables one to see all objects of form. It has three seats, the [spiritual] eye itself being the [primary] seat and the eyeballs being the accessory seats, *dakṣiṇāgni* is in the heart, *gārhapatya* is in the belly and in the face is *āhavanīya*. [In this sacrifice with the three *agnis*], the *puruṣa* is himself the sacrificer; *buddhi* becomes his wife; contentment (*santoṣa*) becomes the vow (*dīkṣā*) taken; the mind and the organs of the senses become the sacrificial vessels; the organs of action *(karmendriyas)* are the sacrificial instruments. In this sacrifice of the body, the several devas who become the sacrificial priests (*ṛtvijs*) perform their parts following the master of the sacrifice, [viz. the true individuality], wherever he goes. In this [sacrifice], the body is the sacrificial place, the skull of the head is the fire-pit, the hairs are the *kuśa* grass; the mouth is the raised platform in sacrifice(*antarvedi*); passion (*kāma*) is the clarified butter; the period of life is the period of sacrifice; sound (*nāda*) produced in the heart (*dahara*) the Sāmveda [recited during the sacrifice]; *vaikharī* is the *yajus* (or Yajurveda hymns); *parā*, *paśyantī*, and *madhyamā* are the *ṛks* (Ṛgveda hymns); cruel words are the *atharvas* (Atharva-veda hymns) and *khilas* (supplementary texts of each Veda); true words are the *vyāhṛtis*. Life, strength, and bile are the sacrificial creatures (*paśus*) and death is the bath which concludes the sacrifice (*avabhṛta*). In this sacrifice, the [three] fires blaze up and then according to [the desires of] the wordly, the devas bless him. All who are living [in this world] are the sacrificers. There is none living who does not perform sacrifice (*yajña*). This body is [created] for *yajña* and arises out of *yajña* and changes according to *yajña*. If this *yajña* is continued in a direction changed [from the right course or is abused], then it leads to an ocean of misery.

In this body, there are sixteen side-teeth, having each a membrane [as its root] and fifteen openings. It (the body) is measured by ninety-six digits. There are in it fourteen *nāḍī* seats and 108 joints. There are seventy-two seats with seventy-two *nāḍīs* between them, of which three are important, viz., *iḍā*, *piṅgalā*, and *suṣumnā*, the fourth is *purītati* and *jīvata*, the fifth. Above the navel, two digits to the left of it, is seated the source of bile. The food taken in is divided into three parts— urine, faeces, and *sāra* (the essence or chyme). The urine dividing itself into two, spreads to the left below the navel. The faeces is in the right and spreads itself over the body. Hence semen and blood are produced from food and drink. In this body, *vāyu* which is moving as *prāṇa* is the *sūtrātman*. Through it, one inspires and expires and moves [his limbs]. Without it, no limb of the body will be animated. Through *vāyu*, the current of blood is driven into the *nāḍīs* from the plexus *(cakra)* of the heart, and those which can be touched [on the body] are easily discernible. The juicy essences [of food] which arise out of digestion enter the womb which is suspended in the stomach of the mother and coming near the child's head nourishes the child's *prāṇa* through the *suṣumnā* [on the crown of head]. *Suṣumnā* is the Brahma-*nāḍī*. *Prāṇa* and others are found there. It (*prāṇa*) descends lower and lower as the time of birth approaches and settles in the heart when the child is born. Through yoga, it should be brought from the middle of the eyebrows to the end of *suṣumnā*, when he becomes the cognizer of the real like the child in the womb. In the body of this nature, ātman is latent and deathless, and is the witness. It lives in this body, being enveloped [by *māyā*]. *Prāṇin* [the *jīva* having *prāṇa*] has identification with the body (*abhimāna*) on account of ignorance. *Ajñāna* which surrounds it is the seed; the internal organ *(antaḥkaraṇa)*, is the sprout and the body is the tree. In this tree [of body], there are eight crores of hairs, eighty hundreds of joints and nine hundreds of tendons. The heart is eight *palas*, the tongue, twelve *palas*, bile, two *palas*, phelgum, one *āḍhaka*, one *kuḍupa* [or 1/4 *prastha*] of *śukra* and two *prasthas* of marrow. One should consider everything as evanescent, like the child in the womb [with its *prāṇa* etc.] stationed in the *suṣumnā* [in the head]. Then he becomes freed and gets no more body. If not, an ignorant man becomes subject to the cycle of rebirths, etc., is exposed like a worm to the drink of urine and faeces, and undergoes in this body the sufferings of hell. Therefore, knowing all this, one should be averse to worldly objects. Thus ends the *mokṣa-śāstra* of Pippalāda—thus ends the *mokṣa-śāstra* of Pippalāda.

Oṃ tat sat is the Upaniṣad

17
Tārasāra Upaniṣad of Śukla Yajurveda

Oṃ. Bṛhaspati asked Yājñavalkya: "That which is called Kurukṣetra is the place of the sacrifice of the devas and the spiritual seat of all beings. Therefore where should one go in order that he may cognize Kurukṣetra, the place of the sacrifice of the devas and the spiritual seat of all beings?" "Avimukta [Benaras] is Kurukṣetra, the place of the sacrifice of the devas and of the study of Brahman, because it is there that Rudra initiates one into the *tāraka* Brahman at death. Through this, one becomes immortal and the enjoyer of *mokṣa*. Therefore, one should always be in the midst of that place Avimukta and should never leave, O reverend sir, Avimukta." Thus said Yājñavalkya.

Then Bhāradvāja asked Yājñavalkya: "What is *tāraka*? What is that which causes one to cross [this mundane existence]." To which Yājñavalkya replied: "*oṃ-namonārāyaṇāya* is the *tārka*. It should be worshipped as *cidātman*. Oṃ is a single syllable and of the nature of matter *(prakṛti)*. '*Nārāyaṇāya*' is of five syllables and is of the nature of Parabrahman. He who knows this becomes immortal. Through Oṃ, is Brahmā produced; through *Na* is

Viṣṇu produced; through *Ma* is Rudra produced; through *Nā* is Īśvara produced; through *Rā* is the universe (*aṇḍa-virāṭ*) produced; through *Ya* is Puruṣa produced; through *Nā* is Bhagavān (Lord) produced; and through *Ya* is Paramātman produced. This eight syllable of Nārāyaṇa is the supreme and the highest reality. Thus is the Ṛgveda with the first foot [or half]. That which is Oṃ is the indestructible, the supreme and Brahman. That alone should be worshipped. It is this that is of the eight subtle syllables. And this becomes eight, being of eight forms. *A* is the first letter; *U* is the second; *M* is the third; *bindu* is the fourth; *nāda* is the fifth; *kāla* is the sixth; *kālātīta* (that beyond *kāla*) is the seventh; and that which is beyond these is the eighth. It is called *tāraka*, because it enables one to cross this mundane existence. Know that *tāraka* alone is Brahman and it alone should be worshipped." The (following) verses may be quoted here: "From the letter *A* came Brahmā named Jāmbavān (the bear). From the letter *U* came Upendra, named Hari. From the letter *M* came Śiva, known as Hanūmān. *Bindu* is named Īśvara and is Śatrughna, the Lord named Bharata and the sound of the conch itself. From *kalā* came the Puruṣa himself as Lakṣmaṇa and the bearer of the earth. *Kalātīta* is known as the goddess Sītā herself. That which is beyond is the Paramātman named Śrī-Rāma and is the highest Puruṣa. All this is the explanation of the letter Oṃ, the past, the present, and the future, and which is other than these (viz.) *tattva*, mantra, colour *(varṇa)*, deity *(devatā)*, metre *(chandas)*, *ṛk*, *kāla*, *śakti*, and creation (*sṛṣṭi*). He who knows this becomes immortal. [Thus is] Yajurveda with the second foot."

Then Bhāradvāja asked Yājñavalkya: "Through what mantra is Paramātman pleased and shows his own ātman [to persons]? Please tell this." Yājñavalkya replied:

"(1st Mantra:) Oṃ. He who is Śrī-Paramātman, Nārāyaṇa, and the Lord described by [the letter] *A* and is Jāmbavān (the bear) and *bhūḥ, bhuvaḥ* and *suvaḥ*: Salutation to him.

"(2nd Mantra:) He who is Paramātman, Nārāyaṇa, and the Lord described by [the letter] *U* and is Upendra [or] Hari and *bhūḥ, bhuvaḥ*, and *suvaḥ*: Salutation to him.

"(3rd Mantra:) Oṃ. He who is Śrī-Paramātman, Nārāyaṇa and the Lord described by [the letter] *M* and is of the form of Śiva [or], Hanumān and *bhūḥ, bhuvaḥ* and *suvaḥ*: Salutation to him.

"(4th Mantra:) Oṃ. He who is Śrī-Paramātman, Nārāyaṇa, the Lord of Śatrughna of the form of *bindu* and the *bhuḥ, bhuvaḥ* and *suvaḥ*: Salutation to him.

"(5th Mantra:) Oṃ. He who is Śrī-Paramātman, Nārāyaṇa, and the Lord, and is Bharata of the form of *nāda* and the *bhūḥ, bhuvaḥ* and *suvaḥ* : Salutation to him.

"(6th Mantra:) Oṃ. He who is Śrī-Paramātman, Nārāyaṇa, and the Lord, and is Lakṣmaṇa of the form of *kalā* and the *bhūḥ, bhuvaḥ* and *suvaḥ*: Salutation to him.

"(7th Mantra:) Oṃ. He who is Śrī-Paramātman, Nārāyaṇa and the Lord and is *kalātīta*, the Goddess Sītā, of the form of *cit* and the *bhūḥ, bhuvaḥ* and *suvaḥ*: Salutation to him."

"(8th Mantra:) Oṃ. He who is Śrī-Paramātmā, Nārāyaṇa and the Lord, that is beyond that [*kalātīta*], is the supreme Puruṣa and is the ancient Puruṣottama, the eternal, the immaculate, the enlightened, the emancipated, the true, the highest bliss, the endless, the secondless and the all-full—that Brahman is myself. I am Rāma and the *bhūḥ, bhuvaḥ* and *suvaḥ*: Salutation to him."

He who has mastered this eightfold mantra is purified by *agni*; he is purified by *vāyu*; he is purified by the sun; he is purified by Śiva; he is known by all the devas. He attains the fruit of reciting Itihāsas, Purāṇas, Rudra (mantras), a hundred thousand times. He who repeatedly remembers [or recites] the eight-syllabled mantra (*aṣṭākṣara*) of Nārāyaṇa, he gains the fruit of the recitation of Gāyatrī a hundred thousand times or of *praṇava* (Oṃ) a myriad of times. He purifies [his ancestors] ten [degrees] above and [his descendants] ten [degrees] below. He attains the state of Nārāyaṇa. He who knows this [attains the state of Nārāyaṇa].

Like the eye [which sees without any obstacle] the things spread [in the sky], the wise ever see this supreme seat of Viṣṇu. Brāhmaṇas who are spiritually awake praise in diverse ways and illuminate the supreme abode of Viṣṇu.

Oṃ tat sat is the Upaniṣad

18

Nārāyaṇa Upaniṣad of Kṛṣṇa Yajurveda

Oṃ. Then Nārāyaṇa, the supreme Puruṣa desired. "I shall create offspring." From Nārāyaṇa emanates *prāṇa*, *manas*, the several organs of sense and action, *ākāśa, vāyu, agni, ap* and *pṛthivī* that supports all. From Nārāyaṇa emanates Brahmā. From Nārāyaṇa emanates Rudra. From Nārāyaṇa emanates Indra. From Nārāyaṇa emanates Prajāpati (the divine progenitor). From Nārāyaṇa emanate the twelve *ādityas*, *rudras*, *vasus* and all the *chandas* (Vedas). From Nārāyaṇa only do all these proceed. Through Nārāyaṇa [they] prosper. In Nārāyaṇa [they] are absorbed. The Ṛgveda teaches this.

Then Nārāyaṇa is eternal. Brahmā is Nārāyaṇa, Śiva is Nārāyaṇa, Indra is Nārāyaṇa, time (*kāla*) is Nārāyaṇa, space (*diś*) is Nārāyaṇa, the intermediate quarters also are Nārāyaṇa; that which is above is Nārāyaṇa, that which is below is Nārāyaṇa, that which is in and out is Nārāyaṇa, the whole universe which existed and will exist is Nārāyaṇa. Nārāyaṇa is the only one that is stainless, sinless, changeless and unnameable and that is pure and divine. He is one without a second. Whoever knows Him thus, becomes Viṣṇu himself. The Yajurveda teaches this.

One should utter "Oṃ" first, then "*namaḥ*," and then "*Nārāyaṇāya*." "Oṃ" [is] a single syllable; "*namaḥ*" contains two syllables: "*Nārāyaṇāya*" contains five syllables. This is the sentence known as the *aṣṭākṣara* of Nārāyaṇa. Whoever studies this *aṣṭākṣara* of Nārāyaṇa and recites it constantly, attains full life and supremacy over men, enjoys the pleasures of royalty and becomes the master of all souls. He attains *mokṣa*; yes, he attains *mokṣa*. The Sāmaveda teaches this.

The yogin having pronounced [the name of] him who is complete bliss, who is Brahma-puruṣa and who is of the nature of *praṇava* (Oṃ)—a combination of *A*, *U*, and *M*—is released from the bondage of birth and mundane existence. He who practises the mantra "*Oṃ-namo-Nārāyaṇāya*" reaches Vaikuṇṭha (the abode of Viṣṇu). It is this lotus [heart]. It is replete with *vijñāna*: It has the brilliance of lightning. The son of Devākī is Brahmaṇya that is Viṣṇu or Brahmā devoted to *tapas*, Vedas, truth and *jñāna*. Madhusūdana is Brahmaṇya. Nārāyaṇa who pervades all elements, who is one only, who is the cause Puruṣa and who is causeless, is known as Parabrahman. The Atharvaṇa Upaniṣad teaches this.

Whoever recites [this Upaniṣad] in the morning destroys the sins committed the night [before]. Whoever recites it in the evening destroys the sins committed during the day. Whoever recites in the morning and evening becomes free from sins, however sinful he may be. Whoever recites [it] in the noon facing the sun is freed from all the five great sins as well as from the minor ones. He derives the good effects of the recitation of all the Vedas. Whoever knows thus attains *sāyujya* of Nārāyaṇa (viz. is absorbed in the essence of Nārāyaṇa). He attains *sāyujya* of Nārāyaṇa.

Oṃ tat sat is the Upaniṣad

19

Kalisantāraṇa Upaniṣad of Kṛṣṇa Yajurveda

At the end of Dvāpara *yuga*, Nārada went to Brahmā and addressed him thus: "O Lord, how shall I, roaming over the earth, be able to cross Kali?" To which Brahmā thus replied: "Well asked. Listen to that which all Śrutis (the Vedas) keep secret and hidden, through which one may cross the mundane existence *(saṃsāra)* of Kali. He shakes off [the evil effects of] Kali through the mere uttering of the name of the Lord Nārāyaṇa, who is the primeval Puruṣa." Again Nārada asked Brahmā: "What is the name?" To which Hiraṇyagarbha (Brahmā) replied thus: [the names are:] "1. Hare, 2. Rāma, 3. Hare, 4. Rāma, 5. Rāma, 6. Rāma, 7. Hare, 8. Hare; 9. Hare, 10. Kṛṣṇa, 11. Hare, 12. Kṛṣṇa, 13. Kṛṣṇa, 14. Kṛṣṇa, 15. Hare, 16. Hare. These sixteen names [of the Lord] are destructive of the evil effects of Kali. No better means than this is to be seen in all the Vedas. These [sixteen names] destroy the veils (*āvaraṇa*) of *jīva* surrounded by the sixteen rays (*kalās*). Then like the sphere of the sun which shines fully after the clouds [screening it] disperse, Parabrahman [alone] shines."

Nārada asked: "O Lord, what are the rules to be observed with reference to it?" To which Brahmā replied that there were no rules for it. Whoever in a pure or an impure state, utters these always, attains the same world of, or proximity with, or the same form of, or absorption into Brahmā.

Whoever utters three and a half *koṭis* (or thirty-five million) times this mantra composed of sixteen names crosses the sin of the murder of a Brāhmaṇa. He becomes purified from the sin of the theft of gold. He becomes purified from the sin of cohabitation with a woman of low caste. He is purified from the sins of wrong done to ancestors, gods and men. Having given up all dharmas, he becomes freed at once from all sins. He is at once released from all bondage. That he is at once released from all bondage.

Oṃ tat sat is the Upaniṣad

20
Bhikṣuka Upaniṣad of Śukla Yajurveda

Among religious mendicants (*bhikṣus*) who long for salvation, (*mokṣa*), there are four kinds, viz., *kuṭīcaka, bahūdaka, haṃsa* and *paramahaṃsa*. Gautama, Bharadvāja, Yājñavalkya, Vasiṣṭha and others belong to the first kind. They take eight mouthfuls [of food daily] and strive after *mokṣa* alone through the path of yoga. The second kind carry three [bamboo] staves [tied together] and a waterpot and wear tuft of hair (*śikhā*), sacred thread (*yajñopavīta*) and red-coloured cloth. They take eight mouthfuls of food in the house of *brahmaṛṣis*, abstain from flesh and alcohol and strive after salvation alone through the path of yoga. Then the *haṃsas* should live not more than a night in a village, five nights in a town and seven nights in a sacred place, partaking daily of cow's urine and cow's dung, observing *cāndrāyaṇa* and striving after *mokṣa* alone through the path of yoga. *Paramahaṃsas* like Saṃvartaka, Āruṇi, Śvetaketu, Jaḍabharata, Dattātreya, Śuka, Vāmadeva, Hārītaka and others take eight mouthfuls and strive after *mokṣa* alone through the path of yoga. They live clothed or naked at the foot of trees, in ruined houses or in burning grounds. With them, there are no dualities as dharma and *adharma*, gain and loss, and purity and impurity. They look upon gold and stone and clods of earth with the same eye [of indifference], live on alms, begging from all without any distinction of caste and look upon everything as ātman alone. Being [naked] as nature made them, being free from the sense of duality and from covetousness, being engaged in pure contemplation (*śukladhyāna*), meditating on ātman and begging at stated times, simply to keep the body and soul together, they reside in ruined houses, temples, straw-huts, ant-hills, the foot of trees, potteries, the places of *agnihotra*, the sand in the bed of rivers, mountain-caves, cavities, the hollows of trees, waterfalls, and *sthaṇḍila* (the level square piece of ground prepared for sacrifice). Having advanced far in the path of Brahman and being pure in mind, they quit this body through the methods prescribed for *paramahaṃsa-sannyāsins*. These are the Paramahaṃsas.

Oṃ tat sat is the Upaniṣad

21

Nāradaparivrājaka Upaniṣad of Atharvaṇaveda

UPAḌEŚA I

Oṃ. Once upon a time, Nārada, the ornament of roaming ascetics *(parivrājakas)*, after roaming over all worlds and cleansing, through merely looking at the places of pilgrimage able to impart rare religious merits, observed, with a mind that had attained purity, without hate, quiescent and patient and indifferent towards all [objects], the forest of Naimiṣa (the modern Nimsār), filled with *ṛṣis* that were engaged in the contemplation of reality and had attained the greatness of the ordained bliss; [there] through the recitation of stories about Hari [Viṣṇu], associated with the musical notes of *Sa*, *Re*, *Ga*, *Ma*, *Pa*, *Dha* and *Ni* [of the gamut], able to impart indifference to objects and to make one look down upon the universe and instilling divine devotion, fixed and movable [or mental and bodily], he entered [the forest], fascinating the crowds of beings—human, animal, *kimpuruṣas*, celestials, *kinnaras*, *apsaras* and *uragas* [collected there]. [Thereupon the] great *ṛṣis* Śāunaka and others who had been engaged for twelve years in *sattra* sacrifice, well-skilled in the recitation of Vedas, the knowers of all and the good practisers of *tapas*, observed Nārada the son of Brahmā and the devotee of the Lord and having risen up, paid their respects to him. Then having respectfully requested him to sit down, they also seated themselves and addressed him thus: "O Lord, son of Brahmā, what is the means of salvation for us? It is meet that it should be communicated [to us]." Thus addressed, Nārada replied to them thus: "One born in a good family and fit to go through the forty-four *saṃskāras*, *upanayana* and others, should, under a teacher to whom he is devoted, study, after the recitation of the Veda of his own division *(śākhā)*, all the different branches of knowledge; then should fulfil, according to the rules ordained, for twelve years, the observance of celibacy *(brahmacarya)*, such as the service of the guru, etc.; then for twenty-five years the order of life *(āśrama)* of a householder *(gṛhastha)*; and for twenty-five years the *āśrama* of a forester *(vānaprastha)*. After thus practising well the fourfold celibacy, the sixfold householder's life, and the fourfold forester's life and having performed all the duties thereof, he should acquire the fourfold means of salvation; thus the *sannyāsin* who gives up the desires along with the *karmas* of mind, speech and body in this *saṃsāra* as well as the *vāsanā* towards the three-fold desire [of son, wife and wealth], and being without malice and endowed with quiescence and patience, undisturbed in the order of life of *paramahaṃsa*, quits the body in the contemplation of reality, is an emancipated person. Such is the Upaniṣad."

UPADEŚA II

All the sages, Śaunaka and others addressing Lord Nārada said thus: "O Lord, please tell us the rules of *sannyāsa*." At which, seeing them, Nārada replied: "It is but meet that we should know the whole truth from the lips of Brahmā himself." After the *sattra* sacrifice was completed, he took the *ṛṣis* along with him to *satyaloka*; and after duly making prostrations to and eulogising Brahmā engaged in meditation upon Brahman, he along with others was duly seated under the order of Brahmā. Then Nārada addressed Brahmā thus: "Thou art guru; thou art father; thou art the knower of the secret of all learning; thou art the knower of all; thou shalt therefore tell me one secret. Who else but thee is fit to tell the secret dear unto me? It is this. Please tell us the rules of the real asceticism (*sannyāsa*)."

Thus prayed to by Nārada, Brahmā surveyed all in the four quarters; and after meditating for one *muhūrta* [48 minutes], and assuring himself that the inquiry was truly for the purpose of escaping from the pain of *saṃsāra*, Brahmā, eyeing Nārada, said thus: "The mystery that was imparted before by Virāṭ-Puruṣa of illimitable form according to the *Puruṣa-Sūkta-Upaniṣad* is now being divulged to you. It is very mysterious. It is fit to be hearkened to with great attention. O Nārada, one born in a good family and obedient to his parents, should, after the performance of *upanayana* according to the rules, find a virtuous guru that is other than his father, is of good custom and habits, of faith, born of good family, a knower of Vedas, a lover of *śāstras*, of [good] qualities and free from duplicity. Having made prostrations and rendered useful service to him he should respectfully acquaint him with his intention. Having studied all departments of knowledge and rendered service for twelve years, he should, under his [the guru's] orders, marry a girl fit for his family and dear unto him. Then having performed for twenty-five years the *karmas* incidental to a householder and attained the status of a Brāhmaṇa that has performed sacrifices and the rest, he should beget a son with the only desire of perpetuating the family. After thus spending twenty-five years in the performance of household dharma, he should bathe thrice daily for twenty-five years and take only one meal in the fourth period; he should live alone in the forest, after giving up his previous wanderings in city and village; and without desire for fruit, should perform the *karmas* incidental to that [forester's] order of life and be without desire for objects seen and heard. Being skilled in the forty *saṃskāras*, he should be devoid of desire for all, have a purified mind, have burnt up desire, jealousy, envy and egoism, and have developed the four means of salvation. Then he becomes fit for *sannyāsa*. Such is the Upaniṣad."

UPADEŚA III

Then Nārada addressed the grandfather thus: "O Lord, by whom, after attaining the qualification of *sannyāsa*, is it fit to be taken?" To which Brahmā replied: "After first expounding the qualifications of *sannyāsa*, the rules of *sannyāsa* will then be stated. Hear carefully. A eunuch, the outcaste, the maimed, the lewd, the deaf, the youth, the dumb, the heretic, the discus-bearer, the *liṅga*-wearer, the forester (*vaikhānasa*), the carrier of Śiva's flag (*haradhvaja)*, the reciter of Vedas for hire, the bald-headed, one without [sacrificial] fire—all these, even though they have attained *vairāgya* are unfit for *sannyāsa*. Even though they have become *sanyāsins*, they are unfit to be initiated into the sacred Vedic sentences (*mahāvākyas*). The *paramahaṃsa-sanyāsin* stated before [as fit to take *sannyāsa*] is the one qualified. It is stated in the Smṛtis that he is a *parivrāṭ*, who is not afraid of others, as others are not afraid of him. The eunuch, the limbless, the blind, the youth, the sinful, the outcaste, the door-keeper, the *vaikhānasa*, the *haradhvaja*-bearer, the discus or *cakrī*-bearer, the *liṅga*-wearer *(liṅgin)*, the heretic the bald-headed, one without fire [sacrifice], one that had undergone *sannyāsa* twice or thrice, the reciter of Vedas for hire—all these are not fit for regular *sannyāsa* but only for *ātura-sannyāsa* [that is *sannyāsa* taken while a person is afflicted, etc.]. What is the opinion of Hindus [*āryas*] on the [fit] time for *ātura-sannyāsa* [being taken]? The time when life [*prāṇa*] is about to rise [out of the body] is called *ātura*. The time other than it is incapable of conferring [upon one] the path of salvation and is not *ātura*. Even in *ātura-sannyāsa*, the wise should, according to rules, initiate themselves into *sannyāsa* after reciting the mantras again and again in the course of respective mantras. There is no difference between regular and *ātura-sannyāsa* in the mantras to be uttered at the time of taking *sannyāsa*. There is no *karma* without mantras; [hence] *karma* needs mantras. Anything done without mantra cannot be termed *karma*. Hence mantras should not be given up. Any *karma* done without mantra is like an offering made in ashes. Through the conciseness [of the performance] of the *karmas*, it is stated to be *ātura-sannyāsa*.

"Therefore, O Muni, the recitation of mantras is stated to be in *ātura-sannyāsa*. One who is always duly doing fire-sacrifice (*agnihoṭra*) should, when he quits [the house] for foreign places through indifference, perform the *prājāpatya* sacrifice in water and then take up *sannyāsa*. After completing in water the observances of *karma* through the mind, or the recitation of mantras, the wise man should attain *sannyāsa*. Else he becomes a fallen man. When, in the mind, indifference to all objects arises, then men should long after *sannyāsa*, [that being the best time for it]; otherwise they are fallen. One who attains *vairāgya* should take *sannyāsa*. One who does not, should remain at home. That vile twice-born with desire, should he take *sannyāsa*, reaches hell. That Brāhamaṇa who is a celibate, who has under control his tongue, sexual organ, stomach and hand, may become a *sannyāsin* without undergoing the ceremony of marriage. Having known *saṃsāra* as one without essence (*sāra*) and not having undergone any marriage on account of the desire to know the *sāra* [or essence of God], they become *sannyāsins* on account of the practice of supreme *vairāgya*. The characteristic of path *(pravṛtti)* is the performance of *karma*; that of *nivṛṭṭi* is *jñāna*. Therefore placing *jñāna* in the forefront, the wise man should take up *sannyāsa*. When the reality of the eternal Parabrahman is understood, then he should take up one staff (*daṇḍa*) and abandon the holy thread and tuft of hair. Then he becomes fit to eat the alms-food [of *sannyāsa*], having become devoted to Paramātman, indifferent to those that are not Paramātman and freed from all desires. He becomes fit to be the eater of alms-food who preserves the same countenance when he is beaten, as when he is worshipped or prostrated to. He becomes fit to be the eater of alms-food who is of the firm certitude that he is no other than the non-dual and indestructible Brahman, otherwise named Vāsudeva. He in whom are existent, control of the organs (*śānti*), control of mind (*śama*), purity [of mind and body], truth (*satya*), contentment (*santoṣa*), straightforwardness (*ārjava*), poverty and non-ostentatiousness should be in the order of life of *kaivalya* [*sannyāsa*]. When one does not, through actions, mind or speech, commit any sinful action to any being, then he becomes fit for eating alms-food. Having become quiescent [through the control of the mind], having practised the ten kinds of dharmas, having, according to rules, studied Vedānta and having paid the three debts [to devas, *ṛṣis* and *pitṛs*], one should take up *sannyāsa*. Courage, fortitude, the control of the body, honesty, purity of [mind and body], control of the [inner] organs, shame, knowledge, truth, and absence of anger—these ten are the characteristics of dharma.

One who does not look back [with pleasure] upon past enjoyments, nor forward into the future, and one who does not rejoice in the present, is fit to become a *sanyāsin*. One who is able to control within, the inner organs and without, the external organs, may be in the order of life of *kaivalya*. One who while in life is not affected by pleasures and pains, as the body is unaffected by them after death, may be in the order of life of *kaivalya*.

"An ascetic of the *paramahaṃsa* [order] shall wear two loin-cloths, one ragged cloth, and one staff. Nothing more is ordained [in his case]. Should he, through desire, wear more than these, he will fall into the hell of Raurava and be born into the womb of an animal. Having stitched together old and clean cloths into one and having coloured it with red [ochre], he should wear it as his upper cloth. He may be with one cloth or even without it. He should roam about alone with the sole vision [of Brahman], devoid of desires; but he may be in one place alone in the rainy season. Having quite abandoned his family, including son and wife, Vedānta, sacrifice and the sacred thread, the ascetic should wander incognito. Having given up all faults, such as passion, anger, pride, desire and delusion, the ascetic (*parivrāṭ*) should become one that owns nothing. He is a *muni* who is devoid of love and hate, who regards equally a clod of earth, stone or gold, who does no injury to any living creature, and is freed from all. That ascetic reaches salvation who is associated with *ātmajñāna*, who is freed from ostentation and egoism, from doing injury and tale-bearing. Through attraction to the senses, he becomes subject to fault, there is no doubt: through their control, he gains perfection. Lust, when enjoyed, is never gratified. Just as fire increases with the oblation [of ghee, etc., poured into it] so also lust waxes strong [with enjoyment]. It should be known that that man who does not rejoice or grieve through hearing, touching eating, seeing, or smelling is a conqueror of the organs (*jitendriya*). He whose speech and mind are well brought under control attains, completely and always, all the fruits of Vedānta.

"That Brāhmaṇa who is always afraid of respect as poison and always longs after disrespect as nectar, sleeps soundly and rises happily even though he is treated with disrespect. He moves about happily in this world. The one who treats him with disrespect perishes. All cruel words should be endured. None should be treated with disrespect. On account of bodily relationship, none should be made inimical. No anger should be directed in turn towards one who is angry. Soft words [only] should be spoken, even when [violently] pulled by another. No untrue words should be uttered, even should afflictions arise to the seven gates [of the body]. One desirous of bliss should dwell in this universe through the aid of ātman alone, intent upon ātman, free from desires and without the desire of blessing [others]. He becomes fit for salvation through the control of the organs, the destruction of love and hate and non-injury to beings. He should abandon [all identification with] this feeble, perishable and impure body of five elements whereof the bones are the pillars, which is strung by the nerves, coated over with flesh and blood, covered up by the skin, is of bad odour, full of urine and faeces, is ever haunted by dotage and miseries and is the seat of all ills. If an ignorant man be fond of this body firmly knit together with flesh, blood, pus, faeces and urine, nerves, fat and bones, he would, *a fortiori*, be fond of hell. That [identification of the body with the self] is alone the seat of the Kālasūtra hell. That is alone the Mahā-vīci-vāgura [hell]. That is alone the Asipatravanaśreṇī [hell]. Such an idea of the body being the self should be strenuously abandoned, though all should perish. That love of the body is not fit to be felt by one intent upon his welfare, just as a low-caste woman eating dog's flesh is unfit to be touched.

"One [fit to reach salvation], after leaving all meritorious actions to those dear to him and all sins to those not dear, attains the eternal Brahman through *dhyāna-yoga*. Such a man, through the ordinances, gives up little by little all associations and being freed from all pairs of opposites, remains in Brahman alone. On account of the accomplishment [of salvation], he should be moving about alone and without any help. He who having understood the effect of being alone never derogates from it, is never left in want. The bowl, the foot of the tree, the tattered robe, the state of being without help, the equality of vision in all these are the characteristics of the emancipated one. One intent upon the welfare of all beings, with a quiescent mind, having the three-knotted staff and bowl and ever devoted to the one [Brahman] after taking up *sannyāsa*, may enter a village. Such one is a alms-taker (*bhikṣu*). Should two unite, it is called *mithuna* [a pair or union]; with three, it becomes a village (*grāma*); with more, it is a city (*nagara*). No city or village or *mithuna* should be made and an ascetic who commits these three [offences] falls from his duty. Through such intercourse [of ascetics], all kinds of talks connected with the king and alms, friendship, tale-bearing and malice occur between them. There is no doubt of it.

"He [the ascetic] should be alone and desireless. He should not converse with anybody. The ascetic should ever be uttering the word Nārāyaṇa in each sentence. Being alone, he should be meditating upon Brahman in all mental, spoken and bodily actions. He should neither rejoice at dying or living. He should be anticipating the time when life will close. He should not be glad of dying; nor should he be glad of living. He should be biding his time like a hireling [for his pay]. An ascetic who plays the part of the dumb, the eunuch, the lame, the blind, the deaf and the idiot is emancipated through the [above six] means. There is no doubt of this. He who has no fondness for eating, saying that this is good and that is bad, who speaks only words that are beneficial, true and moderate is said to be dumb. He is a eunuch who is no more affected by the sight of a sixteen-year-old girl than of a newborn female baby or a hundred-year-old woman. He who does not move about for more than the distance of a *yojana* for alms or for the calls of nature is a lame man. That ascetic (*parivrāṭ*) is said to be a blind man, who whether sitting or walking, has his vision extended to no more than four yokes' distance on the ground. He is said to be deaf who, though hearing words beneficial or non-beneficial, pleasant or painful to the mind, is as if he does not hear them. That clever ascetic is said to be an idiot who is ever in a state of sleep, as it were, having his organs non-agitated by objects, even though near. He should never observe the following six—the scenes of dancing, gambling, lovely women, eatables, enjoyables and women in their monthly course.

"The ascetic should never in thought even think of others with the six [viz.] love, hate, pride, deceit, treachery and the illusion [of confounding them]. To the ascetics, the following six are sinful: cot, white cloth, the stories of women, love towards women, sleep during the day and vehicles. He who is engaged in ātmic contemplation should carefully avoid a long journey. He should ever practise the *Upaniṣadic-vidyā* tending to salvation. The ascetic need not bathe daily. He need not observe fast (*upavāsa*). He need not be one that has studied Vedas. He need not be one that is able to produce a commentary [of scriptures]. He should daily observe acts without sin, deceit, or falsehood. He who, having withdrawn the organs within, like a turtle its limbs [within its shell], is with the actions of the organs and the mind annihilated, without desires, without possessing any object as his own, without dualities, without prostrations, without the oblations to *pitṛ devatās* [they being with desires], without mine or I, without awaiting anything, without the desire to be happy and living in places where men do not live—he alone is emancipated. There is no doubt of this.

"A celibate or householder or forester, who is [ever] vigilant, has *karma*, devotion, and knowledge and is independent, after understanding his peculiar tendency and having become indifferent [to his order of life], may become a householder after ending the celibate life, or may from the householder's life enter the life of a forester, and then the life of an ascetic; or from the life of a celibate or householder or forester may [directly] enter that of an ascetic. The moment, whether he is with religious observance (*vrata*) or not, is *snātaka* or not, or with a discontinued fire-sacrifice or not. On account of that, some perform Prājāpatya sacrifice alone; or Āgneya-sacrifice may be performed. Is not *agni, prāṇa*? Through this alone, one should perform that sacrifice only which is connected with the three *dhātus*. The three *dhātus* are *sattva, rajas* and *tamas* alone. With the mantra, *ayaṃ te yonir ṛtvijo yato jāto arocathāḥ taṃ jānannagnā ārohyathā no vardhyā rayiṃ*. Agni [fire] should be taken in. Thus it is said [in the Śrutis]: *eṣa vā agneryonir yaḥ prāṇaḥ prāṇaṃ gaccha svāṃ yoniṃ gaccha svāhā*. The *agni* from *āhavanīya* should be brought and taken in as before [with the mantras above mentioned]. Should such an *agni* be not obtainable, the oblation (*homa*) should be done in water with the mantra, *āpo vai sarvā devtās sarvābhyo devatābhyo juhomi svāhā*. After performing *homa*, the water should be taken in and sipped. After uttering the mantra, *sājyam haviranāmayaṃ mokṣadam.* He abandons the tuft of hair on the head, the holy thread, father, son, wife, *karma*, Vedic study and mantra and becomes an ascetic. The Śrutis say that a knower of ātman should be engaged in meditation upon Brahman, through the three mantras tending to salvation."

Then Nārada asked Brahmā thus: "How can one, without the body thread, be a Brāhmaṇa?" To which Brahmā replied: "The wise should, after shaving [the head] together with the tuft of hair, cast off the holy thread. He should wear, as his thread (*sūtra*), the indestructible and supreme Brahman. On account of [*sūcanāt*] its being an indication, it [thread] is called *sūtra. Sūtra* is the *paramapada* [supreme seat]. He by whom that *sūtra* is known is a Brāhmaṇa. That *sūtra* [thread of Brahman] in which is strung the whole universe like beads on a string (*sūtra*), should be worn by the yogin that has known yoga and *tattva*. The wise man that is in supreme yoga should abandon the outer thread (*sūtra*). He who wears [in his heart] this *sūtra* of Brāhmic reality is alone Brāhmaṇa. Through wearing this higher *sūtra*, it becomes not a rejected one, not an impure one. Those only whose *sūtra* is internal, having the holy thread as *jñāna* are the real knowers of the *sūtra*; they are said to possess the holy thread (*yajñopavīta*). To those whose tuft of hair (*śikhā*) is *jñāna*, whose holy thread is *jñāna* and whose meditation is upon *jñāna*, *jñāna* alone is supreme. It is said that *jñāna* alone is able to purify. That wise man alone who possesses the *jñāna-śikhā* like the *śikhā* (flame) of fire (*agni*) is said to possess *śikhā* (tuft of hair). Those that have mere *śikhā* are no Brāhmaṇa. The Brāhmaṇas and others that are entitled to perform the Vedic *karmas* are allowed to wear the [external] thread, only as an auxiliary to the *karmas*. It is only Vedic. The knowers of Brahman know that all Brahmaṇya [the state of Brahman] accrues to him only that has the knowledge-tuft of hair (*jñānamaya śikhā*) and the Brahmanful holy thread *(tanmaya upavīta)*.

"Having known it, a Brāhmaṇa should take up *sannyāsa*. Such a *sannyāsin* should be, in order to bear the bodily afflictions, with one cloth, bald-headed and without having anything as being required [for his use]; or according to rules, he may be [naked] as nature made his body, and should abandon his son, friend, wife, trustworthy relatives, etc., as well as all *karmas* and love for the universe, the loin-cloth, staff and covering. Enduring all pairs of opposites without cold or heat, happiness or grief, fame or disgrace, without the six changes, I-ness, malice, pride, ostentation, jealousy, slander of others, love and hate, pleasure and pain, passion, anger, greed and delusion and regarding his body as a mere carcass, without thinking of all the things, internal and external, that are other than self. Without prostrations, without the worship of devas and *pitṛs* and without praise or condemnation, he should wander about of his own accord. He should not receive gold and others. For him there is no invocation or dismissal [of deities], mantra or non-mantra, meditation or worship, aim or non-aim, others or not-others; without having another's or [his own] settled place of residence and having a firm conviction, he should be in a desolate house or at the foot of trees, or in a temple, a plenteous turfed spot, a potter's place or that of *agnihotra* or sacrifice, river, tank, sand-heap, subterranean vault, cave, mountain-rill, the place prepared for sacrifice or forest; or like the naked personages, Śvetaketu, Ṛbhu, Nidāgha, Jaḍabharata, Ṛṣabha, Durvāsas, Samvartaka, Sanatsujāta, Vaideha [Janaka], Vatasiddha, Śuka, Vāmadeva, Dattātreya, Raivataka and Gorakṣa, he should roam about as nature made him, without being recognised and without any means of discovery of his course of life, like a lad or an insane man or a ghost, with the actions of a madman though not mad, after discarding in water the three-knotted staff, the stringed sling [bag], vessel, bowl, waist-string, loin-cloth, stick, and cloth. He should ever be engaged in ātmic deliberation. Being in his natural state without being affected by the pairs, without receiving anything, being ever settled firmly in the Brāhmic path, having a pure mind, eating the food that is obtained without asking, in the palm as vessel, or in another's vessel, in order to merely protect the body at the time required, being of equal mind whether the object is gained or not, without having thought of his own, always meditating upon Brahman, being established in himself (*ātma-niṣṭhā*), having eradicated all actions, virtuous and sinful and having given up all—that one who ever utters *(brahma-praṇava)*, that 'I am Brahman' alone, with the blissful and non-dual *jñāna* and after rising above the three bodies [to Brahman], like the analogy of the wasp and the worm, gives up the body as a *sannyāsin*, is said to have done all his work [in this world]. Such is the Upaniṣad."

UPADEŚA IV

"One who after giving up the world, the Vedas, the objects and the organs is in ātman alone, attains the supreme abode. A good ascetic should not make known his caste, name, clan *(gotra)*, etc., his place and time. the Vedas etc. studied by him, his family, age, history, observance, and conduct. He should neither converse with women nor remember the women he had seen. He should give up all stories connected with women. He should not even see the figure of a woman in a picture. The mind of an ascetic who through delusion adopts the above four things connected with women is necessarily affected and thereby perishes. The following are prohibited in his case: Thirst, malice, falsehood, deceit, greed, delusion, the pleasant and the unpleasant, manual work, lecture, yoga, passion (*kāma*), desire, begging, I-ness, mine-ness, the obstinacy of curing diseases, penance, pilgrimage and the accomplishment of fruits of mantras, and medicines. He who performs these interdicted things, goes into a debased state. A muni who has *mokṣa* as his supreme seat should address such respectful words as 'Please come, please go, please stay and welcome', to one, even though he be his intimate friend. He should neither receive presents, etc., nor ask for them to be given to others. Even in dream, an ascetic should never direct a person [to do work for him]. Even should he witness or hear of the happiness or grief of his wife, brother, son and other relatives, he should not be affected thereby. He should abandon all joy and sorrow.

"To the ascetics controlling their mind, the following are their own duties (*svadharmas*): Harmlessness, truth, honesty, celibacy, non-coveting, humility, high-spiritedness, clearness of mind, steadiness of mind, straightforwardness, non-attachment [to any], service to the guru, faith, patience, bodily restraint, mental restraint, indifference, firm and sweet words, endurance, compassion, shame, *jñāna*, *vijñāna,* yoga, moderate food and courage. That *paramahaṃsa* of an ascetic in the order of life of a *sannyāsin* who is without dualities, always follows the pure *sattvaguṇa* and sees all equally, is no other than the actual Nārāyaṇa himself. He may live one day in a village and five days in a city, but five months in the wintry season. At other times he should live in other places [such as forest, etc.]. He should not live in a village for two days [even]; should he do so, desires and the rest will arise in him and thereby he becomes fit for hell. He should live like a [harmless] worm on the earth with his mind under control and with no settled place of residence, at the end of the village where there are no persons. He may live in the same place in the wintry season. He should roam about on the earth with one or no cloth, with the one vision [of Brahman] alone, with no desires [of objects], with no condemnation of the actions of the wise and with meditation. That yogin of an ascetic should go about, observing the duties of his order of life and with the eyes cast on the earth, in pure places. He should not roam about in night, midday or the two twilight periods in which are places void or difficult to be waded through or likely to injure living creatures. He may live for one day in a village, for three days in a town, for two days in a hamlet and for five days in a city. He may live in the wintry season [longer] in one place surrounded fully by water. The ascetic should regard all creatures as self and dwell upon earth like the blind, the hunchback, the deaf, the insane and the dumb. The *bahūdaka* and the forester should bathe thrice a day. In the case of *haṃsa*, one bath only is ordained; but none in the case of *paramahaṃsa*. In the case of the one having one staff, seven things are ordained, viz. silence, yoga-posture, yoga, endurance, solitariness, desirelessness and equal vision over all. Bathing being not prescribed for *paramahaṃsa*, he should abandon all the modifications of the mind only; what is the difference between the worms and the men that rejoice over this ill-smelling body which is only a collection of skin, flesh, blood, nerves, fat, marrow, bone, offal and urine? What is the body but a collection of all phlegm, etc.? And what are the qualities, the *vāsanā* of the body, effulgence, beauty etc.? [They are opposed to one another.] The ignorant man that is fond of this body, which is but a compound of flesh, blood, the ill-smelling urine and offal, nerve, fat and bone, will be fond of hell too. Though there is no difference between the women's secret parts that cannot be described by words and an [ever] oozing tubular wound, yet through the difference of the mind, [men are deluded]. Such men are said to be without *prāṇa*, [*viz.* dead] though alive. Prostrations to those that sport in that piece of flesh which is rent in twain and tainted with the breaking of the wind, etc. What more revolting thing is there than this?

"To the wise, there is nothing to do, no sign [of identification]. The muni who is without 'mine' and fear, with quiescence, without duality and eating leaf [alone], should ever be in meditation with either loin-cloth or no cloth. A yogin who is thus in meditation becomes fit to be Brahman. Though he may have some signs [of identification to pass under this order of life or that], such signs are useless for gaining mokṣa. The cause of salvation is jñāna alone. He is a [true] Brāhmaṇa who cannot be identified as *sat* good person or *asat*, knower of religious books or not, follower of good conduct or bad conduct. Therefore that learned man who is without signs, a knower of dharma, engaged in the actions of Brahman and a knower of the secret mysteries, should roam about incognito. He should go about on this earth without any caste or order of life and without being [even] doubted [regarding his identity] by any beings, like the blind, the idiot or the mute. Then [even] the angels become fond of him who has a quiescent mind. It is the dictate of the Vedas that the sign [of non-identification] itself is *kaivalya*."

Then Nārada asked the grandfather about the rules of *sannyāsa*. to which Brahmā assented and said: "Before either the *ātura* or regular *sannyāsa* is taken, *kṛcchra* penance should be done and then the eight *śrāddhas*. In each of the [eight] *śrāddhas*, two Brāhmaṇas should be fed, in lieu of *Viśvadevas* called Satyavasu and the *Trimūrtis* called Brahmā, Viṣṇu and Maheśvara, in *deva-śrāddha* first; then in *ṛṣiśrāddha* in lieu of Rājarṣi, and *manuṣyarṣi*; then in *divyaśrāddha*, in lieu of Vasu, Rudra, and Ādityas; then in *manuṣyaśrāddha* in lieu of Sanaka, Sanandana, Sanatkumāra, and Sanatsujāta; then in *bhūtaśrāddha*, in lieu of the five great elements, *pṛthvī*, etc., eye and other organs and the four kinds of collections of *bhūtas*; then in *pitṛśrāddha*, in lieu of father, grandfather and great-grandfather; then in *mātṛśrāddha*, in lieu mother, mother's father and mother's grandfather; and then in *ātmaśrāddha*, in lieu of himself, his father and grandfather or of himself, grandfather and great-grandfather, should his father be alive. He should perform the eight *śrāddhas* in one day, or eight days, with the mantras of his *śākhā* in one *yājñapakṣa* or eight *yājñapakṣas*. Then he should worship and feed the Brāhmaṇas according to the rules contained in *pitṛyajña*. Then offering the *piṇḍas* [balls of rice to the *pitṛs*], he should gladden the Brāhmaṇas with the *tāmbūla* [nut and betel, etc.] presents and dismiss them. Then for the accomplishment of the remaining *karmas*, he should pluck off seven hairs; then again for finishing the rest of the *karmas*, he should hold seven or eight hairs and have the head shaved. Except his arm-pit and secret parts, he should have the hairs of his head, whiskers and moustache and nails shaved. After shaving, he should bathe and perform the evening *sandhyā*, uttering Gāyatrī a thousand times. Then performing *brahmayajña*, he should establish his own fire and acting up to his *śākhā*, he should perform the oblation of ghee according to what is said therein till the *ājya* portion with those [mantras beginning with] ātman, etc.; he should eat thrice the fried rice-powder and then sipping the water, he should maintain the fire; then seated north of the fire on a deer-skin, he should be engaged in the study of Purāṇas; without sleeping, he should bathe at the end of the four *yāmas* and after cooking the oblation of [rice] in the fire he should offer it to the fire in sixteen oblations according to [the mantras of] Puruṣa-Sūkta. Then having done *virajāhoma* and sipped water, he should close it with the gift to Brāhmaṇas [of cloth, golden vessel and cows along with presents of money and then dismiss Brahmā [who had been invoked]. With the prescribed mantra, he should attract *agni* (fire) unto himself. After meditating upon and coming round and prostrating before the fire, he should dismiss it. Then in the morning performing *sandhyā* and uttering Gāyatrī a thousand times, he should make worship (*upasanā*) to the sun. Then descending into water up to the navel, he should make water-offering (*arghya*) to the guardians of the eight quarters; then he should give leave to Gāyatrī, making Sāvitrī enter into *vyāhṛti*.

"The mantra prescribed for this should be uttered through the mind and voice in high, middling, and low tones. With the mantra, *abhayaṃ sarvabhutebhyo mattaḥ sarvaṃ pravartate* the water should be sipped and having taken the water with the two hands, it should be dropped on the east. Having uttered *svāhā* he should pluck his hair [yet left] and uttering the prescribed mantra and having torn off the sacred thread and taken it in the hand with water, should utter *oṃ bhūḥ* 'go to the ocean' and cast them down as oblation in water—*oṃ bhuḥ sannyastaṃ mayā oṃ bhuvaḥ sannyastaṃ mayā oṃ svaḥ sannyastaṃ mayā*. Having uttered thrice and saturated thrice [the water] with [the influence of] the mantra, he should sip the water; and then uttering the mantras *oṃ bhuḥ*, etc., he should cast aside in water the cloth and waist-cord. Having thought himself to be the abdicator of all *karmas*, he, being in the meditation of his own reality as nature made him, should go as before northwards with hands upraised. Should he be a sannyāsin learned [in the Vedas, etc.], he should get himself initiated into *praṇava* from his teacher and go about at his own free will with the thought of there being none other but his self, and feeding his body with fruits, leaves and water, live in mountains, forest and temples. That lover of salvation who after *sannyāsa* roams about naked in all places with his heart full of the enjoyment of ātmic bliss, with fruit of avoidance of *karmas* and maintaining his life with fruits, juice, barks, leaves, roots and water should abandon his body in mountain caves, uttering the *praṇava*. But an aspirant after wisdom, should he become a *sannyāsin*, should, after walking a hundred steps, be addressed by the teacher and other Brāhmaṇas thus: 'O very fortunate person Mahābhāga, stay, wear the staff, cloth and bowl, come to the teacher in order to learn the meaning of *praṇava* mantra *vākya*'. He should then take up the waist-cord, loin-cloth, red-coloured cloth and bowl. A bamboo staff which is not injured from top to bottom, equal, beautiful, and not spotted with black, should be worn by him, after sipping the water and uttering the mantra prescribed for the purpose. Then the bowl should be taken up, after uttering the mantra with the *praṇava* preceding it: *oṃ jagaj jīvanaṃ jivanādhārabhūtaṃ māteva mā mantrayasva sarvadā sarva śaubhya*. Then after first uttering [the mantra] *guhyācchādanaṃ kaupīnaṃ oṃ śītavātoṣṇatrāṇakaraṃ dehaika-rakṣaṇaṃ vastraṃ oṃ,* he should take up the waist-cord, loin-cloth and cloth with the *ācamana* (sipping of water) preceding it.

"Thus consecrated with yoga and thinking that he had done all that should be done, he should be firm in the observances of his order of life. Thus is the Upaniṣad."

UPADEŚA V

Then Nārada said to the grandfather thus: "You said that *sannyāsa* was the liberator of all *karmas*. Now you say again that the *sannyāsin* is one that should be in the observance of his order of life (*āśrama*). [How to reconcile the two?]" To which the grandfather replied thus: "To the *jīva* possessing the body, there are three *avasthās*—the waking, the dreaming, and the dreamless sleeping with *turya* (the fourth). Those beings of *puruṣas* that are subject to these *avasthās* follow the observances, incidental to them of *karma*, *jñāna*, and *vairāgya*." Nārada said: "O Lord, if so, what are the differences of different orders of *sannyāsa*? And what are the differences of their observances? Please tell us truly."

Therefore the difference of *sannyāsas* and the differences of observances were related for the sake of Nārada by Brahmā, after assenting to his [Nārada's] question thus:

"Truly *sannyāsa* is of one kind only. On account of *ajñāna*, inability and non-performance of *karmas* [of persons], it is divided into three and then into four, thus: *vairāgya-sannyāsa, jñāna-sannyāsa, jñānavairāgya-sannyāsa* and *karma-sannyāsa*. The *vairāgya-sanyāsin* is one who becomes an ascetic after being in a vicious condition of lust, etc., and then, becomes disgusted with the objects through his former good *karmas*. A *jñāna-sannyāsin* is one who becomes an ascetic following the four practices of salvation, after controlling the organs through book-wisdom and becoming familiar with the experiences of the world of virtue and vice, after abandoning anger, jealousy, envy, *ahaṅkāra* and all *sannyāsa* productive of identification, after giving up the three *vāsanās* of the body, books and world, which are of the form of desires for women, wealth and earth and after thinking that the whole of the universe should be given up, like vomited food. A *jñānavairāgya-sannyāsin* is one who becomes an ascetic as nature made him after practising and enjoying all and having the body alone remaining, through *jñāna* and *vairāgya*, in the realisation of the reality. A *karma-sannyāsin* is one who though he has no *vairāgya*, becomes an ascetic by regularly passing from one *āśrama* to another, from the celibate, to the householder and then to the forester. A *vairāgya-sannyāsin* is one who becomes an ascetic from the celibate order [directly], being as nature made him.

"[There is another fourfold classification.] The four kinds are: *vidvat-sannyāsa, jñāna-sannyāsa, vividisā-sannyāsa* and *karma-sannyāsa*. In *karma-sannyāsa*, there are two [sub] divisions, *nimitta* [causal] and *animitta* [non-causal]. *Ātura-sannyāsa* [on account of the cause of approaching death, disease, etc.], is *nimitta-sannyāsa*. The *karma* [regular] *sannyāsa* is *animitta*. *Ātura-sannyāsa* is on account of defective *karmas*. When sannyāsa is taken at the time of death, it is called *nimitta*. *Animitta* is that when one becomes duly a *sannyāsin* when the body is strong, [after being convinced] that all created things are subject to destruction, that the body and others should be given up, that all ātmans—each one shining in the pure, dwelling in all, moving in the middle world (*antarikṣa-ākāśa*) as of the form of *vāyu*, in the sacrificial pit as of the form of fire, in the moon, in all men, in the supreme angels, in the form of truth, in *ākāśa*, in the form of the conch, pearl, fish, etc., in water, in the form of grain, etc., on earth, in the form of the limbs of Vedas, in the form of the rivers from the mountains, in the form of truth and the great one—are no other than Brahman and that others are but perishable.

"There are six classes of *sannyāsins—kuṭīcaka, bahūdaka, haṃsa, paramahaṃsa, turīyātīta* and *avadhūta*. *Kuṭīcaka* is one who wears the tuft of hair, holy thread, staff, bowl, loin-cloth and tattered cloth, who worships mother, father and teacher, who has potsherd and sling, who is uttering mantras, who takes food in one and the same place, who wears, vertically, the white earth [on the forehead as sect-mark] and who has a staff. *Bahūdaka* is one who, like *kuṭīcaka* wears the tuft of hair, tattered cloth, etc., as well as the three [sect] marks, but who eats eight morsels of food through getting alms. The *haṃsa* is one who wears matted hair and the three vertical sect-marks and eats the alms-food without any limit [as to the morsel] and wears the bare loin-cloth only. The *paramahaṃsa* is he who is without tuft of hair and holy thread, begs food in one day from five houses, has one loin-cloth, wears one red cloth alone and sacred ashes and has given up all. The *turīyatīta* is one who either may take fruits, eating them with his mouth like cows or if he is an eater of food, may beg food from three houses. The naked man having the body alone has the bodily action [quiescent], like the dead body. Such a one is the *turīyātīta*. The *avadhūta* is he who is without any rules, gets his food [in his mouth] following the course of the boa constrictor, [remaining in one place only and taking any food that may come to its mouth as it is lying there] from all persons except persons of ill-repute and outcastes and is ever engaged in the realisation of the real. Should the *ātura-sannyāsin* be alive [after taking *sannyāsa*], he should take up regular *sannyāsa*. The rules to be observed in the case of the [three], *kuṭīcaka, bahūdaka* and *haṃsa* are the same as for the orders of life from the celibate to the *sannyasin*. For the three, *paramahaṃsa* upwards, they have no waist-cord, loin-cloth, cloth, bowl and staff. They may get food from all castes and should be as nature made them. Such are the rules.

"At the time of the *sannyāsa*, the recitation of the Vedas should be made till the mind is cleared; and after casting aside in water the waist-cord, loin-cloth, staff, cloth, bowl, etc., he should roam about. He should be without even the slightest tattered cloth. He should neither utter anything other than *praṇava*, nor talk, nor hear. He should not study logic or grammar. He should not talk many words: they will but pain his vocal organ. He should not converse with people through the vocal organ. He should not talk in other language [than Samskṛt]. He has no worship of God and no witnessing of festivals; he should be free from pilgrimage. The other rules of ascetics are: The *kuṭīcaka* should beg alms in one house only; for the *bahūdaka*, eight morsels in eight houses; for the *haṃsa*, there is no limit; for *paramahaṃsa*, he should beg with his hand as the vessel in five houses; for the *turīyātīta*, he should eat fruits with his mouth like cows; for *avadhūta*, he should take food like a boa constrictor in all castes. The ascetic should not dwell in one place for many days. He should not make prostrations to any one among the *turīyātīta* and *avadhūta*, even though one is junior, he should not make prostrations to another, a senior who has known the reality. He should not swim with his hands and cross the river. He should not climb up a tree, nor get into a carriage. Nothing should be purchased or sold [by him]. No exchange should be made, no ostentation for him. There is nothing for the ascetic to do. If there is anything for him to do, he will perish. Therefore the only thing he is qualified to do is reflection, etc.

"To the *āturas* and *kuṭīcakas*, the world they attain is *bhūrloka* and *bhuvarloka*; to the *bahūdakas, svargaloka*; to the *haṃsas, tapoloka*; to the *paramahaṃsas, satyaloka*, to the *turīyātīta* and *avadhūta, kaivalya* in ātman according to the analogy of the wasp and the worm through the realisation of reality. It is the command of the Vedas that whatever form the one thinks of at the last [death] moment and before leaving the body, is attained by him and no other. Knowing it thus, he should not be a practiser of anything but the realisation of reality. Through the observance of any other, he goes to the world of that other. To one that has attained *jñāna-vairāgya*, his salvation is in the self, as there is no other observance for him. The same one [ātman] alone is styled *viśva* in the waking state, *taijasa* in the dreaming state and *prājña* in the dreamless sleeping state. Through the difference of states, there is the difference of the agent presiding over them. To the fourteen organs [the ten organs of sense and actions and the four organs of the mind in the states], the outer and inner, modifications (*vṛttis*) are the material cause. There are four *vṛttis*, viz. *manas, buddhi, ahaṅkāra* and *citta*. Through the difference of actions of the *vṛttis*, there arise the difference of separate functions. When [the presiding agent is] in the eyes, there is the waking state; in the throat, the dreaming state; in the heart, the dreamless sleeping state; and in the head, the *turya* [or fourth] state. Knowing these and that the *turya* is the indestructible, one should not hear or see anything in the waking state, as if he were in dreamless sleeping state. To such a one who does not apparently know them, even the dreaming state forms the same [dreamless sleeping] state. Such a one is termed *jīvanmukta*. All the Vedas say that there is salvation to such a one.

"To the ascetic, there should be no desire of this world or the higher. Then he will be one that will practise accordingly. Through the practices of [the study of] books foreign to the realisation of reality, he becomes a useless person like a camel bearing saffron paint. To him, there is no entry into yoga books, no study of *Śāṅkhya* books, no practice of mantra or tantra. Should there be any entry into other books [than the one treating of reality], then it will be like an ornament to a dead body. Like a cobbler, he should be beyond *karma* and knowledge and unfit for salutation and repeating the names of the Lord. He will duly get the benefit of the *karmas* [of his order of life]. Having given up all like the foam [separating itself] from the castor oil, having the mental staff which controls the mind clinging to objects, having the hand as the vessel [for eating] and having the quarters alone as the cloth, the ascetic should go about like a lad, idiot, or ghost. He should neither desire to live nor die. Like a coolie abiding his appointed time [of pay], the ascetic should bide his time [of death]. One who lives by taking alms without [the qualifications of] patience, wisdom, *vairāgya* and the qualification beginning with control of mind (*śama*) is the spoiler of the order of life of an ascetic. There is no salvation obtained through the mere assumption of the staff or making the head bald or other disguise or through ostentatious observances. That man who has *jñāna* as his staff is said to be the *ēkadaṇḍin* [one having Brahman alone as the staff]. An ascetic who, having merely a wooden staff without *jñāna*, eats all [indiscriminately] in all places, goes to the terrible hells called *mahāraurava*. [The sense of] greatness in his case is likened by the *ṛṣis* to the pig's dung. Having given it up, he should move about like a worm. Food and cloth without being begged for by him should be obtained involuntarily through the will of others. A naked [ascetic] may bathe at the wish of another. A man who practises meditation upon the self in the dreaming state as in the waking is said to be the foremost and first of *brahmavādins*. He should neither grieve for things not obtained, nor rejoice at things obtained. With the organs not attached to objects, he should be engaged in the sole protection of life. He should always look down upon the gains obtained with much respect [shown to him]. Through the gains obtained with much respect, the ascetic, though released, becomes bound. What is meant by the protection of life, is this: When the fire [of the hearth in a house] had been extinguished and all have taken food, he may go to the house of caste people that are fit for taking alms from. The yogin who has his hand only as his alms-bowl should not often take alms. He may take [food] standing nor sitting; so in the middle [of taking food], he may sip water. Those who have a pure mind should not overstep the limits like the ocean. The great ones do not give up their self-restraint like the sun. When the muni takes, like a cow, the food with the mouth only [without the use of the hand], he becomes of equal vision to all beings. Then he becomes fit for salvation. He may, for alms, go from a forbidden house to a non-forbidden one. He should go [for alms] to a house where the door is ajar, but not to a house where it is closed. The muni who has a dusty body, an uninhabited house or the foot of a tree as his abode, without anything dear or not dear to him, sleeping where the sun sets, without any fire-worship, without any settled place and with patience and the organs under control, should live without any desire in any place obtained. He who after going to the forest dwells with *jñāna* as the sacrifice and the organs under his mastery and awaits his time [of death], is fit to be of the nature of Brahman. A muni who goes about with no cause for instilling fear into all beings need never have any fear from them. One without any identification with body (*abhimāna*) or egoism or dualities or doubt, never is angry, never hates, never lies through the vocal organ. That person who, having visited all sacred places, does not do any injury to any living creature and gets alms at the proper time, is fit to be of the nature of *Brahman*. He should not associate with a forester or householder. He should conduct himself in such manner as not to be known to others. He should not be glad of anything. He should roam about on earth like a worm, according to the direction pointed out by the sun. He should not do or cause to do works tending to [his] fame or pains or people's benefit. He should not be inclined towards vicious books. He should not live dependent upon any. He should give up all over-disputatious reasoning. He should not join any party [fighting with another]. He should not take any disciples. He should not study many books. He should not discourse. Neither should he commence any works. Without any distinguishing characteristics and without letting others know his opinions, that wise man or *muni*, ever intent upon the *Brāhmic vision*, should exhibit himself to people like an idiot or a lad or a mute person. He should neither do nor talk anything. He should not think of a good or bad thing. Rejoicing in that within himself, the muni should go about like an idiot. He should roam about alone without associating with any and with the senses under control. The clever *jñānin* sporting in ātman, ever delighting in ātman, looking upon all with equal vision like an *ātma-jñānin* and playing like a child, should wander about like an idiot. That learned man versed on *brahma-vidyā* should talk like a madman. He should follow the observances of cows [by eating with the mouth, causing no trouble to anybody]. A good *jñānin* whether pushed, disregarded, slighted, beaten, or hindered by the vicious or burnt by their acts, or having urine and faeces thrown upon him by them or afflicted in various other ways, should always think well of them, though pained, and thus make them lift themselves through their own selves. A yogin whether praised or afflicted by others, never thinks of it in order to reach a superior state in yoga. A yogin who is slighted by people attains a higher state in yoga. A yogin never goes against the actions of the virtuous. He is the same whether people slight him or do not desire his association. He should do all that is right through the actions of mind, speech and body to all beings born out of the embryo or the egg, etc. He should harbour no malice against any and give up all clinging to things. The ascetic, after giving up passion, anger, pride, desire, delusion and other faults should be without fear. Eating alms-food, preserving silence, *tapas*, special meditation, a good *jñāna*, and *vairāgya*—these are said, in the opinion [of the great], to be the dharma of the ascetic. Wearing the red cloth and being ever in *dhyāna-yoga*, he should live either at the foot of a tree, outside the village, or in the temple. Daily he should live upon begging. He should not eat one food alone [from one only]. Till the mind becomes pure, the learned man should thus be moving about. Then when the mind is purified, he may be anywhere as *parivrājaka*. Seeing Janārdana in and out everywhere, preserving, being equal in happiness and pains and with patience, eating whatever comes to hand, equally regarding without any hate, Brāhmaṇa, cow, horse, beasts and others, meditating through the mind upon Viṣṇu that is Paramātman and Īśvara, thinking ever of Brāhmic bliss and thinking himself to be Brahman alone—such a one having known, thus, regarding the staff to be no other than the certitude of the mind as above, having no desire, being naked and having abandoned all *saṃsāra* through the actions ever done through the mind, speech and body, attains salvation, according to the analogy of the wasp and the worm, through the practice of the realisation of reality without ever seeing the universe. Such is the Upaniṣad."

UPADEŚA VI

Nārada, addressing Brahmā, asked: "O Lord! You said of practice (*abhyāsa*) according to the analogy of the wasp and the worm. What is that practice?"

To which the Grandfather replied thus:

"One [viz. an ascetic] should live with true speech and *jñāna-vairāgya* and with the body alone as the remaining [possession]. Know *jñāna* alone as the body, *vairāgya* alone as mental control (*prāṇa śānti*) and bodily control (*dānti*) as the eyes, *manas* alone as the face, *buddhi* alone as *kalā*, parts of effulgence, the twenty-five *tattvas* as the limbs, the *avasthās* as the five great elements, *karma*, *bhakti*, *jñāna* and *vairāgya* as the branches [or parts] and that the waking, dreaming, dreamless sleeping and *turya avasthās* and the fourteen organs as being of the nature of a pillar planted in the mud. Though such is the case, the man who masters these through his *buddhi*, like a boatman regarding the boat immersed in the mire, or the elephant driver regarding the elephant [under his control] and has known that all else beside self is illusory and destructible and become indifferent, should ever utter: 'I am Brahman alone'. He should not know anything as other than self. A *jīvanmukta* who lives thus is a doer of that which should be done. He should not discourse that he is other than Brahman. But he should ever be discoursing: 'I am Brahman'. From the waking, dreaming and dreamless sleeping states, he should reach the *turya* state and then the state beyond *turya* (*turyātīta*). The waking state is in the day; the dreaming in the night and the dreamless sleeping in the midnight. Each *avasthā* [state] has its sub-states. The functions of the fourteen organs, eye and others mutually dependent are the following: The eye perceives forms; the ears, sounds; the tongue perceives tastes; the nose, odours; the vocal organ speaks;

the hand lifts; the leg walks; the anus excretes; the sexual organ enjoys; the skin feels; the *buddhi* perceives objects, being under the control of the organs; through *buddhi*, he understands; through *citta*, he thinks; through *ahaṃkāra*, he says 'I'. All these should be abandoned. Through the identification with the house [the body], he, like a householder, becomes a *jīva,* thinking that the body is itself.

"The *jīva* is dwelling in this body. When he is in the eastern petal [of the heart], he is inclined to virtuous actions; in the south-eastern petal, to sleep and laziness; in the southern petal, to cruel actions; in the south-western petal, to sinful actions; in the western petal to love of sport in the north-western petal, to travelling; in the northern petal, to peace of mind; in the north-eastern petal, to *jñāna*; in [the middle of] the pericarp, to *vairāgya*; in the filament, to ātma-deliberation. Such are the different aspects to be understood [in the heart]. The first living *avasthā* [of *jīva*] is the waking; the second is the dreaming; the third is the dreamless sleeping; the fourth *turya*; that which is not these four is *turyātīta*. The one Lord alone that is witness and without qualities appears [as many] through the difference of *viśva taijasa, prājña* and *taṭastha* [the neutral]. One should [always] utter: 'I am Brahman alone'. Else in the waking state, [he is] in the four states of the waking state and others; in the dreaming state, [he is] in the four states of the dreaming state and others; in the dreamless sleeping state, [he is] in the four states of *turya* and others; to the *turyātīta* that is *nirguṇa*, such states are not. There is only one witness in all the states of *viśva, taijasa* and *prājña*, who is presiding over the gross, the subtle and the causal [bodies]. Is *taṭastha* the seer? Or is he not? As [to *taṭastha*], there is the property of seeing; the *jīva* that is affected by egoism, etc. of agency and enjoyment is not the seer. The one other than *jīva* [viz. *taṭastha*] is not concerned [with egoism, etc.]. If it is said that the *jīva* is not so [concerned with egoism], then it is not a fact. Through the *abhimāna* of the *jīva*, there is the *abhimāna* of the body. And [conversely] through the *abhimāna* of the body, there is the *abhimāna* of the *jīva*. The state of the *jīva* is as a screen [to screen Brahman] like [the pot and house] the pot-*ākāśa* and the house-*ākāśa*. Through such a screen, he reaches self-realisation through the mantra—'*Haṃsa-So'ham*' having the characteristics of inspiration [*Haṃsa*]and expiration [*So'ham*]. Having known thus, if he should give up the identification with the body, then he does not identify himself with the body [i.e., not attain the state of *jīva*]. Such a one is stated to be Brahman. Having given up *abhimāna* and anger, being content with moderate food, having conquered the organs and having controlled the avenues [of the organs], one should make the mind enter into meditation. The yogin who has always controlled [his mind and organs] should ever diligently commence his meditation in empty places, caves and forests. The knower of yoga who is bent upon accomplishing the end should never be engaged in giving feasts to Brāhmaṇas, in *śrāddha* sacrifices, etc., or in going to places of pilgrimages, festivals or crowds. The well-controlled yogin should go about as if people had treated him with disrespect. He should not go against the actions of the wise. That great ascetic is said to be having a three-knotted staff (a *tridaṇḍin*) who holds firmly the three-*daṇḍa* [control] of mind, speech, and body. That ascetic is said to be a supreme person who begs alms-food of worthy Brāhmaṇas, when smoke has ceased and fire has been extinguished [in their houses]. Is he not a degraded ascetic who, though holding the staff and begging food, is without *vairāgya* and is not intent upon the observances of his order? He is an ascetic—not any other—who does not go to the house where he expects to find special alms or which he has already visited. He is said to transcend all castes and orders of life who realises the self-shining supreme *tattva* that is without body and organs, the all-witness, the real *vijñāna* that is of the form of bliss. To the ātman that is of the nature of *jñāna*, such an idea as 'the order of life, etc., is mine,' being generated out of *māyā* in this body, can never exist. He who knows thus through Vedānta is beyond all castes and orders of life. He from whom all castes and orders of life slip away through ātmic vision, transcends them all and remains in ātman alone. That person is said by the knower of the meaning of the Vedas to be beyond caste and order of life (*ativarṇāśramin*) who after crossing all castes and orders of life, abides in ātman alone. Therefore, O Nārada, the castes and orders of life which are foreign [to ātman] are attributed falsely, by the ignorant, to ātman. O Nārada, for those that are *brahma-*

jñānis, there are no rules ordained nor prohibited; there is nothing to be given up or not; similarly nothing else [for them]. Having attained indifference to all objects even up to Brahmā's seat, having destroyed [or done away with] all fondness for everything, as for son, relatives, wife etc., and having faith in the path of salvation and through love of *Vedānta-jñāna*, he should approach a guru who is a knower of Brahman with a gift [in his hand]. Having an equilibrated mind, he should satisfy the guru for a long time through service, etc., and learn with a steady firm mind the meaning of the sentences of the Vedas. Then being devoid of 'I' and 'mine' and of all attractions and having attained peace of mind, etc., he sees ātman in himself. Through observing the faults of *saṃsāra*, there arises indifference. There is no doubt that *sannyāsa* arises in one who becomes disgusted with *saṃsāra*. The aspirant after salvation who is called *paramahaṃsa* should through the hearing, etc., of Vedānta, practise *brahma-jñāna*, which is the direct and chief means of salvation. In order to attain *brahma-jñāna*, the one named *paramahaṃsa* should possess the qualities of the control of mind and body, etc. He should always be one who practises Vedānta, being master of the mind, the body and the organs, being without fear and egoism, with a firm mind, without the pairs [of opposites], without attaching himself to any, having a worn-out loin-cloth and being bald-headed or naked. He should have the great intelligence of the knower of Vedānta, a yogin without 'I' and 'mine' and being equal and friendly to friends and other beings. That *jñānin* alone and none else is able to cross *saṃsāra* who has his mind at peace. With the grace of the guru towards him, be should live with him for one year. He should be careful to observe restraint (*yama*) and religious observance (*niyama*). At the end of that [year], he should attain the supreme *jñāna-yoga*, and roam about on this earth without going against dharma; [or] at the end of one year, he should give up the three orders of life and attain the chief *āśrama* [of *sannyāsa*], as well as the supreme *jñāna-yoga*. Then, taking leave of the guru, he should wander over the earth, having given up association [with wife, etc.] as well as anger and being content with moderate food and having controlled the senses. The householder who does not perform *karma* and the ascetic who performs *karma*—both become fallen through their perverse doings. Each becomes intoxicated through seeing women. Each becomes intoxicated through drinking alcohol. Therefore women, the mere sight of who is poison, should be shunned at a distance. Such things as conversation and proximity with and sight of women dancing, singing, using violence against persons and disputatious arguments should be given up. Therefore O Nārada, to such a one, there is neither bath nor muttering of mantras, nor worship, nor *homa*, nor means of accomplishment, nor any *karma* of fire-sacrifice etc., nor worshipping with flowers, etc., nor *karmas* to the ancestors nor pilgrimages, nor religious observances, nor dharmas, nor *adharmas*, nor any rules of observance, nor any other worldly *karmas*. He should give up all *karmas* and wordly observances. That yogin of an ascetic who is a learned person, having his intelligence directed towards reality, should never injure any worm or insect, bird or tree. O Nārada, roam through the world with vision ever directed inwards, with purity, with mind under control, with a mind that is full of Brahman and all attraction given up within. The sage that goes about alone, does [or should] not dwell in countries where there is no king. [In his case], there is neither praise nor prostration, nor the propitiation of gods or ancestors. Thus the ascetic who has his abode changeful [in body], or changeless [in ātman], should be content with whatever he gets. Thus is the Upaniṣad."

UPADEŚA VII

The grandfather, after eulogising Nārada who asked about the observance of ascetics, replied thus:

"The ascetic who has attained indifference [to objects], should stay in one and the same place in the rainy season [for four months], and then for [the remaining] eight months should wander alone. Then also the ascetic should not stay in one and the same place for more than a day. Like a deer that does not stay in one place on account of fear, he should not stay in one place. He should not create an attraction [in his mind] that may serve as an obstacle to his going about. He should not cross a stream [by swimming] with his hand, nor ascend a tree, nor witness the festival of a god, nor partake of regal food, nor do the external worship of god. Having discarded all things other than the self, he should be with his body emaciated by taking food [from each house] like the bees [from each flower]. He should not increase the fat [in the body]; he should discard ghee like blood. Regarding such royal food as flesh, sandal-coating etc. as offal, the different tastes as the degraded caste, the cloth as a defiled vessel, the oil-bath as sexual union, the gladdening of a friend as urine, desires as cow's flesh, the country known to him as the outcastes' place, gold and women as cobra or deadly poison, the place of assembly as the burning ground the capital of the town as the hell called Kumbhīpāka and royal food as balls of rice offered to the dead, he should be without any worship of God other than the self; and having given up all the actions of the world and his own country, and ever thinking of the bliss of his self, like the bliss arising from the discovery of a lost object, forgetting his country and the fondness for his body, and knowing that his body should be slighted like a carcass, he should dwell away from son, relation and native place, like a thief released from prison. Taking whatever comes to him without effort, ever intent upon the realisation, through meditation, of *brahma-praṇava*, being freed from all *karmas*, having burnt up all passion, anger, greed, delusion, pride, malice, etc., having transcended the three *guṇas*, being without the six human infirmities [hunger, thirst, grief, delusion, old age and death] without the six changes [birth, existence, growth, transformation, decrease and annihilation] speaking the truth and being opposed to all savoury things, he should live for one day in a village, five days in a town, five days in a sacred place and five days in sacred waters. With no settled place of residence and with a firm mind, he should dwell alone in mountain caves without uttering falsehood. Two persons should not join together. Should three join, there is created a village thereby; with four, is formed a city. Therefore he should live alone in a village. In it, the ascetic should not give scope to his fourteen organs. Having attained the wealth of *vairāgya* through non-dissipated *jñāna* and having deliberated within himself that there is none other than the self, he should attain *jīvanmukti*, having seen the reality everywhere. Till *prārabdha-karma* is over, he should understand the four kinds of *svarūpa* [in *tattvamasi*] and should live in the realisation of reality, till his body falls [a prey to death].

To the *kuṭīcaka* there is [prescribed] a bath three times daily; to the *bahūdaka*, twice; to the *haṃsa*, once; to the *paramahaṃsa* there is the mental bath; to the *turyātīta*, there is the holy-ashes bath; to the *avadhūta*, there is the wind as the bath. For the *kuṭīcaka*, there is the vertical sect-mark; for the *bahūdaka*, there is three-lined [horizontal] sect-mark; for the *haṃsa*, both; for the *paramahaṃsa*, there is the holy-ashes sect-mark; for the *turyātīta*, there is the spot-sect-mark; for the *avadhūta* or for the *turyātīta* and *avadhūta* there is none. For the *kuṭīcaka*, shaving takes place once in two months; for the *bahūdaka*, once in four months; for the *haṃsa* and *pramahaṃsa*, none, or if wanted, once in a year; for the *turyātīta* and *avadhūta* none at all. The *kuṭīcaka* should take the food in one [place only]; the *bahūdaka* should take alms [in many places]; for the *haṃsa* and *paramahaṃsa*, the hand is the vessel; the *turyātīta*, it is like the action of the boa constrictor [opening the mouth and taking whatever comes into it]. For the *kuṭīcaka*, there are two cloths; for the *bahūdaka*, there is one cloth; for the *haṃsa* there is a piece of cloth; and the *paramahaṃsa* should be naked or have only a loin-cloth; in the case of the *turyātīta* and *avadhūta*, they should be as nature made them. For the *haṃsa* and *paramahaṃsa*, there is [prescribed] a deerskin, and for no others. For the *kuṭīcaka* and *bahūdaka*, there is the worship of the divine [image]; for the *haṃsa* and *paramahaṃsa* there is mental worship; for the *turyātīta* and *avadhūta*, there is the idea that they alone are Brahman. The *kuṭīcaka* and *bahūdaka* are entitled to mantras and *japas*; the *haṃsa* and *paramahaṃsa*, to *dhyāna* [meditation]; the *turyātīta* and *avadhūta* are entitled to none; but they are entitled to the initiation of the sacred sentences of the Vedas; so also the *paramahaṃsa*. The *kuṭīcaka* and *bahūdaka* are not entitled to initiate others; for them, there is [the uttering of] the mental *praṇava*; for the *haṃsa* and *paramahaṃsa*, there is the internal *praṇava* [in the heart]; for the *turyātīta* and *avadhūta*, there is the *Brahma-praṇava* [always]. For the *kutīcaka* and *bahūdaka*, there is hearing and study (*śravaṇa*); for the *haṃsa* and *paramahaṃsa*, there is *manana* thinking and remembering; for the *turyātīta* and *avadhūta* there is profound meditation ever (*nididhyāsana*). For all these, there is necessarily the meditation upon ātman. Thus the aspirant after salvation should ever be uttering the *praṇava* which enables one to cross *saṃsāra*, and be living as a *jīvanmukta*. Thus the ascetic, according to each one's capacity, should ever be seeking the means to attain *kaivalya*. Such is the Upaniṣad."

UPADEŚA VIII

Then Nārada asked Parameṣṭhin [Brahmā] to enlighten him, who had surrendered himself to him, about *saṃsāra-tāraka* [or that *praṇava* which lifts one out of *saṃsāra*].

Assenting to which, Brahmā began thus: "Oṃkāra that is Brahman is the individual (*vyaṣṭi*) and the cosmic (*samaṣṭi*). What is the individual? What is the cosmic? *Brahma-praṇava* is of three kinds, destructive (*saṃhāra-praṇava*), creative (*sṛṣṭi-praṇava*) and belonging to both (*ubhyātmaka*) *praṇava*, as being of two forms, internal and external. [It is also eight:] *antaḥ-praṇava, vyāvahārika-praṇava, bāhya-praṇava, ārśa-praṇava, ubhyātmaka* or *virāṭ-praṇava, saṃhāra-praṇava, brahma-praṇava*, and *ardhyamātrā praṇava*. O is Brahman. Know that the mantra of the one-syllabled O is *praṇava*. It has the eight differences of *akāra*, *ukāra*, *makāra, ardhamātrā, nāda, bindu, kalā*, and *śakti*. Know it is not four [alone]. *Akāra* is associated with ten thousand limbs: *ukāra*, with one thousand limbs; *makāra* with one hundred limbs; *ardhamātrā* is of the nature of endless limbs. That which is *saguṇa* [associated with *guṇas*] is preservation (*virāṭ*) *praṇava*; that which is *nirguṇa* [not associated with *guṇas*] is destruction (*saṃhāra*) *praṇava*; that which is associated with *guṇas* and is not so associated, is origination (*utpatti*) *praṇava*. *Pluta* [the elongated accent] is *virāṭ*: *plutapluta* is *samhāra*. The *virāṭ-praṇava* is of the form of sixteen *mātrās* and is above the thirty-six *tattvas*. The sixteen *mātrās* are thus: *akāra* is the first *mātrā*; *ukāra* is the second; *makāra* is the third; *ardhamātrā* is the fourth; *nāda* is the fifth; *bindu* is the sixth; *kalā* is the seventh; *kalātīta* is the eighth; *śānti* is the ninth; *śāntyatīta* is the tenth; *unmanī* is the eleventh; *manonmanī* is the twelfth; *purītati* is the thirteenth; *tanumadhyamā* is the fourteenth; *pati* is the fifteenth; *parā* is the sixteenth. Then [again] having sixty-four *mātrās* and their division into the two, *prakṛti* and *puruṣa* and resolving themselves into the one hundred and twenty-eight differences of *mātrās*, it becomes *saguṇa* and *nirguṇa*. Though *brahma-praṇava* is one only, it is the substratum of all the support of the whole universe, of the form of all letters [*akṣaras*], time, Vedas and Śiva. This *Oṃkāra* should be sought after, that is mentioned in the Vedas of the nature of the Upaniṣads. Know that this *Oṃkāra* is the ātman that is indestructible during the three periods of time, past, present and future, able to confer salvation and eulogized by Brahma-sound [Vedas]. Having experienced this one Oṃ as immortal and ageless, and having brought about the Brahma-nature in this body, become convinced that your ātman, associated with the three bodies, is Parabrahman. Through Viśva and other [viz. *taijasa, prājña*, and *turya*] in order, the realisation of Parabrahman should be attained, since ātman is of four kinds through his identification with, and the enjoying of, the gross as well as the enjoyer of the gross, the subtle as well as the enjoyer of the subtle, and through his identification [with the third body] enjoying bliss in the fourth. He has four feet. The one presiding over the waking state is gross; and since he is the enjoyer of the universe (*viśva*) he becomes the gross consciousness (*sthūla-prajñā*). He has nineteen [viz. the five organs of sense, the five organs of action, the five *prāṇas* and the four of the mind] facets and eight parts. He is all pervasive and the Lord. He is the enjoyer of the gross and is the (*caturātman*) called Viśva. He alone is the Puruṣa called Vaiśvānara. He alone is (the conqueror of the universe) Viśvajīt. This is the first foot. When this Lord attains the dreaming condition, he is the subtle consciousness (*sūkṣma-prajña*). O conqueror of all, he is the one having eight limbs, and there is none else. He is the enjoyer of the subtle and is *caturātman*, named *taijasa* and the protector of elements. He alone is the Hiraṇyagarbha, presiding over the gross (or subtle matter rather). He is said to form the second foot. *Suṣupti* [or the dreamless sleep] is that state where one sleeps without any desire and where one sees no dreams. The one identified with this dreamless sleep is *prajñāna-ghana*, is blissful, of the nature of eternal bliss and the ātman in all creatures; yet he is enjoyer of bliss, has consciousness as his [one] foot, is all-pervading, indestructible, *caturātman* and the Lord and is named Prājña, the third foot. He alone is the Lord of all, the knower of all, of subtle thought, the latent one, and the cause of all creation. He alone is the origin and the destruction. These three [states] are obstacles to all creatures obtaining [the final] peace. As is *svapna*, so is *suṣupṭi*, it [also] being said to be illusory. The *caturātman* the fourth, as he is *sat, cit* and the one essence (*ekarasa*), ends as the fourth and follows [upon the heels of each of the above states], is the knower of the means of *vikalpa-jñāna* and is the one following knower (*anujñātṛ*). Having known them, and known as *māyā* the three *vikalpas* of *suṣupṭi*, *svapna* and *āntara* (the inner), even in this state, is he not [to be known as] *sat-cit-ekarasa*. This shall be expressed as differentiated thus: It is not even the gross *prajñā*; nor is it the very subtle *prajñā*; nor is it *prajñā* itself [of the causal body]: O sage neither is it the trifling *prajñā*; nor is it the *non-prajñā*; nor is it the dual *prajñā*; nor is it the internal *prajñā*, though it is without *prajñā*; it is *prajñāna-ghana*. It can never be known by the organs; nor can it be known by the reason; it cannot be grasped by the organs of action. It cannot be proved. It cannot be reached by thought. It cannot be proved by analogy. It can be realised by self-realisation alone. It is with the waking state, etc. It is the auspicious, with changes, without a second. Such a one is thought to be *turya*. This alone is Brahman, *brahma-praṇava*. This should be known. There is no other *turya*. To the aspirants after salvation, it is the support, like the sun everywhere; it is the self-light. As it alone is Brahman, this *brahma-ākāśa* is shining always. Thus is the Upaniṣad."

UPADEŚA IX

Nārada asked: "Who is *brahma-svarūpa*?" To which Brahmā replied thus: "*brahma-svarūpa* is thus: Those who know that 'he [Brahman] is one and I am another' are only animals (*paśus*). The real animals [*paśus*] are no animals. The wise man who knows Brahman thus [as himself, and himself as Brahman] escapes out of the mouth of death. There is no other path to salvation.

Is time the cause [of origination of universes]? Or nature? Or *karma*? Or accident? Or the [great] elements? Or Puruṣa? This should be considered. It is not the union of them. [Then] there is the ātman, but [*jīva*] ātman is not the Lord, as it is subject to pleasures and pains. Those [ṛṣis] following *dhyāna-yoga* have beheld, as the cause, the *devātmanśakti* concealed by its own qualities of that one that presides over all the causes associated with time and ātman. Him [the Universal Soul], we consider as the wheel which has one circumference, which is covered by three [layers], which has sixteen end-parts, which has fifty spokes and twenty counter-spokes, which has six times eight [nails], which has one rope of various forms, which has the threefold path and which has delusion arising from the twofold cause. Him [we worship as a river] which has [water] oozing out of the five currents [of organs], which is terrible and crooked through the five causes [of elements], whose *prāṇas* are the five waves, which has *buddhi* etc., as the root cause, which has five whirlpools, which is impelled by the velocity of the five pains, which has fifty differences [or has the five miseries] and which has the five obstacles. In this wheel of Brahman, which is the support of life and the last abiding place of all beings, and which is infinite, is whirling deluded the *jīva*, thinking that it is different from the one [Lord] ordainer. Being blessed by him, he gains salvation through such [a blessing]. This is declared as Brahman, as the supreme and the indestructible. In it are the three [the enjoyer, the enjoyed and enjoyment]. Hence it is the firm abode [of all]. The knowers of Brahman having known Brahman within [the universe, etc.] attain *samādhi* in Brahman and are absorbed in Brahman. Īśvara upholds this universe, closely associated with the destructible and the indestructible, which are manifest and unmanifest; but the not-ruler of [*jīva*] ātman is bound through the thought of its being the enjoyer; and having known the Lord is freed from all fetters. Both Īśvara and *jīva* are birthless; one [the former], is *jñānin* and the other is *ajñānin* [the latter]. [The goddess of] *Brahmātma-śakti*, is birthless, is alone engaged [in this world], on account of the enjoyment of the enjoyers. Ātman is endless. The universe is his form. He is not the agent. Whoever knows the Brahman that is threefold [as *jīva*, Īśvara and the universe] is released from bondage. It is Pradhāna alone that is destructible. It is Īśvara that is immortal and indestructible. The one Lord [Īśvara] ordains Pradhāna and Puruśa.

"The illusion of the universe disappears through meditation on union [or absorption] and *sattva-bhāva* of Parameśvara always.

Through knowing the Lord, *avidyā* and the rest are destroyed. Through the removal of such pains, there is freedom from birth and death. Through the meditation of that Parameśvara, the third body is acquired after this [physical] body, all wealth is enjoyed, and he attains whatever should be attained. He should know with certitude that all the three things [viz. the enjoyer, the enjoyed and enjoyment] are nothing but Brahman, and are of the nature of his own self. There is none but this to be known. All ātmic knowledge is through only [*tapas*]. That, Brahman contains in itself all excellence. Having known thus, whoever meditates upon the *ātma-svarūpa*, to him where then is grief? Where then is delusion? Therefore the *virāṭ* is the past, present and future time and is of indestructible nature.

"Ātman, that is the atom of atoms and the greatest of the greatest, is in the cave of the heart of all creatures. One without the thought of objects and without grief, knows the ātman capable of neither increase nor decrease through the grace of Īśvara or through the non-attraction to the objects of the senses. He [ātman] walks speedily without legs, lifts objects without hands, sees without eyes and hears without ears. He knows all, but none knows him. He is said to be the foremost *mahāpuruṣa*. Having known ātman that is bodiless in this fleeting body, the great, the all-pervading, the support of all, with incomprehensible power, fit to be known through the meaning, etc., of all the Upaniṣads, the supreme of the supreme, the supreme object fit to be known, the one remaining after all, the all-knowing, the eternal, the foremost of all foremost beings, the ordiner of all, the one fit to be worshipped by all angels, the one without beginning, end and middle, without limit or destruction, the cause of Brahmā, Viṣṇu, and Rudra, the one that has all the universe latent in himself, of the nature of the five elements with the expansion of all the quintuplicated creation, without being enveloped by his own limbs of quintuplicated objects, superior to the supreme, greater than the greatest, of the nature of effulgence, the eternal and the auspicious, the undaunted personage never grieves. One who has neither given up vicious actions, nor controlled his organs, nor mastered his mind, nor given up longing after fruits of actions though the mind is undisturbed, nor brought his mind to one state [or point], will not attain this ātman.

"This [Brahman] is neither internal nor external consciousness; is neither gross, nor *jñāna*, nor *ajñāna*; nor is it the state between the waking and the dreaming states. It cannot be cognised by the organs; is not subject to proof; is within. He who knows that which is by itself alone, is an emancipated person."

The Lord Brahmā said that he becomes an emancipated person. He who knows reality is a *parivraṭ*. Such a *parivrāṭ* roams about alone. Through fear, he is like a terrified deer. He will not be opposed to going anywhere. Having given up all but his body, he will live like a bee and without considering others as foreign to himself; ever meditating upon reality, he attains liberation in himself. Such a *parivrāṭ* will be without delusion, without action or causing others to act, being absolved from teacher, disciple, books, etc. and having abandoned all *saṃsāra*. Such a *parivrāta* roams about thus—without wealth, being happy, able to get wealth [if wanted], having crossed *jñāna* and *ajñāna* as well as happiness and grief, being self-effulgence, being fit to be known by the Vedas, having known all, able to confer *siddhis* and remaining himself as Brahman, the Lord. Such a *parivrāṭ* attains the supreme abode of Viṣṇu, from which a yogin that has gone to it does not return, and where the sun and the moon do not shine. He does not return. Such is *kaivalya*.

Oṃ tat sat is the Upaniṣad

22
Śāṇḍilya Upaniṣad of Atharvaṇaveda

CHAPTER I

Om. Śaṇḍilya questioned Atharvan thus: "Please tell me about the eight parts *(aṅgas)* of yoga which is the means of attaining to ātman."

Atharvan replied: "The eight *aṅgas* of yoga are *yama*, *niyama, āsana, prāṇāyāma, pratyāhāra, dhāraṇā, dhyāna,* and *samādhi*. Of these, *yama* is of ten kinds: and so is *niyama*. There are eight *āsanas*. *Prāṇāyāma* is of three kinds; *pratyāhāra* is of five kinds: so also is *dhāraṇā*. *Dhyāna* is of two kinds, and *samādhi* is of one kind only.

"Under forbearance *(yama)* are ten: *ahiṃsā, satya, asteya, brahmacarya, dayā, ārjava, kṣamā, dhṛti, mitāhāra,* and *śauca*. Of these, *ahiṃsā* is the not causing of pain to any living being at any time through the action of one's mind, speech, or body. *Satya* is the speaking of the truth that conduces to the well-being of creatures, through the actions of one's mind, speech or body. *Asteya* is not coveting of another's property through the actions of one's mind, speech, or body. *Brahmacarya* is refraining from sexual intercourse in all places and in all states in mind, speech or body. *Dayā* is kindliness towards all creatures in all places. *Ārjava* is the preserving of equanimity of mind, speech, or body in the performance or non-performance of the actions ordained or forbidden to be done. *Kṣamā* is the bearing patiently of all pleasant or unpleasant things, such as praise or blows. *Dhṛti* is the preserving of firmness of mind during the period of gain or loss of wealth or relatives. *Mitāhāra* is the taking of oily and sweet food, leaving one-fourth of the stomach empty. *Śauca* is of two kinds, external and internal. Of these, the external is the cleansing of the body by earth and water; the internal is the cleansing of the mind. This [the latter] is to be obtained by means of the knowledge of self *(adhyātmavidyā)*.

"Under religious observances (*niyama*), are ten, viz. *tapas, santoṣa, āstikya, dāna, īśvarapūjana, siddhānta-śravaṇa, hrīḥ, mati, japa,* and *vrata*. Of these *tapas* is the emancipation of the body through the observances of such penances as *kṛcchra, cāndrāyaṇa*, etc., according to rules. *Santoṣa* is being satisfied with whatever comes to us of its own accord. *Āstikya* is the belief in the merits or demerits of actions as stated in the Vedas. *Dāna* is the giving with faith to deserving persons, money, grains, etc., earned lawfully. *Īśvarapūjana* is the worshipping of Viṣṇu, Rudra, etc., with pure mind according to one's power. *Siddhānta-śravaṇa* is the inquiry into the significance of Vedānta, *hrīḥ* is the shame felt in the performance of things contrary to the rules of the Vedas and of society. *Mati* is the faith in the paths laid down by the Vedas. *Japa* is the practising of the mantras into which one is duly initiated by one's spiritual instructor, and which is not against [the rules of] the Vedas. It is of two kinds—the spoken and the mental. The mental is associated with contemplation by the mind. The spoken is of two kinds—the loud and the low. The loud pronunciation gives the reward as stated [in the Vedas]: [while] the low one [gives] a reward thousand times [of that]. The mental [gives] a reward a crore [times of that]. *Vrata* is the regular observance of or the refraining from the actions enjoined or prohibited by the Vedas.

"The postures *(āsanas)* are [chiefly] eight, viz. *svastika, gomukha, padma, vīra, siṃha, bhadra, mukta,* and *mayūra*.

"*Svastika* is the sitting at ease with the body erect, placing each foot between the thighs and knees of the other. *Gomukha* is (the sitting at ease with the body erect), placing the hollow of the left foot under the side of the right posterior and the hollow of the right foot under the side of the left posteriors, resembling a cow's face (*gomukha*). *Padma* is (the sitting at ease with the body erect) placing the back of each foot in the thigh of the other, the right hand grasping the right toe and the left hand the left toe. This, O Śāṇḍilya, is praised by all. *Vīra* is [the sitting at ease with the body erect], placing one foot on the thigh of the other and the other foot underneath the corresponding [opposite thigh]. *Siṃha* is [the sitting at ease with the body erect], pressing the right side [of the thigh] with the hollow of left heel and vice versa. Rest your hands on the knees, spread out the fingers, open your mouth and carefully fix your gaze on the tip of your nose. This is always praised by the yogins. *Siddha* is [the sitting at ease with the body erect], pressing the perineum with the left heel and placing the heel of the right foot above the genital organ, concentrating the mind between the two eyebrows. *Bhadra* is [the sitting at ease with the body erect], pressing the two ankles of the two feet firmly together against the *sīvinī* (viz. lower part of the seed) and binding the knees firmly with the hands. This is the *bhadra* which destroys all diseases and poisons. *Mukta* is [the sitting at ease with the body erect], pressing with the left heel the right side of the tender part of the *sīvinī*, and with the right heel the left side of the tender part of the *sīvinī*. *Mayūra*—(lit., peacock): rest your body upon the ground with both palms and place your elbows on the sides of the navel, lift up the head and feet and remain like a stick in the air, [like the plant balance in gymnastics]. This is the *mayūra* posture which destroys all sins. By these, all the diseases within the body are destroyed; all the poisons are digested. Let the person who is unable to practise all these postures betake himself to any one [of these] which he may find easy and pleasant. He who conquers [or gets mastery over] the postures—he conquers the three worlds. A person who has the practice of *yama* and *niyama* should practise *prāṇāyāma*; by that the *nāḍīs* become purified."

Then Śāṇḍilya questioned Atharvan thus: "By what means are the *nāḍīs* purified? How many are they in number? How do they arise? What vital airs (*vāyus*) are located in them? What are their seats? What are their functions? Whatever is worthy of being known in the body, please tell me." To that Atharvan replied [thus]: "This body is ninety-six digits in length. *Prāṇa* extends twelve digits beyond the body. He who through the practice of yoga reduces his *prāṇa* within his body to make it equal to or not less than the fire in it becomes the greatest of the yogins. In humans, the region of fire which is triangular in form and brilliant as the molten gold is situated in the middle of the body. In four-footed animals, it [fire] is quadrangular. In birds, it is round. In its [the region of fire's] centre, the purifying, beneficial, and subtle flame is situated. Two digits above the anus and two digits below the sexual organ is the centre of the body for humans. For four-footed animals, it is the middle of the heart. For birds, it is the middle of the body. Nine digits from (or above) the centre of the body and four digits in length and breadth is situated an oval form. In its midst is the navel. In it, is situated the wheel (*cakra*) with twelve spokes. In the middle of the *cakra*, the *jīva* (ātman) wanders, driven by its good and bad deeds. As a spider flies to and fro within a web of fine threads, so *prāṇa* moves about here. In this body, the *jīva* rides upon *prāṇa*. Lying in the middle of the navel and above it, is the seat of *kuṇḍalinī*. The *kuṇḍalinī śakti* is of the form of eight *prakṛtis* (matter) and coils itself in eight ways. The movement of vital airs (*vāyus*) checks duly the food and drink all round the body (*skandha*). It closes by its head [the opening of] the *brahmarandhra*, and during the times of [the practice of] yoga is awakened by the fire (in the *apāna*); then it shines with great brilliancy in the *ākāśa* of the heart in the shape of wisdom. Depending upon *kuṇḍalinī* which is situated in the centre, there are fourteen principal *nāḍīs* (viz.) *iḍā*, *piṅgalā*, *suṣumnā*, *sarasvatī vāruṇī*, *pūṣā*, *hastijihvā*, *yaśasvinī*, *viśvodarī*, *kuhūḥ*, *payasvinī*, *alambuṣā*, and *gāndhārī*. Of them, *ṣuṣumnā* is said to be the sustainer of the universe and the path of salvation. Situated at the back of the anus, it is attached to the spinal column and extends to the *brahmarandhra* of the head and is invisible and subtle and is *Vaiṣṇavī* (or has the *śakti* force of Viṣṇu). On the left of *suṣumnā* is situated *iḍā*, and on the right is *piṅgalā*. The moon moves in *iḍā* and the sun in *piṅgalā*. The moon is of the nature of *tamas* and the sun of *rajas*. The poison share is of the sun and the nectar of the moon. They both direct (or indicate) time and *suṣumnā* is the enjoyer (or consumer) of time. To the back and on the side of *suṣumnā* are situated *sarasvatī* and *kuhūḥ* respectively. Between *yaśasvinī* and *kuhūḥ* stands *vāruṇī*. Between *pūśā* and *sarasvatī* lies *payasvinī*. Between *gāndhārī* and *sarasvatī* is situated *yaśasvinī*. In the centre of the navel is *alambuṣā*. In front of *suṣumnā* there is *kuhūḥ*, which proceeds as far as the genital organ. Above and below *kuṇḍalinī* is situated *vāruṇī*, which proceeds everywhere. *Yaśasvinī* which is beautiful (or belonging to the moon), proceeds to the great toes. *Piṅgalā* goes upwards to the right nostril. *payasvinī* goes to right ear. *Sarasvatī* goes to the upper part of the tongue and *śāṅkhinī* to the left ear, [while] *gāndhārī* goes from the back of *iḍā* to the left eye. *Alambuṣā* goes upwards and downwards from the root of the anus. From these fourteen *nāḍīs*, other [minor] *nāḍīs* spring; from them springing others, and from them springing others; so it should be known. As the leaf of the *aśvattha* tree *(Ficus-religiosa)* etc., is covered with minute fibres so also is this body permeated with *nāḍīs*.

"*Prāṇa*, *apāna*, *samāna*, *udāna*, *vyāna*, *nāga*, *kūrma*, *kṛkara*, *devadatta*, and *dhanañjaya*—these ten vital airs (*vāyus*) move in all the *nāḍīs*. *Prāṇa* moves in the nostrils, the throat, the navel, the two great toes and the lower and the upper parts of *kuṇḍalinī*. *Vyāna* moves in the ear, the eye, the loins, the ankles, the nose, the throat and the buttocks. *Apāna* moves in the anus, the genitals, the thighs, the knees, the stomach, the seeds, the loins, the calves, the navel, and the seat of the anus of fire. *Udāna* lives in all the joints and also in the hands and legs. *Samāna* lives, permeating in all parts of the body. Along with the fire in the body, it causes the food and drink taken in, to spread in the body. It moves in the seventy-two thousand *nāḍīs* and pervades all over the body along with the fire. The five *vāyus* beginning with *nāga* go towards the skin, the bones, etc. The *prāṇa* which is in the navel separates the food and drink which is there and brings about the juices (*rasas*) and others. Placing the water above the fire and the food above (or in) the water, it goes to the *apāna* and along with it, fans up the fire in the centre of the body. The fire thus fanned up by the *apāna* gradually increases in brightness in the middle of the body. Then it causes through its flames the water which is brought in the bowels by the *prāṇa* to grow hot. The fire with the water causes the food and condiments, which are placed above, to be boiled to a proper degree. The *prāṇa* separates these into sweat, urine, water, blood, semen, faeces and the like. And along with the *samāna*, it takes the juice (or essence) to all the *nāḍīs* and moves in the body in the shape of breath. The *vāyus* excrete the urine, the faeces, etc., through the nine openings in the body which are connected with the outside air. The functions of *prāṇa* are inspiration, expiration, and cough. Those of *udāna* are keeping the body straight etc. Those of *samāna* are nourishing the body. Those of *nāga* are vomiting etc.; of *kūrma*, the movement of the eyelids; of *kṛkara*, the causing of hunger, etc. of *devadatta*, idle-ness etc., and *dhanañjaya*, phlegm.

"Having thus acquired a thorough knowledge of the seat of the *nāḍīs* and the *vāyus* with their functions, one should begin with the purification of the *nāḍīs*. A person possessed of *yama* and *niyama*, avoiding all company, having finished his course of study, delighting in truth and virtue, having conquered [his] anger, being engaged in the service of his spiritual instructor and having been obedient to his parents and well instructed in all the religious practices and the knowledge of his order of life, should go to a sacred grove abounding in fruits, roots, and water. There he should select a pleasant spot always resounding with the chanting of the Vedas, frequented by the knowers of Brahman that persevere in the duties of their orders of life, and filled with fruits, roots, flowers, and water. [Else] either in a temple or on the banks of a river or in a village or in a town, he should build a beautiful monastery. It should be neither too long nor too high, should have a small door, should be besmeared well with cow-dung and should have every sort of protection. There listening to the exposition of Vedānta, he should begin to practise yoga. In the beginning, having worshipped Vināyaka, he should salute his tutelary deity (*iṣṭa-devatā*) and sitting in any of the above-mentioned postures on a soft seat, facing either the east or the north and having conquered them, the learned man keeping his head and neck erect and fixing his gaze on the tip of his nose, should see the sphere of the moon between his eyebrows and drink the nectar flowing therefrom through his eyes. Inhaling the air through *iḍā* for the space of twelve *mātrās*, he should contemplate on the sphere of fire (= *mūlādhāra cakra* at the level of navel) situated in the belly as surrounded with flames and having as its seed र (RA); then he should exhale it through *piṅgalā*. Again inhaling it through *piṅgalā* and retaining it [within], he should exhale it through *iḍā*. For the period of twenty-eight months, he should practise six times at every sitting through the three *sandhyās* (morning, noon, and evening) and during the intervals. By this, the *nāḍīs* become purified. Then the body becomes light and bright, the [gastric] fire is increased [within] and there is the manifestation of internal sound (*nāda*).

"*Prāṇāyāma* is is said to be the union of *prāṇa* and *apāna*. It is of three kinds—expiration, inspiration, and cessation. They are associated with the letter of the [Samskṛt] alphabet [for the right performance of *prāṇāyāma*]. Therefore *praṇava* (Oṃ) only is said to be *prāṇāyāma*. Sitting in the *padma* posture, the person should meditate that there is at the tip of his nose Gāyatrī, a girl of red complexion surrounded by the numberless rays of the image of the moon and mounted on a swan (*haṃsa*) and having a mace in her hand. She is the visible symbol of the letter *A*. The letter *U* has as its visible symbol Sāvitrī, a young woman of white colour having a disc in her hand and riding on a eagle (*garuḍa*). The letter *M* has as its visible symbol Sarasvatī, an aged woman of black colour riding on a the single letter—the supreme light—the *praṇava* (Oṃ)—is the origin or source of these three letters *A*, *U*, and *M*. Drawing up the air through *iḍā* for the space of sixteen *mātrās*, he should meditate on the letter A during that time; retaining the inspired air for the space of sixty-two *mātrās*, he should meditate on the letter *U* during the time; he should then exhale the inspired air for the space of thirty-two *mātrās*, meditating on the letter *M* during that time. He should practise this in the above order over and over again.

"Then having become firm in the posture and preserved perfect self-control, the yogin should, in order to clear away the impurities of the *suṣumnā*, sit in the lotus posture (*padmāsana*), and having inhaled the air through the left nostril, should retain it as long as he can and should exhale it through the right. Then drawing it again through the right and having retained it, he should exhale it through the left in the order that he should draw it through the same nostril by which he exhaled it before and retained it. In this context, occur [to memory] the following verses: 'In the beginning having inhaled the breath (*prāṇa*) through the left nostril, according to the rule, he should exhale it through the other; then having inhaled the air through the right nostril, should retain it and exhale it through the other.' To those who practise according to these rules through the right and left nostrils, the *nāḍīs* become purified within three months. He should practise cessation of breath at sunrise, in the midday, at sunset and at midnight slowly till eighty [times a day] for four weeks. In the early stages, perspiration is produced; in the middle stage the tremor of the body, and in the last stage levitation in the air. These [results] ensue out of the repression of the breath, while sitting in the lotus (*padma*) posture. When perspiration arises with effort, he should rub his body well. By this, the body becomes firm and light. In the early course of his practice, food with milk and ghee is excellent. One sticking to this rule becomes firm in his practice and gets no burning sensation in the body (*tāpa*). As lions, elephants and tigers are gradually tamed, so also the breath, when rightly managed [comes under control]; else it kills the practitioner.

"He should [as far as is consistent with his health and safety] properly exhale it, properly inhale it or retain it properly. Thus [only] will he attain success. By thus retaining the breath in an approved manner and by the purification of the *nāḍīs*, the brightening of the [gastric] fire, the hearing distinctly of [spiritual] sounds and [good] health result. When the nerve centres have become purified through the regular practice of *prāṇāyāma*, the air easily forces its way up through the mouth of the *suṣumnā* which is in the middle. By the contraction of the muscles of the neck and by the contraction of the one below (viz. *apāna*), the breath (*prāṇa*) goes into the *suṣumnā* which is in the middle from the west *nāḍī*. Drawing up the *apāna* and forcing down the *prāṇa* from the throat, the yogin freed from old age becomes a youth of sixteen.

"Seated in a pleasant posture and drawing up the air through the right nostril and retaining it inside from the top of the hair to the toe nails, he should exhale it through the same nostril. Through it, the brain becomes purified and the diseases in the air *nāḍīs* are destroyed. Drawing up the air through the nostrils with noise [so as to fill the space] from the heart to the neck, and having retained it [within] as long as possible, he should exhale it through the nose. Through this, hunger, thirst, idleness and sleep do not arise.

"Taking in the air through the mouth [wide open] and having retained it as long as possible, he should expel it through the nose. Through this, [such diseases as] *gulma*, *plīha* [both being splenetic diseases], bile and fever as also hunger, etc., are destroyed.

"Now we shall proceed to restraint of breath (*kumbhaka*). It is of two kinds—*sahita* and *kevala*. That which is coupled with expiration and inspiration is called *sahita*. That which is devoid of these is called *kevala* (alone). Until you become perfect in *kevala*, practise *sahita*. To one who has mastered *kevala*, there is nothing unattainable in the three worlds. By *kevala*-restraint of breath, the knowledge of *kuṇḍalinī* arises. Then he becomes lean in body, serene in face and clear-eyed, hears the [spiritual] sounds distinctly, becomes free from all diseases and conquers his seminal fluid (*bindu*), his gastric fire being increased.

"Centring one's mind on an inward object whilst his eyes are looking outside without the shutting and opening of his eyelids, has been called *vaiśṇavī-mudrā*. This is kept hidden in all the tāntric works. With his mind and breath absorbed in an internal object, the yogin, though he does not really see the objects outside and under him, still [appears to] see them with eyes in which the pupils are motionless. This is called *khecarī-mudrā*. It has as its sphere of extension one object and is very beneficial. [Then] the real seat of Viṣṇu, which is void and non-void, dawns on him. With eyes half closed and with a firm mind, fixing his eyes on the tip of his nose and becoming absorbed in the sun and moon, he after remaining thus unshaken [becomes conscious of] the thing which is of the form of light, which is free from all externals, which is resplendent, which is the supreme truth and which is beyond. O Śāṇḍilya, know this to be *tat* (That). Merging the sound in the light and elevating the brows a little, this is of the way of [or is a part of] the former practice. This brings about the state of *unmanī* which causes the destruction of the mind. Therefore he should practise the *khecarī-mudrā*. Then he attains to the state *unmanī* and falls into the yoga sleep (trance). To one who obtains this yoga sleep, time does not exist. Placing the mind in the midst of *śakti* he should centre his mind on *śakti*, and behold the mind with the mind, O Śāṇdilya be happy. Place the ātman in the midst of *ākāsa* and *ākāśa* in the midst of ātman, and having reduced everything to *ākāśa*, do not think of anything else. You should not [then] entertain thoughts, either external or internal. Abandoning all thoughts, become abstract thought itself. As camphor in fire and salt in water become absorbed, so also the mind becomes absorbed in the truth (*tattva*). What is termed mind is the knowledge of everything that is known and its clear apprehension. When the knowledge and the object cognised are lost alike, there is no second path. By its giving up all cognition of objects, it [the mind] is absorbed and when the mind is absorbed, isolation (*kaivalya*) alone remains.

"For the destruction of the *citta*, there are two ways— yoga and *jñāna*. O prince of sages! Yoga is the [forcible] repression of the modification of the mind, and *jñāna* is the thorough inquiry into them. When the modifications of the mind are repressed, it [the mind] verily obtains peace. Just as the actions of the people cease with the stopping of the fluctuations of the sun (viz. with sunset), so when the fluctuations of the mind cease, this cycle of births and deaths comes to an end. [Then] the fluctuations of *prāṇa* are prevented, when one has no longing for this mundane existence or when he has gratified his desires therein—through the study of religious books, the company of good men, indifference [to enjoyments], practice and yoga or long contemplation with intentness on any desired [higher] object or through practising one truth firmly.

"By the repression of the breath through inhalation etc., by continual practice therein which does not cause fatigue, and by meditating in a secluded place, the fluctuations of the mind are arrested. Through the right realisation of the true nature of the sound which is at the extreme end of the pronunciation of the syllable Oṃ (viz. *ardhamātrā*), and when dreamless sleeping state (*suṣupti*) is rightly cognised through consciousness, the fluctuations of *prāṇa* are repressed. When the passage at the root of the palate which is like the bell, (viz. uvula) is closed by the tongue with effort, and when the breath goes up through [the upper hole], then the fluctuations of *prāṇa* are stopped. When the consciousness (*saṃvit*) is merged in *prāṇa*, and when through practice the *prāṇa* goes through the upper hole into the twelfth centre (*dvādaśānta*) above the palate, then the fluctuations of *prāṇa* are stopped. When the eye of consciousness (viz. the spiritual or third eye) becomes calm and clear so as to be able to distinctly see in the transparent *ākāśa* at a distance of twelve digits from the tip of his nose, then the fluctuations of *prāṇa* are stopped. When the thoughts arising in the mind are bound up in the calm contemplation of the world of star or eye (*tāraka*) between one's eyebrows and are [thus] destroyed, then the fluctuations cease. When the knowledge which is of the form of the knowable, which is beneficent and which is untouched by any modifications arises in one and is known as Oṃ only and no other, then the fluctuations of *prāṇa* cease. By the contemplation for a long time of the *ākāśa* which is in the heart, and by the contemplation of the mind free from *vāsānās*, then the fluctuations of *prāṇa* cease. By these methods and various others suggested by [one's] thought and by means of the contact of the many [spiritual] guides, the fluctuations ceases.

"Having by contraction opened the door of *kuṇḍalinī*, one should force open the door of *mokṣa*. Closing with her mouth the door through which one ought to go, the *kuṇḍalinī* sleeps in spiral form and coiled up like a serpent. He who causes this *kuṇḍalinī* to move—he is an emancipated person. If this *kuṇḍalinī* were to sleep in the upper part of the neck of any yogin, it goes towards his emancipation. [If it were to sleep] in the lower part [of the body], it is for the bondage of the ignorant. Leaving the two *nāḍīs, iḍā* and the other (*piṅgalā*), it (*prāṇa*) should move in the *suṣumnā*. That is the supreme seat of Viṣṇu. One should practise control of breath with the concentration of the mind. The mind should not be allowed by a clever man to rest on any other thing. One should not worship Viṣṇu during the day alone. One should not worship Viṣṇu during the night alone; but should always worship him, and should not worship him merely during day and night. The wisdom-producing opening (near uvula) has five passages. O Śāṇḍilya this is the *khecarī-mudrā*; practise it. With one who sits in the *khecarī-mudrā*, the *vāyu* which was flowing before through the left and right *nāḍīs* now flows through the middle one (*suṣumnā*). There is no doubt about it. You should swallow the air through the void (*suṣumnā*) between *iḍā* and *piṅgalā*. In that place is *khecarī-mudrā* situated, and that is the seat of truth. Again that is *khecarī-mudrā* which is situated in the *ākāśa-cakra* [in the head] in the supportless (*nirālamba*) seat between the sun and moon (viz. *iḍā* and *piṅgalā*). When the tongue has been lengthened to the length of a digit (*kalā*) by incision [of the fraenum lingum] and by rubbing and milking it (*viz.* the tongue), fix the gaze between the two eyebrows and close the hole in the skull with the tongue reversed. This is *khecarī-mudrā*. When the tongue and the mind (*citta*) both move in the *ākāśa* (*khecarī*), then the person with his tongue raised up becomes immortal. Firmly pressing the perineum (*yoni*) by the left heel, stretching out the right leg, grasping the feet with both hands and inhaling the air through the nostrils, practise, *kaṇṭha-bandha*, (=holding the air in the throat) retaining the air upwards. By that, all afflictions are destroyed; then poison is digested as if it were nectar. Asthma, splenetic disease, the turning up of the anus and the numbness of the skin are removed. This is the means of conquering *prāṇa* and destroying death. Pressing the *yoni* by the left heel, place the other foot over the left thigh: inhale the air, rest the chin on the chest, contract the yoni and contemplate, [as far as possible], your atmā as situated within your mind. Thus is the direct perception [of truth] attained.

"Inhaling the *prāṇa* from outside and filling the stomach with it, centre the *prāṇa* with the mind in the middle of the navel, at the tip of the nose and at the toes during the sunset and sunrise (*sandhyās*) or at all times. [Thus] the yogin is freed from all diseases and fatigue. By centring his *prāṇa* at the tip of his nose, he obtains mastery over the element of air; by centring it at the middle of his navel, all diseases are destroyed; by centring it at the toes, his body becomes light. He who drinks the air [drawn] through the tongue destroys fatigue, thirst and diseases. He who drinks the air with his mouth during the two *sandhyās* and the last two hours of the night, within three months the auspicious

Sarasvatī (goddess of speech) is present in his speech (*vāc*), viz. he becomes eloquent and learned in his speech. In six months, he is free from all diseases. Drawing the air by the tongue, retain the air at the root of the tongue. The wise man thus drinking nectar enjoys all prosperity. Fixing the self in the ātman itself in the middle of the eyebrows, [having inhaled] through *iḍā* and breaking through that [centre] thirty times, even a sick man is freed from disease. He who draws the air through the *nāḍīs* and retains it for twenty-four minutes in the navel and in the sides of the stomach becomes freed from disease. He who for the space of a month during the three *sandhyās* (sunset, sunrise, and midnight or noon) draws the air through the tongue, pierces thirty times and retains his breath in the middle of his navel, becomes freed from all fevers and poisons. He who retains the *prāṇa* together with the mind at the tip of his nose even for the space of a *muhūrta* (forty-eight minutes), destroys all sins that were committed by him during one hundred births.

"Through the *saṃyama* of *tāra* (Oṃ) he knows all things. By retaining the mind at the tip of his nose, he acquires a knowledge of Indra-world; below that, he acquires a knowledge of Agni-world. Through the *saṃyama* of *citta* in the eye, he gets a knowledge of all worlds: in the ear, a knowledge of Yama world: in the sides of the ear, a knowledge of Nṛṛti-world: in the back of it [the ear], a knowledge of Varuṇa-world: in the left ear, a knowledge of Vāyu-world: in the throat, a knowledge of Soma world: in the left eye, a knowledge of Śiva-world: in the head, a knowledge of Brahmā-world: in the soles of the feet a knowledge of Atala world: in the feet, a knowledge of Vitala world: in the ankles, a knowledge of Nitala [rather Sutala] world: in the calves, a knowledge of Sutala [rather Talātāla] world: in the knees, a knowledge of Mahātala world: in the thighs, a knowledge of Rasātala world: in the loins, a knowledge of Talātala] rather Pātāla] world: in the navel, a knowledge of Bhūrloka (earth-world): in the stomach, a knoweldge of Bhuvar (world): in the heart, a knowledge of Suvar (world): in the place above the heart, a knowledge of Mahar world: in the throat, a knowledge of Jana world: in the middle of the brows, a knowledge of Tapas world: in the head, a knowledge of Satya world.

"By conquering dharma and *adharma*, one knows the past and the future. By centring it on the sound of every creature, a knowledge of the cry [or language] of the animal is produced. By centring it on the past *karma* yet to be enjoyed (*sañcita-karma*), a knowledge of one's previous births arises in him. By centring it on the mind of another, a knowledge of the mind [or thoughts] of other is induced. By centring it on the *kāya-rūpa* [or form of the body], other forms are seen. By fixing it on the strength (*bala*), the strength of persons like Hanūmān is obtained. By fixing it on the sun, a knowledge of the worlds arises. By fixing it on the moon, a knowledge of the constellation is produced. By fixing it on the Dhruva (Polar star) a perception of its motion is induced. By fixing it on his own [self], one acquires the knowledge of Puruṣa; on the navel, he attains a knowledge of the mystical arrangement of all the particles of the body so as to enable a person to wear out his whole *karma* in one life *(kāya-vyūha)*: on the well of the throat, freedom from hunger and thirst arises: on the *kūrma nāḍī* (which is situated in the well of the throat), a firmness [of concentration] takes place. By fixing it on the pupil of the eye (*tārā*), he obtains the sight of the spiritual personages (*siddhas*). By conquering the *ākāśa* in the body, he is able to soar in the *ākāśa*: [in short] by centring the mind in any place, he conquers the *siddhis* appertaining to that place.

"Then comes *pratyāhāra*, which is of five kinds. It is the drawing away of the organs from attaching themselves to the objects of senses. Contemplating upon everything that one sees as ātman is *pratyāhāra*. Renouncing the fruits of one's daily actions is *pratyāhāra*. *Dhāraṇā* in the eighteen important places [mentioned below] is *pratyāhāra*, (viz.) the feet, the toes, the ankles, the calves, the knees, the thigh, the anus, the penis, the navel, the heart, the well of the throat, the palate, the nose, the eyes, the middle of the brows, the forehead, and the head in ascending and descending orders.

"Then [comes] *dhāraṇā*. It is of three kinds, (viz.) fixing the mind in the ātman, bringing the external *ākāśa* into the *ākāśa* of the heart and contemplating the five *mūrtis* (forms of deities) in the five elements—earth, *ap*, fire, *vāyu*, and *ākāśa*.

"Then comes *dhyāna*. It is of two kinds, *saguṇa* (with quality) and *nirguṇa* (without quality). *Saguṇa* is the meditation of a *mūrti*. *Nirguṇa* is on the reality of self.

"*Samādhi* is the union of the individual self (*jīvātman*) and the higher self (Paramātman) without the threefold state, (viz. the knower, the known, and the knowledge). It is of the nature of extreme bliss and pure consciousness.

"Thus ends the first chapter of the Śāṇḍilya Upaniṣad."

CHAPTER II

Then the Brahmarṣi Śāṇḍilya not obtaining the knowledge of Brahman in the four Vedas, approached the Lord Atharvan and asked him: "What is it? Teach me the science of Brahman by which I shall obtain that which is most excellent."

Atharvan replied: "O Śāṇḍilya, Brahman is *satya vijñāna* and *ananta* in which all this [world] is interwoven, warp-wise and woof-wise, from which all originated and into which all are absorbed, and which being known makes everything else known. It is without hands and feet, without eyes and ears, without tongue or without body, and is unreachable and undefinable. From which speech (*vāc*) and mind return, being unable to obtain [or reach] it. It is to be cognised by *jñāna* and yoga. From which, *prajñā* of old sprang. That which is one and non-dual, that which pervades everything like *ākāśa*, which is extremely subtle, without a blemish, actionless, *sat* (be-ness) only, the essence of the bliss of consciousness, beneficent, calm and immortal and which is beyond. That is Brahman. Thou art that. Know that by wisdom. He who is the one, the shining, the giver of the power of ātman, the omniscient, the lord of all, and the inner soul of all beings, who lives in all beings, who is reachable only through yoga and who creates, supports and destroys everything—he is ātman. Know the several worlds in the ātman. Do not grieve, O knower of ātman, thou shalt reach the end of pains."

CHAPTER III

Then Śāṇḍilya questioned Atharvan thus: "From the Brahman that is Oṃ, imperishable, actionless, benefical, *sat* only and supreme, how did this universe arise? How does it exist in it? And how is it absorbed in it? Please dispel this doubt."

Aṭharvan replied: "The Supreme Brahman, the truth, is the imperishable and the actionless. Then from the formless Brahman, three forms [or aspects] arose, (viz.) partless *(niṣkala)*, with parts *(sakala)*, and with and without parts *(sakala-niṣkala)*. That which is *satya vijñāna* and *ānanda*. That which is actionless, without any impurity, omnipresent, extremely subtle, having faces in every direction, undefinable and immortal—that is his *niṣkala* aspect. Maheśvara (the great Lord) who is black and yellow rules, with *avidyā*, *mūlaprakṛti* or *māyā* that is red, white, and black, and that is co-existent with him. This is his *sakala-niṣkala* aspect. Then the Lord desired [or willed] by his spiritual wisdom [thus]: May I become many? may I bring forth? Then from this person who was contemplating and whose desires are fulfilled, three letters sprang up. Three *vyāhṛtis*, (*bhur*, *bhuvaḥ*, *svaḥ*) the three-footed Gāyatrī, the three Vedas, the three devas, the three *varṇas* (colours or castes) and the three fires sprang. That Supreme Lord who is endowed with all kinds of wealth, who is all pervading, who is situated in the hearts of all beings, who is the Lord of *māyā* and whose form is *māyā*—he is Brahmā. He is Viṣṇu: He is Rudra: He is Indra: He is all the devas: He is all the elements or beings (*bhūtas*): He only is before: He only is behind: He only is on our left: He only is on our right: He only is below: He only is above: He only is the all. That form of him as Dattātreya, who is brilliant as fire, resembling the petals of a red lotus and is of four hands, who is mild and shines sinlessly—this is His *sakala* form."

Then Śāṇḍilya questioned Atharvan, "O Lord, that which is *sat* only and the essence of the bliss of consciousness —why is he called Parabrahman?"

Aṭharvan replied: "Because he increases *bṛhati* and causes to increase everything *(bṛhanti)*; so he is called Parabrahman. Why is he called ātman? Since he obtains *(āpnoti)* everything, since he takes back everything and since he is everything, so he is called ātman. Why is he called Maheśvara (the great Lord)? Since by the sound of the words Mahat-Īśa (the great Lord) and by his own power, the great Lord governs everything. Why is he called Dattātreya? Because the Lord being extremely pleased with Atri (*ṛṣi*) who was performing a most difficult penance and who had expressed his desire to see him who is light itself, offered himself (*datta*) as their son, and because the woman Anasūyā was his mother and Atri was his father. Therefore he who knows the [secret] meaning knows everything. He who always contemplates on the supreme that it is himself becomes a knower of Brahman. Here these stanzas (*ślokas*) occur [to memory]. 'He who contemplates always on the Lord of Lords and the ancient thus—as Dattātreya, the beneficent, the calm, of the colour of sapphire, one who delights in his own *māyā* and the Lord who has shaken off everything, as naked and as one whose whole body is besmeared with the holy ashes, who has matted hair, who is the Lord of all, who has four arms, who is bliss in appearance, whose eyes are like full-blown lotus, who is the store of *jñāna* and yoga, who is the spiritual instructor of all the worlds and who is dear to all the yogins, and one who is merciful towards his devotees, who is the witness of all and who is worshipped by all the *siddhas* is freed from all sins and will attain [the Spirit]."

Oṃ tat sat is the Upaniṣad

23
Yogatattva Upaniṣad of Kṛṣṇa Yajurveda

I shall now describe yoga-truth (*yoga-tattva*) for the benefit of yogins who are freed from all sins through the hearing and the studying of it. The Supreme Puruṣa called Viṣṇu, who is the great yogin, the great being and the great *tapasvin*, is seen as a lamp in the path of truth. The Grandfather [Brahmā] having saluted the Lord of the universe [Viṣṇu] and having paid him due respect, asked him [thus]: "Pray, explain to us the truth of yoga which includes in it the eight subservients." To which Hṛṣīkeṣa [the Lord of the senses or Viṣṇu] replied thus: "Listen. I shall explain its truth. All souls are immersed in happiness and sorrow through the snare of *māyā*. *Kaivalya*, the supreme seat, is the path which gives them emancipation, which rends asunder the snare of *māyā*, which is the destroyer of birth, old age and disease and which enables one to overcome death. There are no other path to salvation. Those who go round the net of the śāstras are deluded by that knowledge. It is impossible even for the devas to describe that indescribable state. How can that which is self-shining be illuminated by the śāstras? That alone which is without parts, and stains, and which is quiescent beyond all, and free from decay becomes the self [*jīva*] on account of the results of past virtues and sins. How did that, which is the seat of Paramātman, is eternal and above the state of all existing things, and is of the form of wisdom and without stains, attain the state of *jīva*? A bubble arose in it as in water and in this [bubble] arose *ahaṁkāra*. To it arose a ball [of body] made of the five [elements] and bound by *dhātus*. Know that to be *jīva* which is associated with happiness and misery and hence is the term *jīva* applied to Paramātman which is pure. That *jīva* is considered to be the alone (*kevala*), which is freed from the stains of passion, anger, fear, delusion, greed pride, lust, birth, death, miserliness, swoon, giddiness, hunger, thirst, ambition, shame, fright, heart-burning, grief and gladness.

"So I shall tell you the means of destroying [these] sins. How could *jñāna,* capable of giving *mokṣa* arise certainly without yoga? And even yoga becomes powerless in [securing] *mokṣa* when it is devoid of *jñāna*. So the aspirant after emancipation should practise [firmly] both yoga and *jñāna*. The cycle of births and deaths comes only through *ajñāna* and perishes only through *jñāna*. *Jñāna* alone was originally. It should be known as the only means [of salvation]. That is *jñāna* through which one cognizes [in himself] the real nature of *kaivalya* as the supreme seat, the stainless, the partless and of the nature of *Saccidānanda* without birth, existence and death and without motion and *jñāna*.

"Now I shall proceed to describe yoga to you. Yoga is divided into many kinds on account of its actions: [viz.] *mantra-yoga*, *laya-yoga*, *haṭha-yoga*, and *rāja-yoga*. There are four states common to all these: [viz.] *ārambha*, *ghaṭa*, *paricaya*, *and niṣpatti*. O Brahmā, I shall describe these to you. Listen attentively. One should practise the *mantra-yoga* along with proper intonations of the sounds, [*mātṛikās*] and others for a period of twelve years; then he gradually obtains wisdom along with the *siddhis*, [such as] *aṇiman*, etc. Persons of weak intellect who are the least qualified for yoga practice this. The [second], *laya-yoga* tends towards the absorption of the *citta* and is described in myriads of ways; [one of which is]—one should contemplate upon the Lord who is without parts [even] while walking, sitting, sleeping, or eating. This is called *laya-yoga*. Now hear [the description of] *haṭha-yoga*. This yoga is said to possess [the following] eight subservients, forbearance (*yama*), religious observance (*niyama*), posture (*āsana*), suppression of breath (*prāṇāyāma*), subjugation of the senses (*pratyāhāra*), concentration (*dhāraṇā*), the contemplation (*dhyāna*) on Hari in the middle of the eyebrows and *samādhi* that is the state of equality. *Mahāmudrā, mahābandha* and *khecarī, jālandhara, uḍḍiyāṇa*, and *mūlabandha*, uttering without intermission *praṇava* [Oṃ] for a long time, and hearing the exposition of the supreme truths, *vajrolī, amarolī* and *sahajolī*, which form a triad—all these separately I shall give a true description of. O four-faced one [Brahmā], among [the duties of] *yama,* moderate eating—and not others— forms the principal factor; and non-injury is most important in *niyama*. [The chief postures are] four [viz.] *siddha, padma, siṃha* and *bhadra*. During the early stages of practice, the following obstacles take place, O four-faced one, [viz.] laziness, idle talk, association with bad characters, acquisition of mantras, etc., playing with metals [alchemy] and woman, etc., and mirage. A wise man having found out these should abandon them by the force of his virtues. Then assuming lotus posture, he should practise *prāṇāyāma*. He should erect a beautiful monastery with a very small opening and with no crevices. It should be well plastered with cow-dung or with white cement. It should be carefully free from bugs, mosquitoes and lice. It should be swept well every day with a broom. It should be perfumed with good odours; and fragrant resins should burn in it. Having taken his seat neither too high nor too low on a cloth, deerskin and *kuśa* grass spread one over the other, the wise man should assume the lotus posture and keeping his body erect and his hands folded in respect, should salute his tutelary deity. Then closing the right nostril with his right thumb, he should gradually draw in the air through the left nostril. Having restrained it as long as possible, he should again expel it through the right nostril slowly and not very fast. Then filling the stomach through the right nostril, he should retain it as long as he can and then expel it through the left nostril. Drawing the air through that nostril by which he expels, he should continue this in uninterrupted succession. The time taken in making a round of the knee with the palm of the hand, neither very slowly nor very rapidly and snapping the fingers once is called a *mātrā*. Drawing the air through the left nostril for about sixteen *mātrās* and having retained it [within] for about sixty-four *mātrās*, one should expel it again through the right nostril for about thirty-two *mātrās*. Again fill the right nostril as before [and continue the rest]. Practise cessation of breath four times daily at sunrise, noon, sunset and midnight, till eighty [times are reached]. By continual practice for about three months, the purification of the *nāḍīs* takes place. When the *nāḍīs* have become purified, certain external signs appear on the body of the yogin. I shall proceed to describe them. [They are] lightness of the body, brilliance of complexion, increase of the gastric fire, leanness of the body and along with these, absence of restlessness in the body. The proficient in yoga should abandon the food detrimental to the practice of yoga. He should give up salt, mustard, things sour, hot, pungent or bitter, vegetables, asafoetida, etc., worship of fire, women, walking, bathing at sunrise, emaciation of the body by fasts, etc. During the early stages of practice, food of milk and ghee is ordained; also food consisting of wheat, green pulse and red rice are said to favour the progress. Then he will be able to retain his breath as long as he likes. By thus retaining the breath as long as he likes, cessation of breath without inspiration and expiration (*kevala kumbhaka*) is attained. When *kevala kumbhaka* is attained by one and thus expiration and inspiration are dispensed with, there is nothing unattainable in the three worlds to him. In the commencement [of his practice], sweat is given out; he should wipe it off. Even after that, owing to the retaining of the breath, the person practising it gets phlegm. Then by an increased practice of *dhāraṇā*, sweat arises. As a frog moves by leaps, so the yogin sitting in the lotus posture, moves on the earth. With [further] increased practice, he is able to rise from the ground. He, while seated in lotus posture, levitates. There arises to him the power to perform extraordinary feats. He does [or should] not disclose to others his feats of great powers [in the path]. Any pain, small or great, does not affect the yogin. Then excretions and sleep are diminished; tears, rheum in the eye, salivary flow, sweat and bad smell in the mouth do not arise in him. With still further practice, he acquires great strength by which he attains *bhūcara-siddhi*, which enables him to bring under his control all the creatures that tread this earth; tigers, [mythical] *śarabhas*, elephants, wild bulls or lions die on being struck by the palm of the yogin. He becomes as beautiful as the god of love himself. All females being taken up with the beauty of his person will desire to have intercourse with him. If he so keeps connection, his virility will be lost; so abandoning all copulation with women, he should continue his practice with great assiduity. By the preservation of the semen, a good odour pervades the body of the yogin. Then sitting in a secluded place, he should repeat *praṇava* (Oṃ) with three or prolonged intonation (*plutamātrās*) for the destruction of his former sins. The *praṇava mantra* (Oṃ) destroys all obstacles and all sins. By practising thus he attains the beginning of the first (*ārambha*) state.

"Then follows the second state (*ghaṭa*)—one which is acquired by constantly practising suppression of breath. When a perfect union takes place between *prāṇa* and *apāna*, manas and *buddhi, jīvātman* and Paramātman without opposition, it is called the *ghaṭa* state. I shall describe its signs. He may now practise only for about one-fourth of the period prescribed for practice before. By day and evening, let him practise only for a *yāma* [3 hours]. Let him practise *kevala kumbhaka* once a day. Drawing away completely the organs from the objects of sense during cessation of breath is called *pratyāhāra*. Whatever he sees with his eyes, let him consider as ātman. Whatever he hears with his ears let him consider as ātman. Whatever he smells with his nose let him consider as ātman. Whatever he tastes with his tongue let him consider as ātman. Whatever the yogin touches with his skin let him consider as ātman. The yogin should thus unwearied gratify his organs of sense for a period of one *yāma* every day, with great effort. Then various wonderful powers are attained by the yogin, such as clairvoyance, clairaudience, ability to transport himself to great distances within a moment, great power of speech, ability to take any form, ability to become invisible and the transmutation of iron into gold when the former is smeared over with his excretions.

"That yogin who is constantly practising yoga attains the power to levitate. Then should the wise yogin think that these powers are great obstacles to the attainment of yoga, and so he should never take delight in them. The king of yogins should not exercise his powers before any person whatsoever. He should live in the world as a fool, an idiot or a deaf man, in order to keep his powers concealed. His disciples would, without doubt, request him to show his powers for the gratification of their own desires. One who is actively engaged in one's duties forgets to practise [yoga]; so he should practise day and night without forgetting the words of the guru. To one nothing is gained by useless company, since thereby he does not practise yoga. So one should with great effort practise yoga. Then by this constant practice is gained the *paricaya* state [the third state]. *Vāyu* [or breath] through arduous practice, pierces along with *agni* the *kuṇḍalinī* through thought and enters the *suṣumnā* uninterrupted. When one's *citta* enters *suṣumnā* along with *prāṇa*, it reaches the high seat [of the head probably] along with *prāṇa*.

"There are the five elements, [viz.] *pṛthivī, ap, agni, vāyu* and *ākāśa*. To the body of the five elements, there is the five-fold *dhāraṇā*. From the feet to the knees is said to be the regions of *pṛthivī*, is four-sided in shape, is yellow in colour and has the *varṇa* [or letter] *La*. Carrying the breath with the letter *La* along the region of earth [viz. from the foot to the knees] and contemplating upon Brahmā with four faces and four mouths and of a golden colour, one should perform *dhāraṇā* there for a period of two hours. He then attains mastery over the earth. Death does not trouble him since he has obtained mastery over the earth element. The region of *ap* is said to extend from the knees to the anus. *Āpas* is semi-lunar in shape and white in colour and has *Va* for its seed (*bīja*) letter. Carrying up the breath with the letter *Va* along the region of *ap*, he should contemplate on Nārāyaṇa having four arms and a crowned head, as being the colour of pure crystal, as dressed in orange clothes and as decayless; and practising *dhāraṇā* there for a period of two hours, he is freed from all sins. Then there is no fear for him from water and he does not meet his death in water. From the anus to the heart is said to be the region of *agni*. *Agni* is triangular in shape, of red colour, and has the letter *Ra* for its seed (*bīja*). Raising the breath made resplendent through the letter *Ra* along the region of fire, he should contemplate on Rudra, who has three eyes,who grants all wishes, who is of the colour of the midday sun, who is daubed all over with holy ash and who is of a pleased countenance. Practising *dhāraṇā* there for a period of two hours, he is not burnt by fire even though his body enters the fire-pit. From the heart to the middle of the eyebrows is said to be the region of *vāyu*. *Vāyu* is hexangular in shape, black in colour and shines with the letter *Ya*. Carrying the breath along the region of *vāyu*, he should contemplate on Īśvara, the Omniscient, as possessing faces on all sides; and practising *dhāraṇā* there for two hours, he enters *vāyu* and then *ākāśa*. The yogin does not meet his death through the fear of *vāyu*. From the centre of the eyebrows to the top of the head is said to be the region of *ākāśa*, is circular in shape, smoky in colour and shining with the letter *Ha*. Raising the breath along the region of *ākāśa*, he should contemplate on Sadāśiva in the following manner, as producing happiness, as of the shape of *bindu*, as the great deva, as having the shape of *ākāśa*, as shining like pure crystal, as wearing the rising crescent of the moon on his head, as having five faces, ten heads and three eyes, as being of a pleased countenance, as armed with all weapons, as adorned with all ornaments, as having Umā [the goddess] in one-half of his body, as ready to grant favours, and as the cause of all the causes. By practising *dhāraṇā* in the region of *ākāśa*, he obtains certainly the power of levitating in the *ākāśa* [ether]. Wherever he stays, he enjoys supreme bliss. The proficient in yoga should practise these five *dhāraṇās*. Then his body becomes strong and he does not know death. That great-minded man does not die even during the deluge of Brahmā.

"Then he should practise *dhāraṇā* for a period of six *ghaṭikās* [2 hours, 24 minutes]. Restraining the breath in [the region of] *ākāśa* and contemplating on the deity who grants his wishes—this is said to be *saguṇa dhyāna* capable of giving (the *siddhis*) *aṇimā*, etc. One who is engagd in *nirguṇa dhyāna* attains the stage of *samādhi*. Within twelve days at least, he attains the stage of *samādhi*. Restraining his breath, the wise one becomes an emancipated person. *Samādhi* is that state in which the *jīvātman* (lower self) and the Paramātman (higher self) are differenceless [or of equal state]. If he desires to lay aside his body, he can do so. He will become absorbed in Parabrahman and does not require going out or up (*utkrānti*). But if he does not so desire and if his body is dear to him, he lives in all the worlds possessing the *siddhis* of *aṇimā*, etc. Sometimes he becomes a deva and lives honoured in *svarga*; or he becomes a man or a *yakṣa* through his will. He can also take the form of a lion, tiger, elephant, or horse through his own will. The yogin, becoming the great Lord, can live as long as he likes. There is difference only in the modes of procedure but the result is the same.

"Place the left heel pressed on the anus, stretch the right leg and hold it firmly with both hands. Place the head on the breast and inhale the air slowly. Restrain the breath as long as you can and then slowly breathe out. After practising it with the left foot, practise it with the right. Place the foot that was stretched before on the thigh. This is *mahābandha* and should be practised on both sides. The yogin sitting in *mahābandha* and having inhaled the air with intent mind, should stop the source of *vāyu* [inside] by means of the throat-*mudrā*, and occupying the two sides [of the throat] with speed. This is called *mahāvedha* and is frequently practised by the *siddhas*. With the tongue thrust into the interior cavity of the head [or throat] and with the eyes intent on the spot between the eyebrows, this is called *khecarī-mudrā*. Contracting the muscles of the neck and placing the head with a firm will on the breast, this is called the *jālandhara* [*bandha*] and is a lion to the elephant of death. That *bandha* by which *prāṇa* flies through *suṣumnā* is called *uḍḍiyāṇabandha* by the yogins. Pressing the heel firmly against the anus, contracting the anus and drawing up the *apāna*, this is said to be *yonibandha*. Through *mūlabandha*, *prāṇa* as well as *nāda* and *bindu* are united and give success in yoga: there is no doubt about this. To one practising in a reversed manner [or on both sides] which destroys all diseases, the gastric fire is increased. Therefore a practitioner should collect a large quantity of provisions, [for] if he takes a small quantity of food, the fire [within] will consume his body in a moment.

"On the first day, he should stand on his head with the feet raised up for a moment. He should increase this period gradually every day. Wrinkles and greyness of hair will disappear within three months. He who practises only for a period of a *yāma* [twenty-four minutes] every day conquers time. He who practises *vajrolī* becomes yogin and the repository of all *siddhis*. If the yoga *siddhis* are ever to be attained, he only has them within his reach. He knows the past and the future and certainly moves in the air.

He who drinks of the nectar thus is rendered immortal day by day. He should daily practise *vajrolī*. Then it is called *amarolī*. Then he obtains the *rāja-yoga* and certainly he does not meet with obstacles. When a yogin fulfils his action by *rāja-yoga*, then he certainly obtains discrimination and indifference to objects. Viṣṇu, the great yogin, the grand one of great austerities and the most excellent Puruṣa is seen as a lamp in the path of truth.

"That breast from which one suckled before [in his previous birth] he now presses [in love] and obtains pleasure. He enjoys the same genital organ from which he was born before. She who was once his mother will now be his wife and she who is now wife is [or will be] verily mother. He who is now father will be again son, and he who is now son will be again father. Thus are the egos of this world wandering in the womb of birth and death like a bucket in the wheel of a well and enjoying the worlds. There are the three worlds, three *vedas*, three *sandhyās*, (morning, noon and evening), three *svaras* (sounds), three *agnis* and *guṇas* and all these are placed in the three letters [*AUṂ*]. He who understands that which is indestructible and is the meaning of the three [*AUṂ*]—by him are all these worlds strung. This is the truth, the supreme seat. As the smell in the flower, as the ghee in the milk, as the oil in the gingelly seed and as the gold in the quartz, so is the lotus situated in the heart. Its face is downwards and its stem upwards. Its *bindu* is downwards and in its centre is situated *manas*. By the letter *A*, the lotus becomes expanded; by the letter *U*, it becomes split [or opened], by the letter *M*, it obtains *nāda*; and the *ardhamātrā* (half-metre) is silence. The person engaged in yoga obtains the supreme seat, which is like a pure crystal, which is without parts and which destroys all sins. As a tortoise draws its hands and head within itself, so drawing in air thus and expelling it through the nine holes of the body, he breathes upwards and forwards. Like a lamp in an air-tight jar which is motionless, so that which is seen motionless through the process of yoga in the heart and which is free from turmoil, after having been drawn from the nine holes, is said to be ātman alone."

Oṃ tat sat is the Upaniṣad

24
Dhyānabindu Upaniṣad of Sāmaveda

Even if sin should accumulate to a mountain extending over great distance *(yojana)*, it is destroyed by *dhyāna-yoga*. At no time has been found a destroyer of sins like this. The seed letter (*bīja-akṣara*) is the supreme *bindu*. The spiritual sound (*nāda*) is above it. When that *nāda* ceases along with the letter, then the *nāda*-less is the supreme state. That yogin who considers as the highest that which is above *nāda*, which is unstruck (*anāhata*), has all his doubts destroyed. If the point of a hair be divided into one-hundred thousand parts, this *nāda* is one-half of that still further divided; and when even this is absorbed, the yogin attains to the stainless Brahman. One who is of a firm mind and without the delusion [of sensual pleasures] and ever resting in Brahman, should see like the string [in a rosary of beads] all creatures [as existing] in ātman like odour in flowers, ghee in milk, oil in gingelly seeds and gold in quartz. Again just as the oil depends for its manifestation upon gingelly seeds and odour upon flowers, so does the the individual (*puruṣa*) depend for its existence upon the body, both external and internal. The tree is with parts and its shadow is without parts but with and without parts, ātman exists everywhere.

The one *akṣara* [letter Oṃ] should be contemplated upon as Brahman by all who aspire for emancipation. *Pṛthivī, agni, Ṛgveda, bhūḥ* and Brahmā—all these [are absorbed] when *Akāra* [*A*], the first part [*aṃśa*] of *praṇava* (Oṃ) becomes absorbed. *Antarikṣa, Yajurveda, vāyu, bhuvaḥ* and Viṣṇu, the Janārḍana—all these [are absorbed] when *Ukāra* [*U*], the second *aṃśa* of *praṇava* becomes absorbed. *Dyus*, sun, *Sāmaveda, suvaḥ*, and Maheśvara—all these [are absorbed] when Makāra [*M*], the third *aṃśa* of *praṇava* becomes absorbed. *Akāra* is of yellow (*pīta*) colour and is said to be of *rajoguṇa*; *Ukāra* is of white colour and of *sattvaguṇa*; *Makāra* is of dark colour and of *tamoguṇa*. He who does not know Oṃkāra as having eight parts (*aṅgas*), four feet (*pādas*), three seats (*sthānas*) and five presiding deities (*devatās*) is not a Brāhmaṇa. *Praṇava* is the bow. Ātman is the arrow and Brāhmaṇa is said to be the aim. One should aim at it with great care and then he, like the arrow, becomes one with it. When that highest is cognised, all *karmas* return [from him, viz. do not affect him]. The Vedas have Oṃkāra as their cause. The sounds (*svaras*) have Oṃkāra as their cause. The three worlds with [all] the moving and fixed [ones in them] have Oṃkāra as their cause. The short [accent of Oṃ] burns all sins, the long one is decayless and the bestower of prosperity. United with *ardhamātrā* [half-metre of Oṃ], the *praṇava* becomes the bestower of salvation. That man is the knower of the Vedas who knows that the end [viz. *ardhamātrā*] of *praṇava* should be worshipped [or recited] as uninterrupted as the flow of oil and [resounding] as long as the sound of a bell. One should contemplate upon Oṃkāra as Īśvara resembling an unshaken light, as of the size of a thumb and as motionless in the middle of the pericarp of the lotus of the heart. Taking in *vāyu* through the left nostril and filling the stomach with it, one should contemplate upon Oṃkāra as being in the middle of the body and as surrounded by circling flames. Brahmā is said to be inspiration; Viṣṇu is said to be cessation [of breath], and Rudra is said to be expiration. These are the *devatās* of *prāṇāyāma*. Having made ātman as the [lower] sacrificial wood (*araṇī*) and *praṇava* as the upper *araṇi*, one should see god in secret through the practice of churning which is *dhyāna*. One should practise restraint of breath as much as it lies in his power along with [the uttering of] Oṃkāra sound, until it ceases completely. Those who look upon Oṃ as of the form of *haṃsa* staying in all, shining like crores of suns, being alone, staying in ever going and coming (*gamāgama*) and being devoid of motion—at last such persons are freed from sin. That *manas* which is the author of the actions [viz.], creation, preservation and destruction of the three worlds, is [then] absorbed [in the supreme one]. That is the highest state of Viṣṇu.

The lotus of the heart has eight petals and thirty-two filaments. The sun is in its midst: the moon is in the middle of the sun. *Agni* is in the middle of the moon: the spiritual light (*prabhā*) is in the middle of *agni*. *Pīṭha* (seat) is in the midst of *prabhā*, being set in diverse gems. One should meditate upon the stainless Lord Vāsudeva as being [seated] upon the centre of *pīṭha*, as having Śrīvatsa [black mark] and garland of gems (*kaustubha*) on his chest and as adorned with gems and pearls resembling pure crystal in lustre and as resembling crores of moons in brightness. He should meditate upon Mahā-Viṣṇu as above or in the following manner. [That is] he should meditate with inspiration [of breath] upon Mahā-Viṣṇu as resembling the *aṭasī* flower and as staying in the seat of the navel with four hands; then with restraint of breath, he should meditate in the heart upon Brahmā, the grandfather as being on the lotus with the pale-red (*gaura*) colour of gems and having four faces: then through expiration, he should meditate upon the three-eyed Śiva between the two eyebrows shining like pure crystal, being stainless, destroying all sins, being in that which is like the lotus facing down with its flower [or face] below and the stalk above or like the flower of a plantain tree, being of the form of all Vedas, containing one hundred petals and one hundred leaves and having the pericarp full-expanded. Then he should meditate upon the sun, the moon and the *agni*, one above another. Passing above through the lotus which has the brightness of the sun, moon and *agni*, and taking its *hrīṃ bīja* [letter], one leads his ātman firmly. He is the knower of Vedas who knows the three seats, the three *mātrās*, the three Brahmās, the three *akṣaras* and the three *mātrās* associated with the *ardhamātrā*. He who knows that which is above *bindu*, *nāda* and *kalā* as uninterrupted as the flow of oil and [resounding] as long as the sound of a bell—that man is a knower of the Vedas. Just as a man would draw up [with his mouth] the water through the [pores of the] lotus-stalk, so the yogin treading the path of yoga should draw up the breath. Having made the lotus-sheath of the form of *ardhamātrā*, one should draw up the breath through the stalk [of the *nāḍis suṣumnā, iḍā* and *piṅgalā*] and absorb it in the middle of the eyebrows. He should know that the middle of the eyebrows in the forehead which is also the root of the nose is the seat of nectar. That is the great place of Brahman.

Postures, restraint of breath, subjugation of the senses, *dhāraṇā*, *dhyāna* and *samādhi* are the six parts of yoga. There are as many postures as there are living creatures; and Maheśvara [the great Lord] knows their distinguishing features. *Siddha, bhadra, siṃha* and *padma* are the four [chief] postures. *Mūlādhāra* is the first *cakra*. *Svādhiṣṭhāna* is the second. Between these two is said to be the seat of *yoni* (perineum), having the form of God of love (Kāma). In the *ādhāra* of the anus, there is the lotus of four petals. In its midst is said to be the *yoni* called Kāma and worshipped by the *siddhas*. In the midst of the *yoni* is the *liṅga* facing the west and split at its head like the gem. He who knows this, is a knower of the Vedas. A four-sided figure is situated above *agni* and below the genital organ, of the form of molten gold and shining like streaks of lightning. *Prāṇa* is with its own (*sva*) sound, having *svādhiṣṭhāna* as its seat (*adhiṣṭhāna*), [or since *sva* or *prāṇa* arises from it]. The *cakra svādhiṣṭhāna* is spoken of as the genital organ itself. The *cakra* in the sphere of the navel is called *maṇipūraka*, since the body is pierced through by *vāyu* like gems (*maṇis*) by string. The *jīva* [ego] urged to actions by its past virtuous and sinful *karmas* whirls about in this great *cakra* of twelve spokes, so long as it does not grasp the truth. Above the genital organ and below the navel is *kanda* of the shape of a bird's egg. There arise [from it] *nāḍīs* seventy-two thousand in number. Of these seventy-two are generally known. Of these, the chief ones are ten and carry the *prāṇas*: *iḍā*, *piṅgalā*, *suṣumnā*, *gāndhārī*, *hastijihvā*, *pūṣā*(?), *yaśasvinī*, *alambuṣā*, *kuhū* and *śaṅkhinī* are said to be the ten. This *cakra* of the *nāḍīs* should ever be known by the yogins. The three *nāḍīs iḍā*, *piṅgalā* on the right side, while the *suṣumnā* is in the middle. These three are known to be the paths of *prāṇa*. *Prāṇa*, *apāna*, *samāna*, *udāna*, and *vyāna*; *nāga*, *kūrma*, *kṛkara*, *devadatta* and *dhanañjaya*; of these the first five are called *prāṇas* etc., and last five *nāga*, etc. are called *vāyus* [or sub-*prāṇas*]. All these are situated [or run along] the one thousand *nāḍīs*, [being] in the form of [or producing] life. *Jīva* which is under the influence of *prāṇa* and *apāna* goes up and down. *Jīva* on account of its ever moving by the left and right paths is not visible. Just as a ball struck up, so *jīva* ever tossed by *prāṇa* and *apāna* is never at rest. He is the knower of yoga who knows that *prāṇa* is never at rest. He is the knower of yoga who knows that *prāṇa* always draws itself from *apāna* and *apāna* draws itself from *prāṇa*, like a bird [drawing itself from and yet not freeing itself] from the string [to which it is tied].

The *jīva* comes out with the letter *Ha* and gets in again with the letter *Sa*. Thus *jīva* always utters the mantra *'haṃsa', 'haṃsa'*. The *jīva* always utters the mantra twenty-one thousand and six hundred times in one day and night. This is called Ajapā Gāyatrī and is ever the bestower of *nirvāṇa* to the yogins. Through its very thought, man is freed from sins. Neither in the past nor in the future is there a science equal to this, is *japa* equal to this or a meritorious action equal to this. Parameśvarī [viz. *kuṇḍalinī-śakti*] sleeps shutting with her mouth that door which leads to the decayless Brahma-hole. Being aroused by the contact of *agni* with *manas* and *prāṇa*, she takes the form of a needle and pierces up through *suṣumnā*. The yogin should open with great effort this door which is shut. Then he will pierce the door to salvation by means of *kuṇḍalinī*. Folding firmly the fingers of the hands, assuming firmly the lotus posture, placing the chin firmly on the breast and fixing the mind in dhyāna, one should frequently raise up the *apāna*, fill up with air and then leave the *prāṇa*. Then the wise man gets matchless wisdom through this *śakti*. That yogin who assuming lotus posture worships [i.e. controls] *vāyu* at the door of the *nāḍīs* and then performs restraint of breath is released without doubt. Rubbing off the limbs the sweat arising from fatigue, abandoning all acid, bitter and saltish [food], taking delight in the drinking of milk and *rasa*, practising celibacy, being moderate in eating and ever bent on yoga, the yogin becomes a *siddha* in little more than a year. No inquiry need be made concerning the result. *Kuṇḍalinī śakti*, when it is up in the throat, makes the yogi get *siddhi*. The union of *prāṇa* and *apāna* has the extinction of urine and faeces.

One becomes young even when old through performing *mūla-bandha* always. Pressing the *yoni* by means of the heels and contracting the anus and drawing up the *apāna*—this is called *mūla-bandha*. *Uḍḍiyāṇa-bandha* is so called because it is [like] a great bird that flies up always without rest. One should bring the western part of the stomach above the navel. This *uḍḍiyāṇa-bandha* is a lion to the elephant of death, since it binds the water [or nectar] of the *ākāśa* which arises in the head and flows down. The *jālandhara-bandha* is the destroyer of all the pains of the throat. When this *jālandhara-bandha*, which is the destroyer of the pains of the throat is performed, then nectar does not fall on *agni* nor does the *vāyu* move. When the tongue enters backwards into the hole of the skull, then there is the *mudrā* of vision latent in the eyebrow called *khecarī*. He who knows the *mudrā*, *khecarī* has not disease, death, sleep, hunger, thirst, or swoon. He who practises this *mudrā* is not affected by illness or *karma*; nor is he bound by the limitations of time. Since *citta* moves in the *kha* [*akāśa*] and since the tongue has entered [in the *mudrā*] *kha* [viz. the hole in the mouth], therefore the *muḍrā* is called *khecarī* and worshipped by the *siddhas*. He whose passage above the uvula is closed [with the tongue backwards] by means of *khecarī-mudrā* never loses his virility, even when embraced by a lovely woman. Where is the fear of death, so long as the *bindu* [virility] stays in the body. *Bindu* does not go out of the body, so long as the *khecarī mudra* is practised. [Even] when *bindu* comes down to the sphere of the perineum, it goes up, being prevented and forced up by violent effort through *yoni-mudrā*. This *bindu* is twofold, white and red. The white one is called *śukla* and the red one is said to contain much *rajas*. The *bindu* stays in the seat of the genital organs. The union of these two is attained in the highest body; when *rajas* is roused up by agitating the *śakti* through *vāyu* which unites with the sun, thence is produced the divine form. *Śukla* being united with the moon and *rajas* with the sun, he is a knower of yoga who knows the proper mixture of these two. The cleansing of the accumulated refuse, the unification of the sun and the moon and the complete drying of the essences (*rasas*), this is called

Mahāmudrā. Placing the chin on the breast, pressing the anus by means of the left heel, and seizing [the toe of] the extended right leg by the two hands, one should fill his belly [with air] and should slowly exhale. This is called Mahāmudrā, the destroyer of the sins of men.

Now I shall give a description of ātman. In the seat of the heart is a lotus of eight petals. In its centre is *jīvātman* of the form of *jyotis* and atomic in size, moving in a circular line. In it is located everything. It knows everything. It does everything. It does all these actions attributing everything to its own power, [thinking] I do, I enjoy, I am happy, I am miserable, I am blind, I am lame, I am deaf, I am mute, I am lean, I am stout, etc. When it rests on the eastern petal which is of white (*śveta*) colour, then it has a mind [or is inclined] to dharma with devotion (*bhakti*). When it rests on the south-eastern petal, which is of blood (*rakta*) colour, then it is inclined to sleep and laziness. When it rests on the southern petal, which is of black (*kṛṣṇa*) colour, then it is inclined to hate and anger. When it rests on the south-western petal which is of blue (*nīla*) colour, then it gets desire for sinful or harmful actions. When it rests on the western petal which is of crystal colour, then it is inclined to flirt and amuse. When it rests on the north-western petal which is of ruby colour, then it has a mind to walk, rove and be indifferent (or have *vairāgya*). When it rests on the northern petal which is yellow (*pīta*) colour, then it is inclined to be happy and to be loving. When it rests on the north-eastern petal which is of lapis lazuli (*vaidūrya*) colour, then it is inclined to amassing money, charity and passion. When it stays in the interspace between any two petals, then it gets the wrath arising from diseases generated through [the disturbance of the equilibrium of] *vāyu*, bile and phlegm [in the body]. When it stays in the middle, then it knows everything, sings, dances speaks and is blissful. When the eye is pained [after a day's work], then in order to remove [its] pain, it makes first a circular line and sinks in the middle. The first line is of the colour of *bandhūka* flower [Bassia]. Then is the state of sleep. In the middle of the state of dream, it experiences the ideas of perception, Vedas, inference, possibility, [sacred] words, etc. Then there arises much fatigue. In order to remove this fatigue, it circles the second line and sinks in the middle. The second is of the colour of [the insect] Indragopa [of red or white colour]. Then comes the state of dreamless sleep.

During the dreamless sleep, it has only the thought connected with Parameśvara (the highest Lord) alone. This state is of the nature of eternal wisdom. Afterwards it attains the nature of the highest Lord (Parameśvara). Then it makes a round of the third circle and sinks in the middle. The third circle is of the colour of ruby (*padmarāga*). Then comes the state of *turyātman*. It attains the nature of eternal wisdom. Then one should gradually attain the quiescence of *buddhi* with self-control. Placing the *manas* in ātman, one should think of nothing else. Then causing the union of *prāṇa* and *apāna*, he concentrates his aim upon the whole universe being of the nature of ātman. Then comes the state of *turyātīta* [viz. that state beyond the fourth]. Then everything appears as bliss. He is beyond the pairs [of happiness and pains, etc.]. He stays here as long as he should wear his body. Then he attains the nature of Paramātman and attains emancipation through this means. This alone is the means of knowing ātman.

When breath (*vāyu*) which enters the great passage associated with a hall where four roads meet gets into the half of the well-placed triangle, then is the indestructible *(acyuta)* seen. Above the aforesaid triangle, one should meditate on the five seed (*bīja*) letters of [the elements] *pṛthivi* etc., as also on the five *prāṇas*, the colour of the *bījas* and their position. The letter *Yaṃ* is the *bīja* of *prāṇa* and resembles the blue cloud. The letter *Raṃ* is the *bīja* of *agni*, is of *apāna* and resembles the sun. The letter *Laṃ* is the *bīja* of *pṛthivī*, is of *vyāna* and resemblies *bandhūka* flower. The letter *Vaṃ* is the *bīja* of *jīva* [or *vāyu*], is of *udāna* and is of the colour of the conch. The letter *Haṃ* is the *bīja* of *ākāśa*, is of *samāna*, and is of the colour of crystal. *Prāṇa* stays in the heart, navel, nose ear, foot, finger and other places, travels through the seventy-two thousand *nāḍīs*, stays in the twenty-eight crores of hair-pores and is yet the same everywhere. It is that which is called *jīva*. One should perform the three, expiration, etc., with a firm will and great control: and drawing in everything [with the breath] in slow degrees, he should bind *prāṇa* and *apāna* in the cave of the lotus of the heart and utter *praṇava*, having contracted his throat and the genital organ. From the *mūlādhāra* [to the head] is the *suṣumnā* resembling the shining thread of the lotus. The *nāda* is located in the spinal column (*vīṇādaṇḍa*); that sound from its middle resembles [that of] the conch, etc. When it goes to the passage of the *ākāśa*, it resembles that of the peacock. In the middle of the cave of the skull between the four doors shines ātman, like the sun in the sky. Between the two bows in the cavity of Brahma, one should see Puruṣa with *Śakti* as his own ātman. Then his *manas* is absorbed there. That man attains *kaivalya* who understands the gems, moonlight, *nāda*, *bindu*, and the seat of Maheśvara (the great Lord).

Oṃ tat sat is the Upaniṣad

25
Haṃsa Upaniṣad of Śukla Yajurveda

Gautama addressed Sanatkumāra thus: "O Lord, thou art the knower of all dharmas and art well versed in all śāstras, pray tell me the means by which I may obtain a knowledge of Brahmavidyā."

Sanatkumāra replied thus:

"Hear, O Gautama, that *tattva* as expounded by Pārvatī after inquiring into all dharmas and ascertaining Śiva's opinion. This treatise on the nature of *haṃsa* which gives the fruit of bliss and salvation and which is like a treasure to the yogin, is [a] very mystic [science] and should not be revealed [to the public].

"Now we shall explain the true nature of *haṃsa* and Paramahaṃsa for the benefit of a celibate seeker after Brahman (*brahmacārin*), who has his desires under control, is devoted to his guru and always contemplates, *haṃsa*, and realises thus: It [*haṃsa*] is permeating all bodies like fire [for heat] in all kinds of wood or oil in all kinds of gingelly seeds. Having known [it] thus, one does not meet with death.

"Having contracted the anus [with the heels pressed against it], having raised the breath [*vāyu*] from *mūlādhāra* [*cakra*], having made circuit thrice round *svādhiṣṭhāna*, having gone to *maṇipūraka*, having crossed *anāhata*, having controlled *prāṇa* in *viśuddhi* and then having reached *ājñā*, one contemplates in *brahmarandhra* [in the crown of head], and having meditated there always 'I am of three *mātrās*,' cognises [his self] and becomes formless. The *śisna* [penis] has two sides [left and right from head to foot]. This is that Paramahaṃsa [supreme *haṃsa* or higher self] having the resplendence of crores of suns and by whom all this world is pervaded.

"It [this *haṃsa* which has *buddhi* as vehicle] has eightfold *vṛtti*. [When it is] in the eastern petal, there is the inclination [in a person] to virtuous actions; in the south-eastern petal, there arise sleep, laziness, etc.; in the southern, there is the inclination to cruelty; in the south-western, there is the inclination to sins; in the western, there is the inclination to sensual sport; in the north-western, there arise the desire of passion, walking, and others; in the northern, there arises the desire of passion; in the north-eastern, there arises the desire of amassing money; in the middle [or the interspace between the petals], there is the indifference to material pleasures. In the filament [of the lotus], there arises the waking state; in the pericarp, there arises the dreaming state *(svapna)*; in the seed of pericarp (*bīja*), there arises the dreamless sleeping state (*suṣupti*); when leaving the lotus, there is the fourth state (*ṭurya*). When *haṃsa* is absorbed in spiritual sound (*nāda*), the state beyond the fourth is reached. *Nāda* [which is at the end of sound and beyond speech and mind] is like a pure crystal extending from *mūlādhāra* to *brahmarandhra*. It is that which is spoken of as Brahmā and Paramātman.

[Here the performance of Ajapā Gāyatrī is given].

"Now *haṃsa* is the *ṛṣi*; the metre is Avyakta Gāyatrī; Paramahaṃsa is the presiding deity (*devatā*) '*Ham*' is the *bīja*; 'Sa' is the *śaktī*; *so'ham* is the *kīlaka*. Thus there are six. There are 21,600 *haṃsas* [or breaths] in a day and night. [Salutation to] Sūrya, Soma, Nirañjana [the stainless] and Nirābhāsa [the universeless]. Ajapā māntra. [May] the bodiless and subtle one guide [or illuminate my understanding]. *Vauṣaṭ* to Agni and Soma. Then *aṅganyāsas* and *karanyāsas* should be performed [after the mantras as they are performed before the mantras] in the heart and other [seats]. Having done so, one should contemplate upon *haṃsa* as the ātman in his heart. Agni and Soma are its wings [right and left sides]; Oṃkāra is its head; *Ukāra* and *bindu* are the three eyes and face respectively; Rudra and Rudrāṇī are the feet *kanthaṭa* or the realisation of the oneness of *jīvātman* or *haṃsa*, the lower self with Paramātman or Paramahaṃsa, the higher self is done in two ways, contemplation with an object of adoration and adoration without it.

"After that, *unmanī* is the end of the *ajapā* [mantra]. Having thus reflected upon *manas* by means of this [*haṃsa*], one hears *nāda* after the uttering of this *japa* [mantra] a crore of times. It [*nāda*] is [begun to be heard as] of ten kinds. The first is *cini* [like the sound of that word]; the second is *cini-cini*; the third is the sound of the bell; the fourth is that of the conch; the fifth is that of lute (*tantrī*); the sixth is that sound of cymbals (*tāla*); the seventh is that of flute; the eighth is that of drum (*bheri*); the ninth is that of double drum (*mṛdaṅga*); and the tenth is that of clouds [viz. thunder]. He may experience the tenth without the first nine sounds [through the initation of a guru]. In the first stage, his body becomes *cini-cini*; in the second, there is the breaking (*bhañjana*) [or affecting] in the body; in the third, there is the piercing (*bhedana*); in the fourth, the head shakes; in the fifth, the palate produces saliva; in the sixth, nectar is attained; in the seventh, the knowledge of the hidden [things in the world] arises; in the eighth, *parāvāk* is heard; in the ninth, the body becomes invisible and the pure divine eye is developed; in the tenth, he attains Parabrahman in the presence of [or with] ātman which is Brahman. After that, when *manas* is destroyed, when that which is the source of *saṅkalpa* and *vikalpa* disappears, owing to the destruction of these two and when virtues and sins are burnt away, then he shines as Sadāśiva of the nature of Śakti pervading everywhere, being effulgence in its very essence, the immaculate, the eternal, the stainless, and the most quiescent Oṃ. Thus is the teaching of the Vedas.

Oṃ tat sat is the Upaniṣad

26
Amṛtanāda Upaniṣad
of
Kṛṣṇa Yajurveda

The wise, having studied the śāstras and reflected on them again and again and having come to know Brahman, should abandon them all like a firebrand. Having ascended the car of Oṃ with Viṣṇu (the higher self) as the charioteer, one wishing to go to the seat of Brahmaloka intent on the worship of Rudra, should go in the chariot so long as he can go. Then abandoning the car, he reaches the place of the Lord of the car. Having given up *mātrā*, *liṅga*, and *pada*, he attains subtle *pada* seat or word without vowels or consonants by means of the letter *M* without the accent (*svara*). That is called *pratyāhāra* when one merely thinks of the five objects of sense, such as sound, etc. as also the very unsteady mind and reins of ātman. Subjugation of the sense (*pratyāhāra*), contemplation (*dhyāna*), control of breath (*prāṇāyāma*) concentration (*dhāraṇā*), *tarka* and *samādhi* are said to be the six parts of yoga. Just as the impurities of mountain-minerals are burnt by the blower, so the stains committed by the organs are burned by checking *prāṇa*. Through *prāṇāyāmas* should be burnt the stains; through *dhāraṇā*, the six; through *pratyāhāra*, the [bad] association; and through *dhyāna*, the godless qualities. Having destroyed the sins, one should think of the shining (*rucira*). Cessation, expiration and inspiration—these three are *prāṇāyāmas* of [*recaka, pūraka* and *kumbhaka*] expiration, inspiration and cessation of breath. That is called [one cycle of] *prāṇāyāma* when one repeats with a prolonged (or elongated) breath three times the Gāyatrī with its *vyāhṛtis* and *praṇava* [before it] along with the head (*śiras*) joining after it. Raising up the *vāyu* from the *ākāśa* [region, viz. the heart] and making the body void [of *vāyu*] and empty and uniting [the soul] to the state of void, is called expiration (*recaka*). That is called inspiration (*pūraka*) when one takes in *vāyu*, as a man would take water into his mouth through the lotus-stalk. That is called cessation of breath (*kumbhaka*) when there is no expiration or inspiration and the body is motionless, remaining still in one state. Then he sees forms like the blind, hears sounds like the deaf and sees the body like wood. This is the characteristic of one that has attained much quiescence. That is called *dhāraṇā* when the wise man regards the mind as *saṅkalpa* and merging *saṅkalpa* into ātman, contemplates upon his ātman[alone]. That is called *tarka* when one makes inference which does not conflict with the Vedas. That is called *samādhi* in which one, on attaining it, thinks [all] equal.

Seating himself on the ground on a seat of *kuśa* grass which is pleasant and devoid of all evils, having protected himself mentally [from all influences], uttering *ratha-maṇḍala*, assuming either *padma*, *svastika*, or *bhadra* posture or any other which can be practised easily, facing the north and closing the nostril with the thumb, one should inspire through the other nostril and retain breath inside and preserve the fire (*agni*). Then he should think of the sound [Oṃ] alone. Oṃ, the one letter is Brahman; Oṃ should not be breathed out. Through this divine mantra [Oṃ], it should be done many times to rid himself of impurity. Then as said before, the mantra-knowing wise should regularly meditate, beginning with the navel upwards in the gross, the primary [or less] gross and the subtle [states]. The greatly wise should give up all [sight] seeing across, up or down and should practise yoga always being motionless and without tremor. The union as stated by remaining without tremor in the hollow stalk [viz. *suṣumnā*] alone is *dhāraṇā*. The yoga with ordained duration of twelve *mātrās* is called *dhāraṇā*. That which never decays is *akṣara* [Oṃ] which is without *ghoṣa* [third, fourth, and fifth letters from *K*], consonant, vowel, palatal (guttural, nasal, letter *R* and sibilants). *Prāṇa* travels through [or goes by] that path through which this *akṣara* [Oṃ] goes. Therefore it should be practised daily, in order to pass along that [course]. It is through the opening of the heart, through the opening of *vāyu* [probably navel], through the opening of the head and through the opening of *mokṣa*. They call it cave (*bila*), hole (*suṣira*), or wheel (*maṇḍala*).

[Then about the obstacles of yoga]. A yogin should always avoid fear, anger, laziness, too much sleep or waking and too much food or fasting. If the above rule be well and strictly practised each day, spiritual wisdom will arise of itself in three months without doubt. In four months, he sees the gods; in five months, he attains *kaivalya* at will. There is no doubt.

That which is of the earth is of five moras (*mātrās*) [or it takes five *mātrās* to pronounce *pārthiva-praṇava*]. That which is of water is of four moras (*mātrās*); of *agni*, three moras (*mātrās*); of *vāyu*, two; and of *ākāśa*, one. But he should contemplate that which is with no *mātrās*. Having united ātman with *manas*, one should contemplate upon ātman by means of ātman. *Prāṇā* is thirty digits long [12 digits beyond the body]. Such is the position [or range] of *prāṇas*. That is called *prāṇa* which is the seat of the external *prāṇas*. The breaths by day and night are numbered as 1,13,180[i.e. taking 21,600 for each of the five *prāṇas*, we get 1,08,000: for the five sub-*prāṇas*, 5 X 1036 is 5,180. hence the total is 1,13,180]. [Of the *prāṇas*] the first (viz. *prāṇa*) is pervading the heart; *apāna*, the anus; *samāna*, the navel; *udāna*, the throat; and *vyāna*, all parts of the body. Then come the colours of the five *prāṇas* in order. *Prāṇa* is said to be of the colour of a blood-red gem (or coral); *apāna* which is in the middle is of the colour of Indragopa (an insect of white or red colour); *samāna* is between the colour of pure milk and crystal (or oily and shining), between both [*prāṇa* and *apāna*]: *udāna* is pale white; and *vyāna* resembles the colour of ray of light. That man is never reborn wherever he may die, whose breath goes out of the head after piercing through this *maṇḍala* [of the pineal gland]. That man is never reborn.

Oṃ tat sat is the Upaniṣad

27
Varāha Upaniṣad of Kṛṣṇa Yajurveda

CHAPTER I

The great sage Ṛbhu performed penance for twelve divine (*daiva*) years. At the end of the time, the Lord appeared before him in the form of a boar. He said: "Rise, rise and choose your boon." The sage got up and having prostrated himself before him said: "O Lord, I will not, in any dream wish of thee those things that are desired by the worldly. All the Veda Śāstra, Itihāsas and all the hosts of other sciences, as well as Brahmā and all the other devas, speak of emancipation as resulting from a knowledge of thy nature. So impart to me that science of Brahman which treats of thy nature."

Then the boar-shaped [Lord] Bhagvān said: "Some disputants hold that there are twenty-four principles (*tattvas*),and some thirty- six, whilst others maintain that there are ninety-six. I shall relate them in their order. Listen with an attentive mind. The organs of sense are five, viz. ear, skin, eye and others. The organs of action are five, viz. mouth, hand, leg and others. *Prāṇas* [vital airs] are five(=*prāṇa, apāna, udāna, vyāna* and *samāna*); sound and others [viz. rudimentary principles] are five (sound, touch, form, taste and odour). *Manas, buddhi, citta* and *ahaṃkāra* are four; thus those that know Brahman know these to be the twenty-four *tattvas*. Besides these, the wise hold the quintuplicated elements to be five, viz. earth, water, fire, wind and space; the bodies to be three, viz. the gross, the subtle and the causal; the states of consciousness to be three, viz. the waking, the dreaming and the dreamless sleeping. The munis know the total collection of *tattvas* to be thirty-six [coupled with *jīva*].

"With these *tattvas*, there are six changes viz. existence, birth, growth, transformation, decay and destruction. Hunger, thirst, grief, delusion, old age and death are said to be the six infirmities. Skin, blood, flesh, fat, marrow and bones are said to be the six sheaths. Passion, anger, avarice, delusion, pride and malice are the six kinds of foes. *Viśva, taijasa* and *prajña* in the states of waking, dreaming and dreamless sleeping are the three aspects of the *jīva*. *Sattva, rajas* and *tamas* are three qualities (*guṇas*). *Prārabdha* (=past *karmas* now being enjoyed), *sañcita* (=*karmas* being in store to be enjoyed) and *āgāmin* (*karmas* now produced to be enjoyed) are the three *karmas*. Talking, lifting, walking, excreting and enjoying are the five actions [of the organs of action]; and there are also thought, certainty, egoism, compassion, memory [functions of *manas*, etc.], complacency, sympathy and indifference: the quarters (*diś*), Vāyu, Sūrya, Agni, Indra, Varuṇa, Aśvini devas, Upendra and Mṛtyu (death): and then the moon, the four-faced Brahmā, Rudra, Kṣetrajña, and Īśvara. Thus these are the ninety-six *tattvas*. Those that worship with devotion, me of the form of the boar, who am other than the aggregate of these *tattvas* and am without decay are released from *ajñāna* and its effects and become liberated in this life *(jīvanmuktas)*. Those that know these ninety-six *tattvas* will attain salvation in whatever order of life they may be, whether they have matted hair or are of shaven head or have [only] their tuft of hair on. There is no doubt of this." Thus ends the first chapter.

CHAPTER II

The great Ṛbhu [again] addressed the Lord of Lakṣmī of the form of boar thus: "O Lord, please initiate me into the supreme

Brahmavidyā." Then the Lord who removes the miseries of his devotees being thus questioned, answered thus: "Through [the right observance of] the duties of one's own caste and orders of life, through religious austerities and through the pleasing of the guru [by serving him rightly], arise to persons the four *vairāgyas*, etc. They are the discrimination of the eternal from the non-eternal; indifference to the enjoyments of this and the other worlds; the acquistion of the six virtues, mental restrain (*śama*), etc., and the longing after liberation. These should be practised. Having subdued the sensual organs and having given up the conception of 'mine' in all objects, you should place your consciousness of 'I' in [or identify yourself with] me, who am the witness consciousness. To be born as a human being is difficult—more difficult it is to be born as a male being—and more so is it to be born as a Brāhmaṇa. Even then, if the fool does not cognise through the hearing, etc., of Vedānta, the true nature of the being-consciousness and blisss [of Brahman] that is all-pervading, and that is beyond all caste and orders of life, when will he obtain *mokṣa*? I alone am bliss. There is none other. If there is said to be another, then it is not bliss. There is no such thing as love, except on my account. The love that is on account of me is not natural to me. As I am the seat of supreme love, that 'I am not' is not. He who is sought after by all, saying 'I should become such,' is myself, the all-pervading. How can non-light affect ātman, the self-shining which is no other than the light whence originates the words 'I am not light'. My firm conviction is, whoever knows for certain that [ātman] which is self-shining and has itself no basis [to rest upon], is one of *vijñāna*.

"The universe, *jīva*, Īśvara, *māyā* and others do not really exist, except my full ātman. I have not their characteristics. *Karma* which has *dhāraṇā* and other attributes and is of the form of darkness and *ajñāna* is not fit to touch [or affect] me, who am ātman, the self-resplendent. That man who sees [his] ātman which is all-witness and is beyond all caste and orders of life as of the nature of Brahman, becomes himself Brahman. Whoever sees, through the evidence of Vedānta, this visible universe as the supreme seat which is of the form of light, attains *mokṣa* at once. When that knowledge which dispels the idea that this body [alone] is ātman, arises firmly in one's mind as was before the knowledge that this body [alone] is ātman, then that person, even though he does not desire *mokṣa*, gets it. Therefore how will a person be bound by *karma*, who always enjoys the bliss of Brahman which has the characteristics of *saccidānanda*, and which is other than *ajñāna*? Persons with spiritual eyes see Brahman, that is the witness of the three states, that has the characteristics of be-ness, wisdom and bliss, that is the underlying meaning of the words 'Thou' (*tvam*) and 'I' (*aham*), and that is untouched by all the stains. As a blind man does not see the sun that is shining, so an ignorant person does not see [Brahman]. *Prajñāna* alone is Brahman. It has truth and *prajñāna* as its characteristics. By thus cognising Brahman well, a person becomes immortal. One who knows his own ātman as Brahman, that is bliss, and without duality and qualities (*guṇas*), and that is truth and absolute consiousness, is not afraid of anything. That which is consciousness alone which is all-pervading, which is eternal, which is all-full, which is of the form of bliss and which is indestructible, is the only true Brahman. It is the settled determination of *brahmajñānin* that there is naught else but that. As the world appears dark to the blind and bright to those having good eyes, so this world full of manifold miseries to the ignorant is full of happiness to the wise. In me, of the form of boar, who am infinite and the bliss of absolute consciousness, if there is the conception of non-dualism, where then is bondage? And who is the one to be emancipated? The real nature of all embodied objects is ever the absolute consciousness. Like the pot seen by the eyes, the body and its aggregates are not [viz. do not really exist]. Knowing as ātman, all the moving and fixed worlds that appear as other than ātman, meditate upon them as 'It I am'. Such a person then enjoys his real nature. There is no other to be enjoyed than one-self. If there is anything, then Brahman alone has that attribute. One who is perfect in *brahmajñāna*, though he always sees this established universe, does not see it other than his ātman. By cognising clearly my form, one is not trammelled by *karma*. He is an undaunted person who by his own experience cognises as his own real nature all [the universe and Brahman] that is without the body and the organs of sense—that is the all witness—that is the one noumenal *vijñāna*, that is the blissful ātman [as contrasted with *jīvātman* or the lower self] and that is the self-resplendent. He is one that should be known as 'I' [myself]. O Ṛbhu, may you become he. After this, there will be never any experience of the world. Thereafter there will be never any experience of the wisdom of one's own true nature. One who has thus known fully ātman has neither emancipation nor bondage. Whoever meditates, even for one *muhūrta* (48 minutes) through the cognition of one's own real form, upon him who is dancing as the all-witness, is released from all bondage. Prostrations—prostrations to me who am in all the elements, who am the *cidātman* [viz. ātman of the nature of consciousness] that is eternal and free and who am the *pratyagātman*. O god, you are I. I am you. Prostrations on account of myself and yourself who are infinite and who are *cidātman*, myself being the supreme Īśa [Lord] and yourself being Śiva [of a beneficient nature]. What should I do? Where should I go? What should I reject? [Nothing because] the universe is filled by me as with the waters of the universal deluge. Whoever gives up [fond] love of the external, love of the internal and love of the body and thus gives up all associations, is merged in me. There is no doubt about it. That ascetic (*paramahaṃsa*) who, though living in the world, keeps aloof from human congregation as from a serpent, who regards a beautiful woman as a [living] corpse and the endless sensual objects as poison and who has abandoned all passion and is indifferent towards all objects is not other than Vāsudeva, [viz.] myself. This is truth (*satya*). This is nothing but truth. It is truth alone that is not said. I am Brahman, the truth. There is naught else but I.

"[The word] *'upavāsa'* (lit., dwelling) signifies the dwelling near [or union] of *jīvātman* and Paramātman and not [the religious observance as accepted by the worldly of] emaciating the body through fasts. To the ignorant, what is the use of the mere drying up of the body? By beating about the hole of a snake, can we be said to have killed the big snake within? A man is said to attain indirect (*parokṣa*) wisdom when he knows [theoretically] that there is Brahman; but he is said to attain direct cognition (*sākṣātkāra*) when he knows [or realises] that he is himself Brahman. When a yogin knows his ātman to be the absolute, then he becomes a *jīvanmukta*. To *mahātmans*, to be always in the state 'I am Brahman' conduces to their salvation. There are two words for bondage and *mokṣa*. They are 'mine'. and 'not mine'. Man is bound by 'mine', but he is released by 'not mine'. He should abandon all the thoughts relating to externals and so also with reference to internals. O Ṛbhu having given up all thoughts, you should rest content [in your ātman] ever.

"The whole of the universe is caused through *saṅkalpa* alone. It is only through *saṅkapla* that the universe manifests. Having abandoned the universe, which is of the form of *saṅkalpa* and having fixed your mind upon the one which is changeless (*nirvikalpa*), meditate upon my abode in your heart. O most intelligent being, pass your time in meditating upon me, glorifying me in songs, talking about me to one another and thus devoting yourself entirely to me as the Supreme. Whatever is consciousness (*citta*) in the universe is only *cinmātra*. This universe is *cinmaya* only. You are *cit*. I am *cit*: contemplate upon the worlds also as *cit*. Make the desires nil. Always be without any stain. How then can the bright lamp of *ātmā-vijñāna* arising through the Vedas be affected by the *karma* arising from the ignorance of the actor and the agent? Having given up not-ātman and being in the world unaffected by it, delight only in the *cinmātra* within, ever intent on the one. As the *ākāśa* of the pot and that of the house are both located in the all-pervading *ākāśa*, so the *jīvas* and Īśvara are only evolved out of me, the *cidākāśa* [the void of universal consciousness]. So that which did not exist before the evolution of ātmans [*jīvas* and Īśvara] and that which is rejected at the end [viz. universal deluge] is called *māyā* by *brahmajñānin* through their discrimination. Should *māyā*—and its effects [the universe] be annihilated, there is no state of Īśvara, there is no state of *jīva*. Therefore like the *ākāśa* without its vehicle, I am the immaculate and *cit*."

"The creation, sentient as well as non-sentient from thinking (*īkṣaṇā*) to entry (*praveśa*) [as stated in the Chāndogya-Upaniṣad, Prapāṭhaka VI, Khaṇḍas II and III] of those having the forms of *jīvas* and Īśvara is due to the creation [or illusion] of Īśvara; while the wordly existence (*saṃsāra*) from the waking state to salvation is due to the creation of *jīva*. So the *karmas* ordained in the sacrifice [called] *triṇācaka* [so called after Naciketas of the Kaṭha-Upaniṣad] to yoga are dependent upon the illusion of Īśvara; while [the systems from] Lokāyata (atheistical system) to *Śāṅkhya,* rest on the illusion of *jīva*. Therefore aspirants after salvation should never make their heads enter into the field of controversy regarding *jīva* and Īśvara. But with an undisturbed mind, the *tattvas* of Brahman should be investigated. Those who do not cognise the *tattva* of the secondless Brahman are all deluded persons only. Whence [then] is salvation to them? Whence then is happiness [to them] in this universe? What if they have the thoughts of the superiority and inferiority [of Īśvara and *jīva*]? Will sovereignty and mendicancy [experienced by a person] in the dreaming state affect him in his waking state? When *buddhi* is absorbed in *ajñāna*, then it is termed, by the wise, sleep. Whence then is sleep to me who have not *ajñāna* and its effects? When *buddhi* is in full bloom, then it is said to be the waking state (*jāgrat*). As I have no changes, etc., there is no waking state to me. The moving about of *buddhi* in the subtle *nāḍīs* constitutes the dreaming state. In me without the act of moving about, there is no dreaming. Then at the time of *suṣupti* when all things are absorbed, enveloped by *tamas*, he then enjoys the highest bliss of his own nature in an invisible state. If he sees everything as *cit* without any difference, he alone is an actual *vijñānin*. He alone is Śiva. He alone is Hari. He alone is Brahmā. This mundane existence which is an ocean of sorrow, is nothing but a long-lived dream or an illusion of the mind or a long-lived reign of the mind. From rising from sleep till going to bed, the one Brahman alone should be contemplated upon. By causing to be absorbed, this universe which is but a superimposition, the *citta* partakes of my nature. Having annihilated all the six powerful enemies, through their destruction, he becomes the non-dual one like the scent-elephant. Whether the body perishes now or lasts the age of moon and stars, what matters it to me having *cit* alone as my body? What matters it to the *ākāśa* in the pot, whether it [the pot] is destroyed now or exists for a long time. While the slough of a serpent lies cast off lifeless in its hole, it [the serpent] does not evince any affection towards it. Likewise the wise do not identify themselves with their gross and subtle bodies. If the delusive knowledge [that the universe is real] with its cause should be destroyed by the fire of *ātmajñāna*, the wise man becomes bodiless, through the idea 'It [Brahman] is not this; It is not this'. Through the study of the śāstras, the knowledge of reality perishes. Through direct perception of truth, one's fitness for action [in the universe] ceases. With the cessation of *prārabdha*, the destruction of the manifestation [of the universe] takes place. *Māyā* is thus destroyed in a threefold manner. If within himself no identification [of *jīva*] with Brahman takes place, the state [of the separateness] of *jīva* does not perish. If the non-dual one is truly discerned, then all affinities [for objects] ceases. With the cessation of *prārabdha* [arising from the cessation of affinities], there is that of the body. Therefore it is certain that *māyā* perishes thus entirely.

"If it is said that all the universe is, that Brahman alone is that of the nature of *sat*. If it is said that the universe shines, then it is Brahman alone that shines. [The mirage of] all the water in an oasis is really no other than the oasis itself. Through inquiry of one's self, the three worlds [above, below and middle] are only of the nature of *cit*. In Brahman, which is one and alone, the essence of whose nature is absolute consciousness and which is remote from the difference of *jīva*, Īśvara and guru, there is no *ajñāna*. Such being the case, where then is the occasion for the universe there? I am that Brahman which is all full. While the full moon of wisdom is robbed of its lustre by the Rāhu [one of the two nodes of the moon] of delusion, all actions such as the rites of bathing, alms-giving and sacrifice performed during the time of eclipse are all fruitless. As salt dissolved in water becomes one, so if ātman and *manas* become identified, it is termed *samādhi*. Without the grace of a good [perfect] guru, the abandonment of sensual objects is very difficult to attain; so also the perception of [divine] truth and the attainment of one's true state. Then the state of being in one's own self shines of its own accord in a yogin in who *jñānaśakti* has dawned and who has abandoned all *karmas*. The [property of] fluctuation is natural to mecury and mind. If either mercury is bound [or consolidated] or mind is bound [or controlled], what then on this earth cannot be accomplished? He who obtains *mūrcchā* [either controlling the breath through *prāṇāyāma* or the consolidation of mercury through some alchemical means leading in both cases to *siddhis*] cures all diseases. The dead are brought to life again. He who has bound [his mind or mercury] is able to move on the air. Therefore mercury and mind confer upon one the state of Brahman. The master of the organs (*indriyas*) is mind (*manas*). The master of manas is *prāṇa*. The master of *prāṇa* is *laya* [absorption yoga]. Therefore *laya-yoga* should be practised. To the yogins, *laya* [*-yoga*] is said to be without actions and changes. This *laya* (absorption) of mind which is above speech and in which one has to abandon all *saṅkalpas* and to give up completely all actions, should be known through one's own [experience]. As an actress, though subject [or dancing in harmony] to music, cymbals and other musical instruments of time, has her mind intent upon the protection of the pot on her head, so the yogin, though intent for the time being upon the hosts of objects, never leaves the mind contemplating on Brahman. The person who desires all the wealth of yoga should, after having given up all thoughts, practise with a subdued mind, concentration on spiritual sound (*nāda*) alone."

CHAPTER III

"The One Principle cannot at any time become of manifold forms. As I am the partless, there is none else but myself. Whatever is seen and whatever is heard is no other than Brahman. I am that Parabrahman, which is the eternal, the immaculate, the free, the one, the undivided bliss, the non-dual, the truth, the wisdom and the endless. I am of the nature of bliss, I am of undivided wisdom; I am the supreme of the supreme; I am the resplendent absolute consciousness. As the clouds do not touch the *ākāśa*, so the miseries attendant on mundane existence do not affect me. Know all to be the happiness through the annihilation of sorrow and all to be of the nature of be-ness (*sat*) through the annihilation of not-be-ness (*asat*). It is only the nature of consciousness (*cit*) that is associated with this visible universe. Therefore my form is partless. To an exalted yogin, there is neither birth nor death, nor going [to other spheres], nor returning [to earth]; there is no stain or purity or knowledge but [the universe] shines to him as absolute consciousness. Practise always silence 'I am [viz. that you yourself are] Parabrahman' which is truth and absolute consciousness, which is undivided and non-dual, which is invisible, which is stainless, which is pure, which is secondless and which is beneficent. It [Brahman] is not subject to birth and death, happiness and misery. It is not subject to caste, law, family and clan (*gotra*). Practise silence—I am *cit* which is *vivarta-upādāna* [viz. the illusory cause] of the universe. Always practise silence—I am [viz. you are] the Brahman, that is the full, the secondless, the undivided consciousness which has neither the relationship nor the differences existing in the universe and which partakes of the essence of the non-dual and the supreme *sat* and *cit*.

"That which always is and that which preserves the same nature during the three periods of time, unaffected by anything, is my eternal form of *sat*. Even the state of happiness which is eternal without vehicles (*upādhis*) and which is superior to all the happiness derivable from *suṣupti* is of my bliss only. As by the rays of the sun, thick gloom is soon destroyed, so darkness, the cause of rebirth is destroyed by Hari [Viṣṇu] viz. the sun's lustre. Through the contemplation and worship of my [Hari's] feet, every person is delivered from his ignorance. The means of destroying deaths and births is only through the contemplation of my feet. As a lover of wealth praises the cause of the universe, who will not be delivered from bondage?

"As in the presence of the sun the world of its own accord begins to perform its actions, so in my presence all the worlds are animated to action. As to the mother-of-pearl, the illusory conception of silver is falsely attributed, so to me is falsely attributed through *māyā* this universe which is composed of *mahat*, etc. I am not with those differences that are [observable] in the body of low caste men, the body of a cow, etc., the fixed ones, the bodies of brāhmaṇas and others. As to a person, even after being relieved from the misconception of the directions, the [same miconception of] direction continues [as before], just so is to me the universe though destroyed by *vijñāna*. Therefore the universe is not. I am neither the body nor the organs of sense and action, nor *prāṇas*, nor *manas*, nor *buddhi*, nor *ahaṅkāra*, nor *citta*, nor *māyā*, nor the universe including *ākāśa* and others. Neither am I the actor, the enjoyer, nor he who causes the enjoyment. I am Brahman that is *cit, sat* and *ānanda* alone and that is Janārdana [Viṣṇu].

"As, through the fluctuation of water, the sun [reflected therein] moves, so ātman arises in this mundane existence through its mere connection with *ahaṃkāra*. The is mudane existence has *citta* as its root. This [*citta*] should be cleansed by repeated effort. How is it you have your confidence in the greatness of *citta*? Alas, where is all the wealth of the kings! Where are the Brahmās? Where are all the worlds? All old ones are gone. Many fresh evolutions have occurred. Many crores of Brahmās have passed away. Many kings have flitted away like particles of dust. Even to a *jñānin*, the love of the body may arise through the demoniacal (*asura*) nature. If the *asura* nature should arise in a wise man, his knowledge of truth becomes fruitless. Should *rajas* and others generated in us be burnt by the fire of discriminative [divine] wisdom, how can they germinate again? Just as a very intelligent person delights in the shortcomings of another, so if one finds out his own faults [and corrects them] who will not be relieved from bondage? O Lord of munis, only he who has not *ātmajñāna* and who is not an emancipated person, longs after *siddhis*. He attains such *siddhis* through medicine, [or wealth], mantras, religious works, time and skill. In the eyes of an *ātmajñānin*, one who has his sight solely on ātman and one who is content with ātman [the higher self] through [his] ātman[or the lower self], never follows [the dictates of] *avidyā*. Whatever exists in this world, he knows to be of the nature of *avidyā*. How then will an *ātmajñānīn* who has relinquished *avidyā* be immersed in[or affected by] it. Though medicine, mantras, religious work, time and skill [or mystical expressions] lead to the development of *siddhis*, yet they cannot in any way help one to attain the seat of Paramātman. How then can one who is an *ātmajñānin* and who is without his mind be said to long after *siddhis*, while all the actions of his desires are controlled?"

CHAPTER IV

On another occasion Nidāgha asked Lord Ṛbhu to enlighten him as to the characteristics of *jīvanmukti*. To which Ṛbhu replied in the affirmative and said the following:

"In the seven stages of development of wisdom [or *bhumikās*] there are four kinds of *jīvanmuktas*. Of these the first stage is good desire (*śubheccā*), the second is inquiry (*vicāraṇā*); the third is or pertaining to the thinned mind (*tanumānasī*); the fourth is the attainment of purity (*sattvāpatti*); the fifth is non-attachment (*asaṃsakti*); the sixth is the analysis of objects (*padārthabhāvanā*) and the seventh is the fourth or final stage (*turya*). The *bhūmikā* which is of the form of *praṇava* [Oṃ] is formed of [or is divided into] *akāra—A*, *ukāra—U*, *makāra—M*, and *ardhamātrā*. *Akāra* and others are of four kinds on account of the difference of gross (*sthūla*), subtle (*sūkṣma*), seed or causal (*bīja*) and witness (*sākṣin*). Their *avasthās* are four: waking, dreaming, dreamless sleeping and fourth (*turya*). He who is in [or the entity that identifies itself with] the waking state in the gross *aṃśa* [essence] of *akāra* is named Viśva; in the subtle essence, he is termed Taijasa; in the *bīja* essence, he is termed Prājña; and in the *sākṣin* essence, he is termed Turya.

He who is in the dreaming state [or the entity which identifies itself with the dreaming state] in the gross essence of *ukāra* is Viśva; in the subtle essence, he is termed Taijasa; in the *bīja* essence, is termed Prājña; and in the *sākṣin* essence, he is termed Turya.

"He who is in the *suṣupti* state in the gross essence of *makāra* is termed Viśva; in the subtle essence, Taijasa; in the *bīja* essence, he is termed Prājña; and in the *sākṣin* essence, he is termed Turya.

"He who is in the *turya* state in the gross essence of *ardhamātrā* is termed Turya-Viśva. In the subtle, he is termed Taijasa; in the *bīja* essence he is termed Prājña; and in the *sākṣīn* essence, he is termed Turya-turya.

"The *turya* essence of *akāra* is [or embraces] the first, second and third [*bhūmikās* or stages of the seven]. The *turya* essence of *ukāra* embraces the fourth *bhūmikā*. The *turya* essence of *makāra* embraces the fifth *bhūmikā*. The *turya* essence of *ardhamātrā* is the sixth stage. Beyond this is the seventh stage.

"One who functions in the [first] three *bhūmikās* is called *mumukṣu*; one who functions in the fourth *bhūmikā* is called a *brahmavit*; one who functions in the fifth *bhūmikā* is called a *brahmavidvara*; one who functions in the sixth *bhūmikā* is called *brāhmavidvarīya*; and one is the seventh *bhūmikā* is called a *brahmavidvariṣṭa*. With reference, to this, there are verses:

"*Śubhecchā* is said to be the first *jñānabhūmi* [or stage of wisdom]; *vicāraṇā*, the second; *tanumānasī*, the third; *sattvāpatti*, the fourth; then come *asaṃsakti* as the fifth, *padārthabhāvanā* as the sixth and *turya* as the seventh.

"The desire that arises in one through sheer *vairāgya* [after resolving] 'Shall I be ignorant? I will be seen with the śāstras and the wise [or I will study the books and be with the wise]' is termed by the wise as *śubhechchā*. The association with the wise and śāstras and the following of the right path preceding the practice of indifference is termed *vicāraṇā*. That stage wherein the hankering after sensual objects is thinned through the first and second stages is said to be within the range of sensual objects through the exercise in the [above] three stages, the purified *citta* rests on ātman which is of the nature of *sat* is called *sattvāpatti*. The light [or manifestation] of *sattvaguṇa* that is firmly rooted, [in one] without any desire for the fruits of actions through the practice in the above four stages is termed *asaṃsakti*. That stage wherein through the practice in the [above] five stages one, having found delight in ātman, has no conception of the internals or externals [though before him] and engages in actions only when impelled to do so by others is termed *padārthabhāvanā*, the sixth stage. The stage wherein after exceedingly long practice in the [above] six stages one is [immovably] fixed in the contemplation of ātman alone without the difference [of the universe] is the seventh stage called *turya*. The three stages beginning with *śubhecchā* are said to be attained with [or amidst] difference and non-differences. [Because] the universe one sees in the waking state he thinks to be really existent. When the mind is firmly fixed on the non-dual one and the conception of duality is put down, then he sees this universe as a dream through his union with the four stages. As the autumnal cloud being dispersed vanishes, so this universe perishes. O Nidāgha, be convinced that such a person has only *sattva* remaining. Then having ascended the fifth stage called *suṣuptipada* (dreamless sleeping seat), he remains simply in the non-dual state, being freed from all the [various] differences. Having always introvision though ever participating in external actions, those that are engaged in the practice of this [sixth stage] are seen like one sleeping when fatigued [*viz.* being freed from all affinities].

[Lastly] the seventh stage which is the ancient and which is called *gūḍhasupti* (secret sleep) is generally attained. Then one remains in that secondless state without fear and with his consciousness almost annihilated where there is neither *sat* nor *asat*, neither self nor not-self. Like an empty pot in the *ākāśa*, there is void both within and without; like a filled vessel in the midst of an ocean, he is full both within and without. Do not become either the knower or the known. May you become the reality which remains after all thoughts are given up. Having discarded [all the distinctions of] the seer, the sight and the seen with their affinities, meditate solely upon ātman which shines as the supreme Light.

"He is said to be an emancipated person (*jīvanmukta*) in whom, though participating in the material concerns of the world, the universe is not seen to exist like the invisible *ākāśa*. He is said to be a *jīvanmukta*, the light of whose mind never sets or rises in misery or happiness and who does not seek to change that happiness to him [viz. either to diminish his misery or increase his happiness]. He is said to be a *jīvanmukta* who though in his *suṣupṭi* is awake and to whom the waking state is unknown and who is free from the affinities [of objects].

"He is said to be a *jīvanmukta* whose heart is pure like *ākāśa*, though acting [as if] in consonance to love, hatred, fear and others. He is said to be a *jīvanmukta* who has not the conception of his being the actor and whose *buddhi* is not attached to material objects, whether he performs actions or not. He is said to be a *jīvanmukta*, of whom people are not afraid, who is not afraid of people and who has given up joy, anger and fear. He is said to be a *jīvanmukta* who, though participating in all the illusory objects, is cool amidst them and is a full ātman, [being] as if they belonged to others. O sage, he is called a *jīvanmukta* who, having eradicated all the desires of his *citta*, is [fully] content with me who am the ātman of all. He is said to be a *jīvanmukta* in whose *citta* do not dawn [the distinctions of] the universe, I, he, thou and others that are visible and unreal. Through the path of the guru and śāstras, enter soon *sat*—the Brahman that is immutable, great, full and without objects—and be firmly seated there. Śiva alone is Guru; Śiva alone is Vedas; Śiva alone is Lord; Śiva alone is I; Śiva alone is all. There is none other than Śiva. The undaunted Brāhmaṇa having known him [Śiva] should attain wisdom. One need not utter many words as they but injure the organ of speech.

"[The *ṛṣi*] Śuka is an emancipated person (a *mukta*). [The *ṛṣi*] Vāmadeva is a *mukta*. There are no others [who have attained emancipation] than through these [viz. two paths of these two *ṛṣis*]. Those brave men who follow the path of Śuka in this world become immediately emancipated (*sadyomukta*) after [the body wears away]; while those who always follow the path of Vāmadeva in this world are subject again and again to rebirths and attain gradual emancipation, through yoga, Sāṅkhya and *karmas* associated with *sattva*. Thus there are two paths laid down by the Lord of Devas [viz.] the Śuka and Vāmadeva paths. The Śuka path is called the bird's path; while the Vāmadeva which [passes stage after stage] is called the ant's path [is direct]. Those persons that have cognised the true nature of their ātman through the mandatory and prohibitory injunctions [of the Vedas], the inquiry into [the true meaning of] *mahāvākyas* [the sacred sentences of the Vedas] the *samādhi* of *Sāṅkhya-yoga* or through the intense self-absorption when one loses one's consciousness of individuality (*samprajñāta samādhi*) and have thereby purified themselves, attain the supreme seat through the Śuka path. Having through *haṭha-yoga* practice with the pain caused by *yama*, postures, etc. become liable to the ever recurring obstacles caused by *aṇimā* and other [*siddhis*] and having not obtained good results, one is born again in a great family and practises yoga through his previous [*kārmic*] affinities. Then through the practice of yoga during many lives, he attains salvation [viz.] the supreme seat of Viṣṇu through the Vāmadeva path. Thus there are two paths that lead to the attainment of Brahman and that are beneficent. The one confers instantaneous salvation and the other confers gradual salvation.

"To one that sees [all] as the one [Brahman], where is delusion? Where is sorrow? Those that are under the eyes of those whose *buddhi* is solely occupied with the truth [of Brahman] that is the end of all experience, are released from all heinous sins. All beings inhabiting heaven and earth that fall under the vision of *brahmavits* are at once emancipated from the sins committed during many crores of births."

CHAPTER V

Then Nidāgha asked Lord Ṛbhu to enlighten him as to the rules [to be observed] in the practice of yoga. Accordingly he [the Lord] said thus:

"The body is composed of the five elements. It is filled with five spheres (*maṇḍalas*). That which is hard is *pṛthivī* [earth], that which is liquid is *ap*: that which is bright is *tejas* [fire]; motion is the property of *vāyu*; that which pervades everywhere is *ākāśa*. All these should be known by an aspirant after yoga. Through the blowing of *vāyu maṇḍala* in this body, [there are caused] 21,600 breaths every day and night. If there is a diminution in the *pṛthivī maṇḍala*, there arise folds in the body; if there is diminution in the essence of *ap*, there arises gradually greyness of hair; if there is diminution in the essence of *tejas*, there is loss of hunger and lustre; if there is diminution in the essence of *vāyu*, there is incessant tremor; if there is diminution in the essence of *ākāśa*, one dies. The *jīvita* [viz. *prāṇa*] which possesses these elements having no place to rest [in the body] owing to the diminution of the elements, rises up like birds flying up in the air. It is for this reason that it is called *uḍḍiyāna* [lit., flying up]. With reference to this, there is said to be a *bandha* [binding, also meaning a posture called *uḍḍiyāna-bandha*, by which this flight can be arrested]. This *uḍḍiyāna-bandha* is to [or does away with] death, as a lion to an elephant. Its experience is in the body, as also the *bandha*. Its binding [in the body] is hurtful. If there is agitation of *agni* [fire within the belly], then there will be caused much pain. Therefore this [*uḍḍiyānabandha*] should not be practised by one who is hungry or who has urgency to make water or void excrement. He should take many times in small quantities proper and moderate food. He should practise *mantra-yoga*, *laya-yoga* and *haṭha-yoga*, through mild, middling and transcendental methods [or periods] respectively. *Laya-yoga*, *mantra-yoga* and *haṭha-yogas* have each [the same] eight subservients. They are forbearance (*yama*), religious restraint (*niyama*), posture (*āsana*), breath control (*prāṇāyāma*), subjugation of the senses (*pratyāhāra*), contemplation (*dhāraṇā*), meditation (*dhyāna*), and intense self-absorption (*samādhi*). [Of these], *yama* is of ten kinds. They are non-injury, truth, non-coveting, continence, compassion, straightforwardness, patience, courage, moderate eating and purity [bodily and mental]. *Niyama* is of ten kinds. They are religious austerities (*tapas*), contentment, belief in the existence of God or Vedas, charity, worship of Īśvara, listening to the exposition of religious doctrines, modesty, a [good] intellect, reciting of prayers (*japa*), and religious observances (*vrata*). There are eleven postures beginning with *cakra*. *Cakra*, *padma*, *kūrma*, *mayūra*, *kukkuṭa*, *vīra, svastika*, *bhadra*, *siṃha*, *mukta*, and *gomukha*, are the postures enumerated by the knowers of yoga. Placing the left ankle on the right thigh and the right ankle on the left thigh and keeping the body erect [while sitting] is the posture *cakra*. *Prāṇāyāma* should be practised again and again in the following order, viz. inspiration, restraint of breath and expiration. The *prāṇāyāma* is done through the *nāḍīs* (nerves). Hence it is called the *nāḍīs* themselves.

"The body of every sentient being is ninety-six digits long. In the middle of the body, two digits above the anus and two digits below the sexual organ, is the centre of the body [called *mūlādhāra* or sacral plexus]. Nine digits above the genitals, there is *kaṇḍa* of *nāḍīs* which revolves oval-shaped, four digits high and four digits broad. It is surrounded by fat, flesh, bone and blood. In it, is situated a *nāḍī-cakra* [wheel of nerves] having twelve spokes. *Kuṇḍalī*, by which this body is supported, is there. It is covering by its face the *brahmaranḍhra* [viz. the cavity of Brahmā] of *suṣumnā*. [By the side] of *suṣumnā* dwell the *nāḍīs alambuṣā* and *kuhū*. In the next two [spokes] are *vāruṇā* and *yaśasvinī*. On the spoke south of *suṣumnā* is, in regular course, *piṅgalā*. On the next two spokes, are *pūṣa* and *payasvatī*. On the spoke west of *suṣumnā* is the *nāḍī* called *sarasvatī*. On the next two spokes are *śaṅkhinī* and *gāndhārī*. To the north of *suṣumnā* dwells *iḍā*; in the next is *hastijihvā*; in the next is *viśvodarā*. In these spokes of the wheel, the twelve *nāḍīs* carry the twelve *vāyus* from left to right [to the different parts of the body]. The *nāḍīs* are like [i.e., woven like the warp and woof of] cloth. They are said to have different colours. The central portion of the cloth [here the collection of the *nāḍīs*] is called the *nābhicakra* [navel plexus]. *jvalantī*, *nādarūpiṇī*, *pararandhrā* and *suṣumnā* are called the [basic] supports of spiritual sound. These four *nāḍīs* are of ruby colour. The central portion of *brahmarandhra* is again and again covered by *kuṇḍalī*. Thus ten *vāyus* move in these *nāḍīs*. A wise man who has understood the course of *nāḍīs* and *vāyus* should, after keeping his neck and body erect with his mouth closed, contemplate immovably upon *turyaka* [ātman] at the tip of his nose, in the centre of his heart and in the middle of *bindu*, [lit. germ] and should see, with a tranquil mind through the [mental] eyes, the nectar flowing from there. Having closed the anus and drawn up the *vāyu* and caused it to rise through [the repetition of] *praṇava* [Oṃ], he should complete with *Śrī-bīja*. He should contemplate upon his ātman as Śrī [or Parāśakti] and as being bathed by nectar. This is *kāla-vañchana* [lit., time illusion]. It is said to be the most important of all. Whatever is thought of by the mind is accomplished by the mind itself. [Then] fire (*agni*) will flame in water (*jala*) and in the flame [of *agni*] will arise the branches and blossoms. Then the words uttered and the actions done regarding the universe are not in vain. By checking the *bindu* in the path, by making the fire flame up in the water and by causing the water to dry up, the body is made firm. Having contracted simultaneously the anus and the womb (*yoni*) united together, he should draw up *apāna* and unite with it *samāna*. He should contemplate upon his ātman as Śiva and then as being bathed by nectar. In the central part of each spoke, the yogin should commence to concentrate *bala* (strength). He should try to go up by the union of *prāṇa* and *apāna*. This most important yoga brightens up in the body the path of *siddhis*. As a dam across the water serves as an obstacle to the floods, so it should ever be known by the yogins that the *chāyā* of the body is [to *jīva*]. This *bandha* is said of all *nāḍīs*. Through the grace of this *bandha*, the goddess becomes visible. This *bandha* of four feet serves as a check to the three paths. This brightens up the path through which the *siddhas* obtained [their *siddhis*]. If with *prāṇa* is made to rise up soon *udāna*, this *bandha* checking all *nāḍīs* goes up. This is called *sampuṭayoga* or *mūlabandha*. Through the practising of this yoga, the three *bandhas* are mastered. By practising day and night intermittently at any convenient time, the *vāyu* will come under his control. With the control of *vāyu*, *agni* [the gastric fire] in the body will increase daily. With increase of *agni*, food etc., will be easily digested. Should food be properly digested, there is increase of essence of food (*rasa*). With the daily increase of *rasa*, there is the increase of spiritual substances (*dhātus*). With the increase of *dhātus*, there is the increase of wisdom in the body. Thus all the sins collected together during many crores of births are burnt up.

"In the centre of the anus and the genitals, there is the triangular *mūlādhāra*. It illumines the seat of Śiva of the form of *bindu*. There is located the *parāśakti* named *kuṇḍalinī*. From that seat, *vāyu* arises. From that seat, *agni* becomes increased. From that seat, *bindu* originates and *nāda* becomes increased. From that seat, *haṃsa* is born. From that seat, *manas* is born. The six *cakras* beginning with *mūlādhāra* are said to be the seat of Śakti (Goddess). From the neck to the top of the head is said to the seat of Śambhu [Śiva]. To the *nāḍīs*, the body is the support [or vehicle]; to *prāṇa*, the *nāḍīs* are the support; to *jīva*, prāṇa is the dwelling place; to *haṃsa*, *jīva* is the support; to Śakti, *haṃsa* is the seat of the moving and fixed universe.

"Being without distraction and of a calm mind, one should practise *prāṇāyāma*. Even a person who is well-skilled in the practice of the three *bandhas* should try always to cognise with a true heart that principle which should be known and is the cause of all objects and their attributes. Both expiration and inspiration should [be stopped and made to] rest in restraint of breath [alone]. He should depend solely on Brahman which is the highest aim of all visibles. [The giving out of] all external objects is said to be expiration (*recaka*). The [taking in of the] spiritual knowledge of the śāstras is said to be inspiration (*pūraka*) and [the keeping to oneself of] such knowledge is said to be restraint of breath (*kumbhaka*). He is an emancipated person who practises thus such a *citta*. There is no doubt about it. Through *kumbhaka*, it [the mind] should be controlled, and through *kumbhaka* alone it should be filled up within. It is only through *kumbhaka* that *kumbhaka* should be firmly mastered. Within it is Paramaśiva. That [*vāyu*] which in non-motionless should be shaken again through throat-posture (*kaṇṭha-mudrā*). Having checked the course of *vāyu*, having become perfect in the practice of expiration and restraint of breath and having planted evenly on the ground the two hands and the two feet, one should pierce the four seats through *vāyu* through the three yogas. He should shake Mahāmeru with the aid of forces (*prakṛtis*)at the mouth of *vāyu*. The two pits (cavities) being drawn, *vāyu* throbs quickly. The union of moon, sun and agni should be known on account of nectar. Through the motion of Meru, the devatās who stay in the centre of Meru move. At first in his *brahma-granthi*, there is produced soon a hole [or passage]. Then having pierced *brahma-granthi*, he pierces *viṣṇu-granthi*: then he pierces *rudra-granthi*. Then to the yogin comes *vedha* [piercing] through his liberation from the impurities of delusion, through the religious ceremonies [performed] in various births, through the grace of gurus and devatās and through the practice of yoga.

"In the *maṇḍala* of *suṣumnā* [situated between *idā* and *piṅgalā*], *vāyu* should be made to rise up through the feature known as *mudrā-bandha*. The short pronunciation (*hrasva*) of *praṇava* frees [one] from from sins: its long pronunciation (*dirgha*) confers [on one] *mokṣa*. So also its pronunciation in very long tone (*āpyāyana* or *pluta svara*). He is a knower of Veda, who through the above-mentioned three ways of pronunciation knows the end of *praṇava* which is beyond the power of speech, like the never ceasing flow of oil or the long-drawn bell-sound. The short *svara* goes to *bindu*. The long *svara* goes to *brahmarandhra*; the *pluta* to *dvādaśānta* [twelfth centre]. The mantras should be uttered on account of getting *mantra siddhis*. This *praṇava* [Oṃ] will remove all obstacles. It will remove all sins. Of this, are four [states] *bhūmikās* predicated, viz. *ārambha*, *ghāta*, *paricaya*, and *niṣpatti*. *Ārambha* is that state in which one having abandoned external *karmas* performed by the three organs [mind, speech and body], is always engaged in mental *karma* only. It is said by the wise that the *ghāta* state is that in which *vāyu* having forced an opening on the western side and being full, is firmly fixed there. *Paricaya* state is that in which *vāyu* is firmly fixed to *ākāśa*, neither associated with *jīva* nor not, while the body is immovable. It is said that *niṣpatti* state is that in which there takes place creation and dissolution through ātman or that state in which a yogin, having become a *jīvanmukta*, performs yoga without effort.

"Whoever recites this Upaniṣad becomes immaculate like *agni*. Like *vāyu*, he becomes pure. He becomes freed from the sin of drinking alcohol. He becomes freed from the sin of the theft of gold. He becomes a *jīvanmukta*. This is what is said by the Ṛgveda. Like the eye pervading the *ākāśa* [seeing without effort everything above], a wise man sees [always] the supreme seat of Viṣṇu. The Brāhmaṇas who have always their spiritual eyes wide open, praise and illuminate in diverse ways the spiritual seat of Viṣṇu."

Oṃ tat sat is the Upaniṣad

28

Maṇḍalabrāhmaṇa Upaniṣad of Śukla Yajurveda

BRĀHMAṆA I

Oṃ. The great muni Yājñavalkya went to Ādityaloka [the sun's world] and saluting him [the Puruṣa of the sun] said: "O reverend sir, describe to me the ātma-*tattva* [the truth of ātman]."

[To which], Nārāyaṇa [viz. the Puruṣa of the sun] replied: "I shall describe the eightfold yoga together with *jñāna*. The conquering of cold and heat as well as hunger and sleep, the preserving of patience and unruffledness and the restraining of the organs [from sensual objects]—all these come under *yama*. Devotion to one's guru, love of the true path, enjoyment of objects producing happiness, internal satisfaction, freedom from association, living in a retired place and the controlling of the *manas* and the not longing after the fruits of actions and a state of *vairāgya*—all these constitute *niyama*. The sitting in any posture pleasant to one and clothed in tatters [or bark] is prescribed for posture (*āsana*). Inspiration, restraint of breath and expiration, which have respectively 16, 64 and 32 [*mātrās*] constitute restraint of breath (*prāṇāyāma*).The restraining of the mind from the objects of senses is subjugation of the senses (*pratyāhāra*). The contemplation of the oneness of consciousness in all objects is *dhyāna*. The mind having been drawn away from the objects of the senses, the fixing of the consciousness (*caitanya*) [on one alone] is *dhāraṇā*. The forgetting of oneself in *dhyāna* is *samādhi*. He who thus knows the eight subtle parts of yoga attains salvation.

"The body has five stains [viz.] passion, anger, outbreathing, fear and sleep. The removal of these can be effected respectively by absence of *saṅkalpa*, forgiveness, moderate food, carefulness and a spiritual sight of *tattvas*. In order to cross the ocean of *saṃsāra* where sleep and fear are the serpents, injury etc. are the waves, thirst (*triśna*) is the whirpool and wife is the mire, one should adhere to the subtle path and overstepping *tattva* and other *guṇas* should look out for *tāraka*. *Tāraka* is Brahman which being in the middle of the two eyebrows, is of the nature of the spiritual effulgence of *saccidānanda*. The [spiritual] seeing through the three kinds of introvision [or the three *lakṣyas*] is the means to it [Brahman]. *Suṣumnā* which is from the *mūlādhāra* to *brahmarandhra* has the radiance of the sun. In the centre of it, is *kuṇḍalinī* shining like crores of lighting and subtle as the thread in the lotus-stalk. *Tamas* is destroyed there. Through seeing it, all sins are destroyed. When the two ears are closed by the tips of the forefingers, a booming sound (*phūtkāra*) is heard. When the mind is fixed on it, it sees a blue light between the eyes as also in the heart. This is internal introvision (*antarlakṣya*). In the external introvision (*bahirlakṣya*) one sees in order before his nose at distance of 4, 6, 8, 10 and 12 digits, the space of blue colour, then a colour resembling indigo-black (*śyāma*) and then shining as red (*rakta*) wave and then with the two yellow and orange red (*pīta*) colours. Then he is a yogin. When one looks at the external space, moving the eyes and sees streaks of light at the corners of his eyes, then his vision can be made steady. When one sees spiritual light (*jyotis*) above his head 12 digits in length, then he attains the state of nectar. In the *madhyalakṣya* (the middle one), one sees the variegated colours of the morning as if the sun, the moon and the fire have joined together in the *ākāśa* that is without them. Then he comes to have their nature [of light]. Through practice, he becomes one with *ākāśa*, devoid of all *guṇas* and peculiarities. At first *ākāśa* with its shining stars becomes to him *para-ākāśa* as dark as *tamas* itself and he becomes one with *para-ākāśa* shining with stars and deep as *tamas*. [Then] he becomes one with *mahā-ākāśa* resplendent [as] with the fire of the deluge. Then he becomes one with *tattva-ākāśa*, lighted with the brightness which is the highest and the best of all. Then he becomes one with *sūrya-ākāśa*, brightened by a crore of suns. By practising thus, he becomes one with them. He who knows them becomes thus.

"Know that yoga is twofold through its division into the earlier (*pūrva*) and the later (*uttara*). The earlier is *tāraka* and the later is the mindless (*amanaska*). *Tāraka* is divided into *mūrti* (with limitation) and *amūrti* (without limitation). That is *mūrti tāraka* which goes to the end of the senses [or exists till the senses are conquered]. That is *amūrti tāraka* which goes beyond the two eyebrows [above the senses]. Both these should be performed through *manas*. Internal vision (*antardṛṣṭi*) association with *manas* comes to aid *tāraka*. Spiritual light (*tejas*) appears in the hole between the two eyebrows. This *tāraka* is the earlier one. The later is *amanaska*. The great light (*jyotis*) is above the root of the palate. By seeing it, one gets the *siddhis*, *aṇimā* etc. *Śāmbhavī-mudrā* occurs when the spiritual vision (*lakṣya*) is internal while the [physical] eyes are seeing externally without winking. This is the great science which is concealed in all the Tantras. When this is known, one does not stay in *saṃsāra*. Its worship [or practice] gives salvation. *Antarlakṣya* is of the nature of water *jyotis* (*jalajyotis*). It is known by the great *ṛṣis* and is invisible both to the internal and external senses.

"*Sahasrāra* [viz. the thousand-petalled lotus in the crown of head] *jalajyotis* is the *antarlakṣya*. Some say the form of Puruṣa in the cave of *buddhi*, beautiful in all its parts, is *antarlakṣya*. Some again say that the all-quiescent Nīlakaṇṭha accompanied by Umā [his wife] and having five mouths and latent in the midst of the sphere in the brain is *antarlakṣya*, whilst others say that the Puruṣa of the dimension of a thumb is *antarlakṣya*. A few again say *antarlakṣya* is the one self made supreme through introvision in the state of a *jīvanmukta*. All the different statements made above pertain to ātman alone. He alone is a Brahmaniṣṭha who sees that the above *lakṣya* is the pure ātman. The *jīva* which is the twenty-fifth *tattva*, having abandoned the twenty-four *tattvas*, becomes a *jīvanmukta* through the conviction that the twenty-sixth *tattva* [viz.] Paramātman is 'I' alone. Becoming one with *antarlakṣya* [Brahma] in the emancipated state by means of *antarlakṣya* [introvision], *jīva* becomes one with the partless sphere of *paramākāśa*."

Thus ends the first Brāhmaṇa.

BRĀHMAṆA II

Then Yājñavalkya asked the Puruṣa in the sphere of the sun: "O Lord, *antarlakṣya* has been described many times, but it has never been understood by me [clearly]. Pray describe it to me." He replied: "It is the source of the five elements, has the lustre of many [streaks of] lightning, and has four seats having [or rising from] 'That' [Brahman]. In its midst, there arises the manifestation of *tattva*. It is very hidden and unmanifested. It can be known [only] by one who has got into the boat of *jñāna*. It is the object of both external (*bahir*) and internal (*antar*) *lakṣyas*. In its midst is absorbed the whole world. It is the vast partless universe beyond *nāda, bindu* and *kalā*. Above it [viz. the sphere of *agni*] is the sphere of the sun; in its midst is the sphere of the nectary moon; in its midst is the sphere of the partless spiritual effulgence of Brahman (*Brahma-tejas*). It has the brightness of *śukla* [white light] like the ray of lightning. It alone has the characteristic of *śāmbhavī*. In seeing this, there are three kinds of sight (*dṛṣṭi*), viz. *amā* [the new moon], *pratipaṭ* [the first day of lunar fortnight], and *pūrṇimā* [the full moon]. The sight of *amā* is the one [seen] with closed eyes. That with half opened eye is *pratipat*; while that with fully opened eyes is *pūrṇimā*. Of these, the practice of *pūrṇimā* should be resorted to. Its aim (*lakṣya*) is the tip of the nose. Then is seen a deep darkness at the root of the palate. By practising thus, a light (*jyotis*) of the form of an endless sphere is seen. This alone is Brahman, the *saccidānanda*. When the mind is absorbed in bliss thus naturally produced, then does *śāmbhavī*, take place. She [*śāmbhavī*] alone is called *khecarī*. By practising it [viz. the *mudrā*], a man obtains firmness of mind. Through it, he obtains firmess of *vāyu*. The following are the signs: first it is seen like a star; then a reflecting [or dazzling] diamond; then the sphere of full moon; then the sphere of the brightness of nine gems; then the sphere of the midday sun; then the sphere of the flame of fire *agni*; all these are seen in order.

"[Thus much for the light in first stage.] Then there is the light in the western direction [in the *uttara* or second stage]. Then the lustres of crystal, smoke, *bindu*, *nāda*, *kalā*, star, firefly, lamp, eye gold, and nine gems, etc. are seen. This alone is the form of *praṇava*. Having united *prāṇa* and *apāna* and holding the breath in *kumbhaka*, one should fix his concentration at the tip of his nose and making *ṣaṇmukhī* [*mudrā*] with the fingers of both his hands, one hears the sound of *praṇava* [Oṃ] in which *manas* becomes absorbed. Such a man has not even the touch of *karma*. The *karma* of *sandhyāvandana* [or the daily prayers] is verily performed at the rising or setting of the sun. As there is no rising or setting [but only the ever shining] of the sun of *cit* [the higher consciousness] in the heart of a man who knows thus, he has no *karma* to perform. Rising above [the conception of] day and night through the annihilation of sound and time, he becomes one with Brahman through the all-full *jñāna* and the attaining of the state of *unmanī* [the state above *manas*]. Through the state of *unmanī*, he becomes *amanaska* [or without *manas*].

"Not being troubled by any thoughts [of the world] then constitutes the *dhyāna*. The abandoning of all *karmas* constitutes invocation of god (*āvāhana*). Being firm in the unshaken [spiritual] wisdom constitutes the offering of water for washing the feet of god (*pādya*). Preserving the state of *amanaska* [when *manas* is offered as sacrifice] constitutes the offering of water as oblation (*arghya*). Being in a state of eternal brightness and shoreless nectar constitutes bathing (*snāna*). The contemplation of ātman as present in all constitutes [the application to the idol of] sandal. The remaining in the real state of the spiritual eye (*dṛk*) is [the worshipping with] non-broken rice (*akṣata*). The attaining of consciousness (*cit*) is [the worshipping with] flower; the real state of fire (*agni*) of *cit* is the buring of incense (*dhūpa*); the state of the sun of *cit* is the light waved before the image (*dīpa*). The union of oneself with the nectar of full moon is the offering of food etc.

(*naivedya*). The immobility in that state [of the ego being one with all] is going round the image (*pradakṣiṇā*). The conception of 'I am He' is prostration (*namaskāra*). The silence [then] is the praise (*stuti*). The all-contentment [or serenity then] is giving leave to god (*visarjana*) or finishing worship . [This is the worship of ātman by all Rāja-yogins]. He who knows this knows all.

"When the three, the knower, the known and the knowledge (*tripuṭi*) are thus dispelled, he becomes the *kaivalya jyotis* without existence (*bhāva*) or non-existence (*abhāva*), full and motionless, like the ocean without the tides or like the lamp without the wind. He becomes a knower of Brahman (*brahmavit*) by cognising the end of the sleeping state, even while in the waking state. Through the [same] mind absorbed in *suṣupti* as also in *samādhi*, there is much difference between them. [In the former case] as the mind is absorbed in *tamas*, it does not become the means of salvation, [but] in *samādhi* as the modifications of *tamas* in him are rooted away, the mind raises itself to the nature of the partless. All that is no other than witness-consciousness of the higher self *(sākṣicaitanya)* into which the absorption of the whole universe takes place, inasmuch as the universe is but a delusion [or creation] of the mind and is therefore not different from it. Though the universe appears perhaps as outside of the mind, still it is unreal. He who knows Brahman and who is the sole enjoyer of brāhmic bliss which is eternal and has dawned once [for all in him]—that man becomes one with Brahman. He in whom *saṅkalpa* perishes has got *mukti* in his hand. Therefore one becomes an emancipated person through the contemplation of Paramātman. Having given up both *bhāva* and *abhāva*, one becomes a *jīvanmukta* by leaving off again and again in all states wisdom (*jñāna*) and object of wisdom (*jñeya*), meditation (*dhyāna*) and object of meditation (*dhyeya*), the aim (*lakṣya*) and non-aim (*alakṣya*), the visible (*dṛśya*) and the non-visible (*adṛśya*) and reasoning (*ūha*) and negative reasoning (*apoha*). He who knows this knows all.

"There are five states (*avasthās*), viz. waking (*jāgrat*), dreaming (*svapna*), dreamless sleeping (*suṣupti*), the *turya* [fourth] and that beyond the fourth (*turyātīta*). The ego (*jīva*) that is engaged in the waking state becomes attached to the worldly (*pravṛtti*) path and is the participator of hell (*naraka*) as the fruit of sins. He desires heaven (*svarga*) as the fruit of his virtuous actions. This very same person becomes [afterwards] indifferent to all these saying, "Enough of the births tending to actions, the fruits of which tend to bondage till the end of this mundane existence." Then he pursues the [return path] *nivṛtti* with a view to attaining emancipation. And this person then takes refuge in a spiritual instructor in order to cross this mundane existence. Giving up passion and others, he does only that which he is asked to do. Then having acquired the four means to salvation (*sādhanas*), he attains, in the middle of the lotus of his heart, the reality of *antarlakṣya* that is but the *sat* of the Lord and begins to recognise [or recollect] the bliss of Brahman which he has left [or enjoyed] in his *suṣupti* state. At last he attains this state of discrimination [thus]: 'I think I am the non-dual one only. I was in *ajñāna* for some time [in the waking state and called therefore Viśva]. I became somehow [or involuntarily] a *taijasa* for some time [in the dreaming state] through the reflection [in that state] of the affinities of the forgotten waking state; and now I am a *prājña* through the disappearance of those two states. Therefore I am one only. I [appear] as more than one through the differences of state and place. And there is nothing of difference of class besides me.' Having expelled even the smack of the difference [of conception] between 'I' and 'That' through the thought 'I am the pure and the secondless Brahman', and having attained the path of salvation which is of the nature of Parabrahman, after having become one with it through the *dhyāna* of the sun's sphere as shining within himself, he becomes fully ripened for getting salvation. *Saṅkalpa* and others are the causes of the bondage of the mind; and the mind devoid of these becomes fit for salvation. Possessing such a mind free from all [*saṅkalpa*, etc.,] and withdrawing himself from the outer world of sight and others and so keeping himself out of the odour of the universe, he looks upon all the world as ātman, abandons the conception of 'I', thinks 'I am Brahman' and considers all these as ātman. Through these, he becomes one who has done his duty.

"The yogin is one that has realised Brahman that is all-full beyond *turya*. They [the people] extol him as Brahman; and becoming the object of the praise of the whole world, he wanders, over different countries. Placing the *bindu* in the *ākāśa*, of Paramātman and pursuing the path of the partless bliss produced by the pure, secondless, stainless and innate yoga sleep of *amanaska*, he becomes an emancipated person. When compared to it, the bliss of Indra and others is very little. He who gets this bliss is the supreme yogin."

Thus ends the second Brāhmaṇa.

BRĀHMAṆA III

The great sage Yājñavalkya then asked the Puruṣa in the sphere [of the sun]: "O Lord, though the nature of *amanaska* has been defined [by you], yet I forget it [or do not understand it clearly]. Therefore pray explain it again to me." Accordingly the Puruṣa said: "This *amanaska* is a great secret. By knowing this, one becomes a person who has done his duty. One should look upon it as Paramātman associated with *śāmbhavī-mudrā* and should know also those that can be known through a [thorough] cognition of them. Then seeing Parabrahman in his own ātman as the Lord of all, the immeasurable, the birthless, the auspicious, the supreme *ākāśa*, the supportless, the secondless, the only goal of Brahmā, Viṣṇu and Rudra and the cause of all and assuring himself that he who plays in the cave [of the heart] is such a one, he shoud raise himself above the dualities of existence and non-existence; and knowing the experience of the *unmanī* of his *manas*, he then attains the state of Parabrahman which is motionless as a lamp in a windless place, having reached the ocean of brāhmic bliss by means of the river of *amanaska-yoga* through the destruction of all his senses. Then he resembles a dry tree. Having lost all [idea of] the universe through the disappearance of growth, sleep, disease, expiration and inspiration, his body being always steady, he comes to have a supreme quiescence, being devoid of the movements of his *manas* and becomes absorbed in Paramātman. The destruction of *manas* takes place after the destruction of the collective senses, like the cow's udder [that shrivels up] after the milk has been drawn. It is this that is *amanaska*. By following this, one becomes always pure and becomes one that has done his duty, having been filled with the partless bliss by means of the path of *tāraka-yoga* through the initiation into the sacred sentences 'I am Paramātman', 'That art thou', 'I am thou alone,' 'Thou art I alone', etc.

"When his *manas* is immersed in the *ākāśa* and he becomes all-full, and when he attains the *unmanī* state, having abandoned all his collective senses, he conquers all sorrows and impurities through the partless bliss, having attained the fruits of *kaivalya*, ripened through the collective merits gathered in all his previous lives and thinking always 'I am Brahman', becomes one that has done his duty. 'I am thou alone. There is no difference between thee and me owing to the fullness of Paramātman'." Saying thus, he [the Puruṣa of the sun] embraced his pupil and made him understand it.

Thus ends the third Brāhmaṇa.

BRĀHMAṆA IV

Then Yājñavalkya addressed the Puruṣa in the sphere [of the sun] thus: "Pray explain to me in detail the nature of the fivefold division of *ākāśa*." He replied: "There are five [viz.] *ākāśa, parākāśa, mahākāśa, sūryākāśa* and *paramākāśa*. That which is of the nature of darkness, both in and out, is the first *ākāśa*. That which has the fire of the deluge, both in and out, is truly *mahākāśa*. That which has the brightness of the sun, both in and out, is *sūryākāśa*. That brightness which is indescribable, all-pervading and of the nature of unrivalled bliss is *paramākāśa*. By cognising these according to this description, one becomes of their nature. He is a yogin only in name, who does not cognise well the nine *cakras*, the six *ādhāras*, the three *lakṣyas* and the five *ākāśa*. Thus ends the fourth Brāhmaṇa.

Thus ends the fourth Brāhmaṇa.

BRĀHMAṆA V

"The *manas* influenced by worldly objects is liable to bondage; and that [*manas*] which is not so influenced by these is fit for salvation. Hence all the world becomes an object of *citta*; whereas the same *citta* when it is supportless and well-ripe in the state of *unmanī*, becomes worthy of absorption in Brahman [*laya*]. This absorption you should learn from me who am the all-full. I alone am the cause of the absorption of *manas*. The *manas* is within the spiritual light (*jyotis*) which again is latent in the spiritual sound which pertains to the heart [*anāhaṭa*] sound. That *manas* which is the agent of creation, preservation, and destruction of the three worlds—that same *manas* becomes absorbed in that which is the highest seat of Viṣṇu; through such an absorption, one gets the pure and secondless state, owing to the absence of difference then. This alone is the highest truth. He who knows this, will wander in the world like a lad or an idiot or a demon or a simpleton. By practising this *amanaska*, one is ever contented, his urine and faeces become diminished, his food becomes lessened; he becomes strong in body and his limbs are free from disease and sleep. Then his breath and eyes being motionless, he realises Brahman and attains the nature of bliss.

"That ascetic who is intent on drinking the nectar of Brahman produced by the long practice of this kind of *samādhi*, becomes a *paramahaṃsa* [ascetic] or an *avadhūta*. By seeing him, all the world becomes pure, and even an illiterate person who serves him is freed from bondage. He [the ascetic] enables the members of his family, for one hundred and one generations, to cross the ocean of *saṃsāra*; and his mother, father, wife and children—all these are similarly freed."

Oṃ tat sat is the Upaniṣad

29
Nādabindu Upaniṣad of Ṛgveda

The syllable *A* is considered to be its [the bird Oṃ's] right wing, *U*, its left: *M*, its tail; and the *ardhamātrā* [half-metre] is said to be its head.

The [*rājasic* and *tāmasic*] qualities, its feet upwards[to the loins] *sattva*, its [main] body; dharma is considererd to be its right eye, and *adharma*, its left.

The *bhūrloka* is situated in its feet; the *bhuvarloka*, in its knees; the *suvarloka*, in its loins; and the *maharloka*, in its navel.

In its heart is situated the *janoloka*; the *tapoloka* in its throat, and the *satyaloka* in the centre of the forehead between the eyebrows.

Then the *mātrā* [or mantra] beyond the *sahasrāra* [thousand rayed] is explained.

An adept in yoga who bestrides the *haṃsa* [bird] thus [viz. contemplates on Oṃ] is not affected by *kārmic* influences or by tens of crores of sins.

The first *mātrā* has *agni* as its presiding deity [devatā]; the second, *vāyu* as its devatā; the next *mātrā* is resplendent like the sphere of the sun and the last, the *ardhamātrā* the wise know as belonging to Varuṇa [the presiding deity of water].

Each of these *mātrās* has indeed three parts (*kalās*). This is called Oṃkāra. Know it by means of the *dhāraṇās*, viz. concentration on each of the twelve *kalās*, or the variation of the *mātrās* produced by the difference of intonation [*svaras*]. The first *mātrā* is called *ghoṣiṇī*; the second, *vidyunmālī* [or *vidyun-mātrā*]; the third, *pataṅginī*; the fourth, *vāyuveginī* the fifth, *nāmadheyā* the sixth, *aindrī*; the seventh, *vaiṣṇavī* the eighth, *śāṅkarī*; the ninth, *mahatī*; the tenth, *dhṛti* the eleventh, *nārī* and the twelfth, *brāhmī*.

If a person happens to die in the first *mātrā* [while contemplating on it], he is born again as a great emperor in Bhāratavarṣa.

If in the second *mātrā*, he becomes an illustrious *yakṣa*; if in the third *mātrā*, a *vidyādhara*; if in the fourth, a *gandharva* [these three being the celestial hosts].

If he happens to die in the fifth, viz. *ardhamātrā*, he lives in the world of the moon, with the rank of a deva greatly glorified there.

If in the sixth, he merges into Indra; if in the seventh, he reaches the seat of Viṣṇu; if in the eighth, Rudra, the Lord of all creatures.

If in the ninth, in *maharloka*; if in the tenth, in *janoloka* if in the eleventh, *tapoloka*, and if in the twelfth, he attains the eternal state of Brahmā.

That which is beyond these, [viz.] Parabrahman which is beyond [the above *mātrās*], the pure, the all-pervading, beyond *kalās*, the ever resplendent and the source of all lights (*jyotis*) should be known.

When the mind goes beyond the organs and the *guṇas* and is absorbed, having no separate existence and no mental action, then [the guru] should instruct him [as to his further course of development].

That person always engaged in its contemplation and always absorbed in it should gradually leave off his body [or family] following the course of yoga and avoiding all interaction with society.

Then he, being freed from the bonds of *karma* and the existence as a *jīva* and being pure, enjoys the supreme bliss by his attaining of the state of Brahmā.

O intelligent man, spend your life always in the knowing of the supreme bliss, enjoying the whole of your *prārabdha* [that portion of past *karma* now being enjoyed] without making any complaint [of it].

Even after knowledge of ātman [*ātmajñāna*] has awakened [in one], *prārabdha* does not leave [him]; but he does not feel *prārabdha* after the dawning of knowledge of truth (*tattvajñāna*) because the body and other things are unreal (*asat*), like the things seen in a dream to one on awaking from it.

That [portion of the] *karma* which is done in former births and called *prārabdha* does not at all affect the person (*tattvajñānin*), as there is no rebirth to him.

As the body that exists in the dreaming state is untrue, so is this body. Where then is rebirth to a thing that is illusory? How can a thing have any existence, when there is no birth [to it]?

As the clay is the material cause of the pot, so one learns from Vedānta that *ajñāna* is the material cause of the universe: and when *ajñāna* ceases to exist, where then is the cosmos?

As a person through illusion mistakes a rope for a serpent, so the fool not knowing the eternal truth (*satya*) sees the world [to be true].

When he knows it to be a piece of rope, the illusory idea of a serpent vanishes.

So when he knows the eternal substratum of everything and all the universe becomes [therefore] void [to him], where then is *prārabdha* to him, the body being a part of the world? Therefore the word *prārabdha* is accepted to enlighten the ignorant [only].

Then as *prārabdha* has, in course of time, worn out, he who is the sound resulting from the union of *praṇava* with Brahman who is the absolute effulgence itself, and who is the bestower of all good, shines himself like the sun at the dispersion of the clouds.

The yogin being in the *siddhāsana* [posture] and practising the *viaṣṇavī-mudrā*, should always hear the internal sound through the right ear.

The sound which he thus practises makes him deaf to all external sounds. Having overcome all obstacles, he enters the *turya* state within fifteen days.

At the beginning of his practice, he hears many loud sounds. They gradually increase in pitch and are heard more and more subtly.

At first, the sounds are like those proceeding from the ocean, clouds, kettle-drum, and cataracts: in the middle [stage] those proceeding from a musical instrument, bell and horn.

At the last stage, those proceeding from tinkling bells, flute, *(vīṇā)* a musical instrument and bees. Thus he hears many such sounds more and more subtle.

When he comes to that stage when the sound of the great kettle-drum is being heard, he should try to distinguish only sounds more and more subtle.

He may change his concentration from the gross sound to the subtle or from the subtle to the gross, but he should not allow his mind to be diverted from them towards others.

The mind having at first concentrated itself on any one sound fixes firmly to that and is absorbed in it.

If [the mind] becoming insensible to the external impressions, it becomes one with the sound as milk with water, and then becomes rapidly absorbed in *cidākāśa* [the void where consciousness prevails].

Being indifferent towards all objects, the yogin having controlled his passions, should by continual practice concentrate his attention upon the sound which destroys the mind.

Having abandoned all thoughts and being freed from all actions, he should always concentrate his attention on the sound, and [then] his *citta* becomes absorbed in it.

Just as the bee drinking the honey [alone] does not care for the odour, so the *citta* which is always absorbed in sound, does not long for sensual objects, as it is bound by the sweet smell of *nāda* and has abandoned its flitting nature.

The serpent serves the purpose of a sharp goad to control the maddened elephant—*citta* which roves in the pleasure-garden of the sensual objects.

It serves the purpose of a snare for binding the deer—*citta*. It also serves the purpose of a shore to the ocean waves of *citta*.

The sound proceeding from *praṇava* which is Brahman is of the nature of effulgence; the mind becomes absorbed in it; that is the supreme seat of Viṣṇu.

The sound exists till there is the *ākāśic* conception [*ākāśa-saṅkalpa*]. Beyond this, is the soundless (*aśabda*) Parabrahman which is Paramātman.

The mind exists so long as there is sound, but with its [sound's] cessation, there is the state called *unmanī* of *manas* [viz. the state of being above the mind].

This sound is absorbed in the *akṣara* (indestructible) and the soundless state is the supreme seat.

The mind, which along with *prāṇa* [*vāyu*], has [its] *kārmic* affinities destroyed by the constant concentration upon *nāda,* is absorbed in the unstained one. There is no doubt of it.

Many myriads of *nādas* and many more of *bindus*—[all] become absorbed in the *brahma-praṇava* sound.

Being freed from all states and all thoughts whatever, the yogin remains like one dead. He is a *mukta*. There is no doubt about this.

After that, he does not at any time hear the sounds of conch or large kettle-drum (*dundubhi*).

The body in the state of *unmanī* is certainly like a log and does not feel heat or cold, joy or sorrow.

The yogin's *citta,* having given up fame or disgrace, is in *samādhi* above the three states.

Being freed from the waking and the sleeping states, he attains to his true state.

When the [spiritual] sight becomes fixed without any object to be seen, when the *prāṇa* [*vāyu*] becomes still without any effort, and when the *citta* becomes firm without any support, he becomes of the form of the internal sound of Brahma-Praṇava.

Oṃ tat sat is the Upaniṣad

30
Yogakuṇḍalī Upaniṣad
of
Kṛṣṇa Yajurveda

Citta has two causes, *vāsanās* and *vāyu* (*prāṇa*). If one of them is controlled, then both are controlled. Of these two, a person should control *vāyu* (*prāṇa*) always through moderate food, postures, and thirdly *śakti-cāla* [viz. the awakening of the *kuṇḍalinī*] I shall explain the nature of these. Listen to it, O Gautama. One should take sweet and nutritious food, leaving a fourth [of his stomach unfilled] in order to please Śiva [the patron of yogins]. This is called moderate food. Posture herein required is of two kinds, *padma* and *vajra*. Placing the two heels over the two opposite thighs (repectively) is the *padma* [posture] which is destroyer of all sins. Placing one heel below the genital organ (*mūlakanda*) and the other over it and sitting with the neck, body and head erect is the *vajra* posture. The *śakti* (mentioned above) is only *kuṇḍalinī*. A wise man should take it up from its place (viz. the navel, upwards) to the middle of the eyebrows. This is called *śakti-cāla*. In practising it, two things are necessary, *sarasvatī-cālana* and the restraint of breath (*prāṇa*). Then through practice, *kuṇḍalinī* (which is spiral) becomes straightened. Of these two, I shall explain to you first *sarasvatī-cālana*. It is said by the wise of old that *sarasvatī* is no other than Arundhatī. It is only by rousing her up that the *kuṇḍalinī* is awakend. When breath (*prāṇa*) is passing through [one's] *iḍā* (left nostril), he should assume firmly *padma*-posture and should lengthen [inwards] 4 digits the *ākāśa* of 12 digits. Then the wise man should bind the [*sarasvatī*] *nāḍī* by means of this lengthened [breath] and holding firmly together [both his ribs near the navel] by means of the forefingers and thumbs of both hands, (one hand on each side) should stir up *kuṇḍalinī* with all his might from right to left often and often; for a period of two *muhūrtas* (48 minutes), he should be stirring it up fearlessly. Then he should draw up a little when *kuṇḍalinī* enters *suṣumnā*. By this means, *kuṇḍalinī* enters the mouth of *suṣumnā*. *Prāṇa* [also] having left [that place] enters of itself the *suṣumnā* [along with *kuṇḍalinī*]. By compressing the neck, one should also expand the navel. Then by shaking *sarasvatī*, *prāṇa* goes above [to] the chest. Through the contraction of the neck, *prāṇa* goes above from the chest. *Sarasvatī* who has sound in her womb should be shaken [or thrown into vibration] each day. Therefore by merely shaking it, one is cured of diseases. *gulma* (a splenetic disease), *jalodara* (dropsy), *plīha* (a splenetic disease) and all other diseases arising within the belly, are undoubtedly destroyed by shaking this *śakti*.

I shall now briefly describe to you *prāṇāyāma*. *Prāṇa* is the *vāyu* that moves in the body and its restraint within is known as *kumbhaka*. It is of two kinds, *sahita* and *kevala*. One should practise *sahita* till he gets *kevala*. There are four *bhedas* (lit., piercings), viz. *sūrya, ujjāyī, śītalī*, and *bhastrī*. The *kumbhaka* associated with these four is called *sahita kumbhaka*.

Being seated in the *padma* posture upon a pure and pleasant seat which gives ease and is neither too high nor too low, and in a place which is pure, lovely and free from pebbles, etc., and which for the length of a bow is free from cold, fire and water, one should shake [or throw into vibration] *Sarasvatī*; slowly inhaling the breath from outside, as long as he desires, through the right nostril, he should exhale it through the left nostril. He should exhale it after purifying his skull (by forcing the breath up). This destroys the four kinds of evils caused by *vāyu* as also by intestinal worms. This should be done often and it is this which is spoken of as *sūryabheda*.

Closing the mouth and drawing up slowly the breath as before with the nose through both the *nāḍīs* (or nostrils) and retaining it in the space between the heart and the neck, one should exhale it through the left nostril. This destroys the heat caused in the head as well as the phlegm in the throat. It removes all diseases, purifies the body and increases the [gastric] fire within. It removes also the evils arising in the *nāḍīs, jalodara* (waterbelly or dropsy) and *dhātus*. This *kumbhaka* is called *ujjāyī* and may be practised [even] when walking or standing.

Drawing up the breath as before through the tongue with (the hissing sound of) *sa* and retaining it as before, the wise man should slowly exhale it through (both) the nostrils. This is called *śītalī kumbhaka* and destroys diseases, such as *gulma, plīha*, consumption, bile, fever, thirst and poison.

Seated in the *padma* posture with belly and neck erect, the wise man should close the mouth and exhale with care through the nostrils. Then he should inhale a little with speech up to the heart, so that the breath may fill the space with noise between the neck and skull. Then he should exhale in the same way and inhale often and often. Just as the bellows of a smith are moved [viz. stuffed with air within and the air is let out], so he should inhale through the right nostril. If his belly is full of *vāyu*, then he should press well his nostrils with all his fingers except his forefinger and performing *kumbhaka* as before, should exhale through the left nostril. This frees one from diseases of fire in [or inflammation of] the throat, increases the gastric fire within, enables one to know the *kuṇḍalīnī*, produces purity, removing sins, gives happiness and pleasure and destroys phlegm which is the bolt [or obstacle] to the door at the mouth of *brahmanāḍī* [viz. *suṣumnā*]. It pierces also the three knots (*brahmagranthi*, *viṣṇugranthi* and *rudragranthi*) differentiated through the three *guṇas*. This *kumbhaka* is known as *bhastrī* and should especially be performed.

Through these four ways when *kumbhaka* is near [or is about to be performed], the sinless yogin should practise the three kinds of postures (*bandhas*). The first is called *mūla-bandha*. The second is called *uḍḍiyāna*, and the third is *jālandhara*. Their nature will be thus described. Breath (*apāna*) which has a downward tendency is forced up by one bending down. This process is called *mūla-bandha*. When *apāna* is raised up and reaches the sphere of fire (*agni*), then the flame of *agni* grows long, being blown about by *vāyu*. Then *agni* and *apāna* come to [commingle with] *prāṇa* in a heated state. Through this *agni* which is very fiery, there arises in the body the flaming [or the fire] which rouses the sleeping *kuṇḍalinī* through its heat. Then this *kuṇḍalinī* makes a hissing noise, becomes erect like a serpent beaten with stick and enters the hole of *brahmanāḍī* (*suṣumnā*). Therefore yogins should daily practise *mūla-bandha* often. *Uḍḍiyāna* should be performed at the end of *kumbhaka* and at the beginning of expiration. Because *prāṇa uḍḍīyate* (viz. goes up) the *suṣumnā* in this *bandha*, therefore it is called *uḍḍiyāna* by the yogins. Being seated in the *vajra* posture and holding firmly the two toes by the two hands, he should press at the *kāṇḍa* at the place near the two ankles. Then he should gradually upbear the thread (*tāna*) which is on the western side first to the upper part of abdomen above the navel, then to the heart and then to the neck. When *prāṇa* reaches the junction (*sandhi*) of navel, slowly it removes the impurities [or diseases] in the navel. Therefore this should be frequently practised. The *bandha* called *jālandhara* should be practised at the end of *kumbhaka*. This *jālandhara* is of the form of the contraction of the neck and is an impediment to the passage of *vāyu* [upwards]. When the neck is contracted at once by bending downwards [so that the chin may touch the breast] *prāṇa* goes through *brahmanāḍī* on the western *tāna* in the middle. Assuming the seat as mentioned before, one should stir up *sarasvatī* and control *prāṇa*. On the first day *kumbhaka* should be done four times; on the second day it should be done ten times and then five times separately; on the third day, twenty times will do and afterwards *kumbhaka* should be performed with three *bandhas* and with an increase of five times each day.

Diseases are generated in one's body through the following causes, viz. sleeping in daytime, late vigils over night, excess of sexual intercourse, moving in crowd, the checking of the discharge of urine and faeces, the evil of unwholesome food and laborious mental operation with *prāṇa*. If a yogin is afraid of such diseases [when attacked by them], he says, "My diseases have arisen from my practice of yoga." Then he will discontinue this practice. This is said to be the first obstacle to yoga. The second [obstacle] is doubt; the third is carelessness; the fourth, laziness; the fifth, sleep; the sixth, the not leaving of objects [of sense]; the seventh, erroneous perception; the eighth, sensual objects; the ninth, want of faith (*anāshā*); and the tenth, the failure to attain the truth of yoga. A wise man should abandon these ten obstacles after great deliberation. The practice of *prāṇāyāma* should be performed daily with the mind firmly fixed on truth. Then *citta* is absorbed in *suṣumnā*, and *prāṇa* [therefore] never moves. When the impurities [of *citta*] are thus removed and *prāṇa* is absorbed in *suṣumnā*, he becomes a [true] yogin. *Apāna*, which has a downward tendency should be raised up with effort by the contraction [of the anus], and this is spoken of as *mūla-bandha*. *Apāna* thus raised up mixes with *agni* and then they go up quickly to the seat of *prāṇa*. Then *prāṇa* and *apāna* uniting with one another go to *kuṇḍalinī*, which is coiled up and asleep. *Kuṇḍalinī* being heated by *agni* and stirred up by *vāyu*, extends her body in the mouth of *suṣumnā*, pierces the *brahmagranthi* formed of *rajas* and flashes at once like lightning at the mouth of *suṣumnā*. Then it goes up at once through *viṣṇugranthi* to the heart. Then it goes up through *rudragranthi* and above it to the middle of the eyebrows. Having pierced this place it goes up to the sphere of the moon. It dries up the moisture produced by the moon in the *anāhata cakra* having sixteen petals. When the blood is agitated through the speed of *prāṇa* it becomes bile from its contact with the sun, after which it goes to the sphere of the moon where it becomes of the nature of the flow of pure phlegm. How does it [blood] which is very cold become hot when it flows there? [Since] at the same time the intense white form of moon is speedily heated. Then being agitated, it goes up. Through taking in this, *citta* which was moving amidst sensual objects externally, is restrained there. The novice enjoying this high state attains peace and becomes devoted to ātman. *Kuṇḍalinī* assumes the eight forms of *prakṛti* (*mūla-prakṛti, mahat, ahaṃkāra* and the five elements) and attains Śiva by encircling him and dissolves itself in Śiva. Thus *rajas-śukla* (seminal fluid) which rises up goes to Śiva along with *marut* (*vāyu*); *prāṇa* and *apāna* which are always produced become equal. *Prāṇa* flows in all things, great and small, describable or indescribable, as fire in gold. Then this body which is composed of elements (*ādhibhautika*) becomes divine (*ādhidaivata*) (relating to a tutelar deity) and is thus purified. Then it attains the stage of being able to convey to other bodies the deity appointed by God (*ativāhika*). Then the body being freed from the inert state becomes stainless and of the nature of *cit*. In it, the *ativāhika* becomes the chief of all, being of the nature of that. Like the conception of the snake in a rope, so the idea of the release from wife and *saṃsāra* is the delusion of time. Whatever appears is unreal. Whatever is absorbed is unreal. Like the illusory conception of silver in the mother-of-pearl, so is the idea of man and woman. The microcosm and the macrocosm are one and the same; so also the *liṅga* and *sūtrātman*, substance (*svabhāva*) and form and the self-resplendent light and *cidātman*.

The *śakti* named *kuṇḍalinī*, which is like a thread in the lotus and is resplendent, is biting with the upper end of its mouth at the root of the lotus, the *mūlakāṇḍa*. Taking hold of its tail with its mouth, it is in contact with the hole of *brahmarandhra* (of *suṣumnā*). If a person seated in the *padma* posture and having accustomed himself to the contraction of his anus makes his *vāyu* go upward with the mind intent on *kumbhaka*, then *agni* comes to *svādhiṣṭhāna* flaming, owing to the blowing of *vāyu*. From the blowing of *vāyu* and *agni*, the chief (*kuṇḍalinī*) pierces open the *brahmagranthi* and then *viṣṇugranthi*. Then it pierces *rudragranthi*, after that, [all] the six lotuses [or plexuses]. Then Śakti is happy with Śiva in 1,000 lotus seat (*sahasrāra kamala*). This should be known as the highest state (*avasthā*) and it alone is the giver of final beatitude. Thus ends the first chapter.

CHAPTER II

I shall hereafter describe the science called *khecarī* which is such that one who knows it is freed from old age and death in this world. One who is subject to the pains of death, disease and old age should, O sage, on knowing this science make his mind firm and practise *khecarī*. One should regard that person as his guru on earth who knows *khecarī*, the destroyer of old age and death, both from knowing the meaning of books and practice and should perform it with all his heart. The science of *khecarī* is not easily attainable, as also its practice. Its practice and *melana* (viz. the secret practice revealed by adapts at initiation) are not accomplished simultaneously. Those that are bent upon practice alone do not get *melana*. Only some get the practice, O Brāhmaṇa, after several births, but *melana* is not obtained even after a hundred births. Having undergone the practice after several births, some [solitary] yogin gets the *melana* in some future birth as the result of his practice. When a yogin gets this *melana* from the lips of his guru, then he obtains the *siddhis* mentioned in several books. When a man gets this *melana* through books and the significance, then he attains the state of Śiva freed from all rebirth. Even gurus may not be able to know this without books. Therefore this science is very difficult to master. An ascetic should wander over the earth so long as he fails to get the *siddhi* in his hand [viz. mastered the psychical powers]. Therefore one should regard as Acyuta (Viṣṇu) the person who imparts the *melana*, as also him who gives out the science. Having got this science from me, you should not reveal it to others. Therefore one who knows this should protect it with all his efforts [viz. should never give it out except to persons who deserve it]. O Brāhmaṇa, one should go to the place where lives the guru, who is able to teach the divine yoga and there learn from him the science *khecarī*, and being then well taught by him should at first practise it carefully. By means of this science, a person will attain the *siddhi* of *khecarī*. Joining with *khecarī śakti* [viz. *kuṇḍalinī śakti*] by means [of the science] of *khecarī* which contains the *bīja* [letter] of *khecarī*, one becomes the lord of *khecaras* and lives always amongst them. *Khecarī bīja* (seed-letter) is spoken of as *agni* encircled with water and as the abode of *khecaras* (devas). Through this yoga, *siddhi* is mastered. The ninth (*bīja*) letter of *somāṃśa* (or moon part) should also be pronounced in the reverse order. Then a letter composed of three *aṃśas* of the form of the moon has been described; and after that, the eighth letter should be pronounced in the reverse order; then consider it as the supreme and its beginning as the fifth, and this is said to be peaks (*kūṭa*) of the several parts, of the moon. This which tends to the accomplishment of all yogas, should be learnt through the initiation of a guru. He who recites this twelve times every day, will not get even in sleep that illusion (*māya*) which is born in his body and which is the source of all vicious deeds. He who recites this five lakhs times with very great care—to him the science of *khecarī* will reveal itself. All obstacles vanish and the devas are pleased. The destruction of *valīpalita* (viz. wrinkles and greyness of hair) will take place without doubt. Having acquired this great science, one should practise it afterwards. If not, O Brāhmaṇa, he will suffer without getting any *siddhi* in the path of *khecarī*. If one does not get this nectar-like science in this practice, he should get it in the beginning of *melana* and recite it always; [else] one who is without it never gets *siddhi*. As soon as he gets this science, he should practise it; and then the sage will soon get the *siddhi*. Having drawn out the tongue from the root of the palate, a knower of self should clear the impurity [of the tongue] for seven days according to the advice of his guru. He should take a sharp knife which is oiled and cleaned and which resembles the leaf of the plant *snuhī* (Euphorbia antiquorum) and should cut for the space of a hair (the Fraenum Lingui). Having powdered rock-salt (*saindhava*) and sea-salt (*pathya*), he should apply it to the place. On the seventh day, he should again cut for the space of a hair. Thus for the space of six months, he should continue it always gradually with great care. In six months, *śiro-bandha* (at the head), which is at the root of the tongue is destroyed. Then the yogin [who knows timely action] should encircle with *śīro-vastra* (lit., the cloth of the head) the deity presiding over speech (the Vāgīśvarī) and should draw [it] up. Again by daily drawing it up for six months, it comes, O sage, as far as the middle of the eyebrows and obliquely up to the opening of the ears; having gradually practised, it goes to the root of the chin. Then in three years, it goes up easily to the end of the hair [of the head]. It goes up obliquely to *śākha* and downwards to the well of the throat. In another three years, it occupies *brahmarandhra* and stops there without doubt. Crosswise it goes up to the top of the head and downwards to the well of the throat. Gradually it opens the great adamantine door in the head. The rare science of *khecarī bīja* has been explained before. One should perform the six parts (*aṅgas*) of this mantra by pronouncing it in six different intonations. One should do this in order to attain all the *siddhis*; and this *kara-nyāsa* should be done gradually and not all at a time, since the body of one who does it all at once will soon decay. Therefore it should be practised, O best of sages, little by little. When the tongue goes to the *brahmarandhra* through the outer path, then one should place the tongue after moving the bolt of Brahmā which cannot be mastered by the devas. On doing this for three years with the point of the finger, he should make the tongue enter within: then it enters *brahmadvāra*. On entering the *brahmadvāra*, one should practise churning (*manthana*) well. Some intelligent men attain *siddhi* even without *manthana*. One who is versed in *khecarī* mantra accomplishes it without *manthana*. By doing the *japa* and *manthana*, one reaps the fruits soon. By connecting a wire made of gold, silver or iron with the nostrils by means of a thread soaked in milk, one should restrain his breath in his heart and seated in a convenient posture with his eyes concentrated between his eyebrows, he should perform *manthana* slowly. In six months, the state of *manthana* becomes natural like sleep in children. And it is not advisable to do *manthana* always. It should be done [once] only in every month. A yogin should not revolve his tongue in the path. After doing this for twelve years, *siddhi* is surely obtained. Then he sees the whole universe in his body as not being different from self. This path of the *ūrdhvakuṇḍalinī* (the arousal of *kuṇḍalinī*), O chief of kings, conquers the macrocosm. Thus ends the second chapter.

CHAPTER III

Melanamantra— Hrīṃ (ह्रीं), Bhaṃ (भं), Śaṃ (शं), Ṣaṃ (षं), Phaṃ (फं), Saṃ (सं) and Kṣaṃ (क्षं).

The lotus-born (Brahmā) said:

"O Śaṅkara, [among] new moon (the first day of the lunar fortnight) and full moon, which is spoken of as its [mantra's] sign? In the first day of lunar fortnight and during new moon and full moon [days], it should be made firm and there is no other way (or time). A man longs for an object through passion and is infatuated with passion for objects. One should always leave these two and seek the stainless (*nirañjana*). He should abandon everything else which he thinks is favourable to himself. Keeping the *manas* in the midst of *śakti*, and *śakti* in of midst of *manas*, one should look into *manas* by means of *manas*. Then he leaves even the highest stage. *Manas* alone is the *bindu*, the cause of creation and preservation. It is only through *manas* that *bindu* is produced, like the curd from milk. The organs of *manas* is not that which is situated in the middle of *bandhana*. *Bandhana* is there where *śakti* is between the sun and moon. Having known *suṣumnā* and its piercing (*bheda*) and making the *vāyu* go in the middle, one should stand in the seat of *bindu* and close the nostrils. Having known *vāyu*, the above-mentioned *bindu* and the *sattva-prakṛti* as well as the six *cakras*, one should enter the *sukhamaṇḍala* [*viz*. the *sahasrāra*, the sphere of joy]. There are six *cakras*. *Mūlādhāra* is in the anus; *svādhiṣṭhāna* is near the genital organ; *maṇipūraka* is in the navel; *anāhata* is in the heart; *viśuddhi* is at the root of the neck and *ājñā* is in the head (between the two eyebrows). Having known these six *maṇḍalas* (spheres), one should enter the *sukhamaṇḍala*, drawing up the *vāyu* and should send it upwards. He who practises thus [the control of] *vāyu* becomes one with the macrocosm (*brahmāṇḍa*). He should practise (or master) *vāyu, bindu, citta*, and *cakra*.

Yogins attain the nectar of equality through *samādhi* alone. Just as the fire latent in [sacrificial] wood does not appear without burning, so the lamp of wisdom does not arise without the practice of yoga (*abhyāsa* yoga). The fire placed in a vessel does not give light outside. When the vessel is broken, its light appears without. One's body is spoken of as the vessel, and the seat of "That" is the fire within; and when it [the body] is broken through the words of a guru, the light of *brahmajñāna* becomes resplendent. With the guru as the helmsman, one crosses the subtle body and the ocean of *saṃsāra* through the affinities of practice. That power of speech (*vāc*) which sprouts in *parā*, gives forth two leaves in *paśyantī*, buds forth in *madhyamā* and blossoms in *vaikharī*—that *vāc* which has before been described, reaches the stage of the absorption of sound reversing the above order [viz. beginning with *vaikharī* etc.] Whoever thinks that he who is the great lord of that *vāc*, who is the undifferentiated and who is the illuminator of that *vāc* is self; whoever thinks over thus, is never affected by words, high or low (or good or bad). The three [aspects of consciousness], *viśva*, *taijasa*, and *prajñā* [in man], the three Virāṭ, Hiraṇyagarbha and Īśvara in the universe, the egg of the universe, the egg of man and the seven worlds—all these in turn are absorbed in *pratyagātma* through the absorption of their respective vehicles (*upādhis*). The egg being heated by the fire of *jñāna* is absorbed with its cause (*kāraṇa*) into Paramātman (Universal Self). Then it becomes one with Parabrahman. It is then neither steadiness nor depth, neither light nor darkness, neither describable nor distinguishable. *Sat* (be-ness) alone remains. One should think of ātman as being within the body like a light in a vessel. Ātman is of the dimensions of a thumb, is a light without smoke and without form, is shining within [the body] and is undifferentiated and immutable.

The *vijñānātman* that dwells in this body is deluded by *māyā* during the states of waking, dreaming, and dreamless sleep; but after many births, owing to the effect of good *karma*, it wishes to attain its own state. Who am I? How has this stain of mundane existence accrued to me? What becomes in the dreamless sleep of me who am engaged in business in the waking and dreaming states? Just as a bale of cotton is burnt by fire, so the *cidābhāsa* which is the result of non-wisdom, is burnt by the [wise] thoughts like the above and by its own supreme illumination. The outer burning [of body as done in the world] is no burning at all. When the wordly wisdom is destroyed, *pratyagātman* that is in the ether of the heart *(dahara ākāśa)* obtains *vijñāna*, diffusing itself everywhere and burns in an instant *jñānamaya* and *manomaya* (sheaths). After this, he himself shines always within, like a light within a vessel.

That sage who contemplates thus till sleep and till death is to be known as a *jīvanmukta*. Having done what ought to be done, he is a fortunate person. And having given up [even] the state of a *jīvanmukta*, he attains *videhamukti* (emancipation in a disembodied state), after his body wears off. He attains the state, as if of moving in the air. Then that alone remains which is soundless, touchless, formless and deathless, which is the essence (*rasa*), eternal, and odourless, which has neither beginning nor end, which is greater than the great and which is permanent, stainless, and decayless.

Oṃ tat sat is the Upaniṣad

GLOSSARY

Adhibhautika one of the three kinds of pain, caused by other beings external to the self.

Adhidaivika one of the three kinds of pain, caused by deities; planetary influences.

Adhikāra a disciple's competency to practise spiritual discipline; authority.

Adhyāropa erroneous transferring of a statement from one thing to another; wrong attribution.

Adhyātma pertaining to the inner development of consciousness.

Agni fire.

Ajapa Mantra the involuntary repetition of a sacred formula.

Anāhata cakra a fifth element, along with earth, water, fire and air often regarded as the heart centre in the subtle body.

Anāhata Śabda unstruck sound.

Annamaya see **Kośa.**

Antaryāmin the dweller within pervading in all things.

Antaḥkaraṇa the inner cognitive instrument consisting of the fourfold inner faculties consisting of *manas*, *buddhi*, *ahaṃkāra* and *citta*.

Aṇimā power (*siddhi*) to become small as an atom through yoga.

Ap the material element of water.

Apavāda refutation, contradiction.

Apāna one of the energies that goes downwards, controlling the vital air in the abdominal region.

Apoha to remove or heal; to keep away from one's self (in disputation) or arguing.

Apsaras one of the celestial nymphs dancing in the court of Indra.

Asamprajñāta-Samādhi a cognitive samādhi wherein there is total cessation of *vṛttis*, *karmas* and their friction.

Aum the three sounds which compose the root mantra, Oṃ.

Avadhūta a rebel renunciate.

Avikalpa non-differentiated, non-fictitious.

Avyakta unmanifested, *prakṛti* in the process of evolution.

Ādhāra literary, support, *six-ādhāras*, or six supports of the subtle body.

Āgamas sacred tantric scriptures.

Āhvanīya fire 'offering fire' placed in the east of the sacrificial area.

Ājñā cakra centre between eyebows in the subtle body.

Ākāśa generally ether, a kind of matter subtler than air.

Ānanda essential principle of joy, bliss, spiritual ecstacy, state of unity.

Āraṇyaka forest teaching, the third part of each of the Vedas.

Āsana steady posture, yogic pose, a condition of balance and poise.

Āvaraṇa-Śakti the energy that veils and limits the primal unity of the absolute principle.

Āśrama a hermitage or dwelling place dedicated to spiritual pursuits.

Bandha muscular flexion; yogic practice in which certain organs of the body are 'locked' in a position.

Bhāva emotion; aesthetic state or feeling which enlivens the senses, the vehicle of *rasa*.

Bhāvanā cultivated concentration.

Bindu dot, a sacred symbol of the universe in its unmanifested form, in tantra also equated with semen.

Bīja mantra a seed sound formula corresponding to a particular psychic potentiality. Tantra texts state that the universe has evolved out of the fifty original *bīja* mantras which correspond to the fifty letters of the Sanskrit alphabet.

Bhūta any of the five elemental conditions of matter.

Bhūtādi rudimentary matter devoid of physical substance.

Brahmacarya celibacy; control of passion.

Brahman the absolute Reality, transcendental or pure consciousness, not to be confused with Brahmā. The single transcendent Reality which is '*Sat*', existence, consciousness and bliss.

Brahmarandhra the cakra on the crown of the head.

Brahmavit knower of Reality.

Brahmā the first god of the Hindu trinity, the creator.

Brahmānanda the bliss of Reality.

Buddhi intellect, the principle of intelligence which reveals knowledge, primary evolute of *prakṛti* in the Sāṃkhya system.

Caitanya pure consciousness, an attribute of the spiritual self.

Cakra centre of psychic power, literally 'wheel' or 'circle': technically the psychic centres of energy situated along Suṣumnā in the subtle human body, also known as *padmas* (lotus).

Caṇḍāla a member of the lowest class of persons among the Hindus, formerly regarded as untouchables.

Cit the principle of pure consciousness, awareness of the spiritual self.

Cit-śakti consciousness as power, the supreme energy.

Citta basic mental awareness.

Citt-ākāśa mental or physical inner space.

Dakṣina Agni 'southern fire' placed in the south of the sacrificial area.

Dama restrain.

Dhairya steadfastness and patience.

Dhāraṇā concentration.

Dhātu a constituent of the body, such as blood, flesh, bones, the three humours (air, phlegm and bile), etc.

Dhyāna meditation, sustained inner concentration beginning with concrete and ending with abstract awareness.

Dīkṣā initiation by a guru.

Ekadaṇḍīn 'bearing one staff'; name of a class of monks.

Ekāgratā one-pointed.

Ekānta silence.

Gāyatrī 'she who chants', a metre of twenty-four syllables in three divisions (*pāda*), the most famous mantra in the Vedas.

Gotra exogenous lineage traced in the paternal line from one of the ancient sages.

Grāhapatya fire the 'householder's fire', lit from the domestic fire, which the householder maintains throughout his life.

Guṇa the three qualities or an evolute of Prakṛti ; *Sattva*, purity and illumination, *Rajas*, dynamic activity and *Tamas*, inertia.

Haṃsa 'swan' the supreme spirit identified with the universal Reality; a class of ascetic who has realized the highest truth; one of the vital airs resoluble into the mantra *aham sa* 'I am that'. See **Prāṇa.**

Hanumān is the incarnation of *vāyu*, one of the elements of Śiva.

Haṭhayoga incorporating bodily disciplines leading to psychic development.

Hiraṇyagarbha 'golden womb', the first seed of creation produced by the self-existent Reality.

Iḍā the left subtle *nādi*, or psychic channel, coiling round the Suṣumṇā and ending at the left nostril.

Indriyas the ten faculties of sensation and perception in the human body: five "knowing" agents, *jñānendriyas* - hearing, touching, seeing, tasting and smelling; five "action" agents, *karmendriyas* - walking, handling, speaking, procreation and evacuation.

Iśītva the power of lordship, a *siddhi*.

Jāgrata the waking consciousness.

Janoloka see **Loka**.

Japa constant repetition, either silently or audibly, of a mantra.

Jīva individual self.

Jīvan-mukta liberated in this life; spiritually free but still manifest in human form.

Jīvātman the individual self.

Jñāna self-knowledge, knowledge of the Absolute through meditation.

Kaivalya final self-realization of one's self as being identical with Reality; isolation of the self from material impediments.

Kalā any single part of a whole; time; the power that conditions or limits the existence of unchangeable elements in matter.

Kalpa aeon; a 'day' of Brahmā, the creator; a cycle of creation and dissolution.

Karanyāsa the ritual of infusing the divine energies of the deities on the fingers and the palms of hands.

Karma action or obligation in the hope of future recompense. There are three types of *karmas*: *prārabdha,* which has commenced in a previous life; *sañcita*, accumulated through successive lives and *āgamī,* that are yet to fructify in future.

Kaustubha a precious jewel obtained with thirteen other precious things at the churning of the ocean. The jewel adorns the breast of Viṣṇu and Kṛṣṇa.

Kāraṇa cause, instrument, source, wine in tantric cakra-pūjā, ritual of union.

Kāraṇa-śarira causal body.

Kālāgni the lowest plane (*bhuvana*) of existence.

Khecarī-mudrā a yogic posture in which the tongue is thrust up to close the nasal orifice.

Kīlaka a wedge. In the Ajapā mantra '*Haṃsa-so'ham*', *So'ham* is the wedge to which the whole mantra is fastened.

Kleśa affliction, impurity, said to be of five kinds: ignorance (*avidyā*), 'I'hood (*asmitā*), attraction (*rāga*), aversion (*dveṣa*), fear of death (*ahiniveśa*).

Kośa sheath; an individual human being is conceived of having five sheaths or *kośas*: the tangible physical body (Annamaya); the sheath of vital air (Prāṇamaya), the sheath of mind (Manomaya); the sheath of cognitive process (Vijñānamaya) and the subtlest of all, the sheath of bliss (Ānandamaya).

Kṣiti the earth element.

Kumāra is the son of Śiva called Kārtikēya, the six-faced, symbolizing the six-faced Mars in one sense.

Kumbhaka retention of breath during the practice of prāṇāyama.

Kuṇḍalinī dormant psychic power lying coiled up like a serpent at the base of the spine.

Kūṭastha 'highest position' immovable or unchangeable, immortal soul who has attained the highest perfection of yoga.

Laghimā power (*siddhi*) to attain weightlessness through yogic practice.

Lakṣya the object of meditation, the state of concentration that is aimed for.

Laya dissolution of the universe and its phenomena to its source.

Liṅga-śarīra the causal body, totality of subtle or psychic body.

Loka world spheres with celestial, atmospheric and terrestrial planes. Its seven subdivisions are: 1. Brahmaloka, the abode of Brahma, 2. Tapa-loka, the abode of Virāj, 3. Janar-loka, the abode of Brahmā's son, 4. Mahar-loka, the abode of Prajāpatis, 5. Svar-loka, the abode of gods, 6. Bhuvar-loka, the atmospheric sphere, the abode of ancestors, and 7. Bhur-loka, the earth and the terrisrial region (see Tala).

Maharloka the fourth of the seven worlds which rise above the other. See **Loka**.

Mahat the universal *buddhi*.

Malas impurities that bind the soul from birth to birth.

Manas the active mind, the mental faculty of coordination, reasoning, assimilation, an evolute of Sāṃkhya.

Mantra sacred formula based on the principle that sound has a spiritual significance and power, incantation.

Mahāmudrā 'supreme posture' in which the practitioner sits with the left heel pressed against the perinium with the right leg stretched outward and holding the right foot with both hands. The nine orifices of the body are contracted and the chin is pressed closely to the chest (*jalandhara-mudrā*) for the control of breath.

Mahāraurava one of the eight hot hells.

Mahātala name of the lower most regions, sixth or seventh, under the earth, inhabited by the Nāgas.

Mahāvākya the twelve sacred utterances of the Upaniṣads such as *tat tvamsi,* (you are That); *aham brahmasmi* (I am Brahman), etc.

Mahimā the power (*siddhi*) to become large.

Maṇipura cakra the navel centre in the subtle body.

Mātrā the time occupied in circling the knee once with the palm of the hand and snapping the fingers. The four *mātrās* are subdivided into twelve by their having each three *svaras*, *udātta*, *anudātta*, and *svarīta*.

Māyā the potent power of Brahman with two fold manifestation, to veil and reveal; the limiting principle; illusion of the real nature of the world appearance.

Melana esoteric practice of attaining the state of union in yoga, known only to the initiator.

Mokṣa liberation from *saṃsāra*.

Muhūrta an auspicious moment calculated on the basis of current positioning and configuration of planets.

Mumukṣa one who has a desire for spiritual liberation.

Mūlādhāra cakra the root cakra at the base of the spinal column in the subtle body.

Mūdrā seal; finger gesture; yogic control of certain organs as an aid to concentration which produces psycho-physical responses.

Nāda motion, vibrational energy manifesting as sound; primeval and inner sound.

Nāda-bindu primal vibration; the seed sound out of which the universe emanates.

Nāḍī psychic or astral nerve channel in the physical body.

Nārayaṇa an aspect of Viṣṇu.

Nirbīja samādhi seedless *samādhi* without objects of concentration.

Nirvāṇa final emancipation.

Nirvikalpa non-discursive awareness.

Niśādas forest dwellers; people of lower ranks of society, from primal communities.

Nivṛtti withdrawal from life.

Niyama control, yogic discipline of the mind and body.

Ojas vital energy.

Oṃ seed mantra compounded of three sounds, a, u, m, embracing all the secrets of the cosmos which are, as it were, gathered to a point within it.

Palam a very small unit of time.

Param haṃsa supreme realization of the yogi.

Param the supreme.

Paramātman the supreme self.

Parāvāk the unmanifest vibratory movement of cosmic sound.

Pañca-ākāśa five interior states of contemplation: *parā-ākāśa*, dark as *tamas*; *mahā-ākāśa*, resplendent as fire of deluge;

tattva-ākāśa, lit with brightness; *sūrya-ākāśa*, bright as crore of suns.

Pañcabhūtas five gross elements; earth, water, fire, air, ether or space.

Paśyanti literally 'seeing'; sound emerging towards the visible.

Pātāla the subterranean regions, see **Tala**.

Piṅgalā the subtle channel on the right side of the subtle body.

Prakṛti counterpart of Puruṣa, creative energy, the source of objectivity referred to as the primeval female or Nature.

Prakṛtis the eight *prakṛtis* are *mūlaprakṛtī*, *mahaṭ*, *ahaṅkāra*, and the five elements; the sixteen *vikāras* of *Prakṛti* are the five organs of the senses, the five organs of action, the five *prāṇas* and *antaḥkaraṇa*.

Praṇva the primal sound.

Pratyāhara withdrawal of senses from their objects.

Pravṛtti inclination, manifestation, active liberation while in life.

Prāṇa life force, the vital energy of the cosmos; the vital energy regulated by five-fold *prāṇas,* each of which governs an energy flow: *prāṇa,* regulates inhalation; *apāna,* the lower breath, exhalation and excretion; *samāna,* the middle breath, digestion and distribution of energies and nutrients; *udāna,* the upward movement of *prāṇa,* and *vyāna,* regulates the entire nervous system and blood flow.

Prāṇāyāma yogic breath control.

Prārabdha-karma see Karma.

Purāṇas 'old', ancient Hindu scriptures expounding in legendary form the powers and deeds of gods and goddesses.

Puruṣa pure consciousness, counterpart of Nature or *Prakṛti.*

Puruṣa-prakṛti consciousness in relation to Nature, male-female, static-kinetic.

Rajas the principle of motion, a constituent of *Prakṛti*; female seed, menstrual flow.

Rasa essence of a thing, aesthetic delight, the substance of aesthetic experience, pleasure in the pure source of feeling.

Rasātala see **Loka.**

Retas physical substance.

Rudragranthi one of the knots that Kuṇḍalinī has to pierce in its ascent.

Sahasrāra cakra the psychic centre symbolized by the thousand-petalled lotus above the head where the Kuṇḍalinī Śakti unites with Śiva.

Samprajñāta Samādhi the lower level samādhi that requires supportive objects.

Sāṃkhya 'enumeration', one of the oldest schools of Indian philosophy started by sage Kapila. See **Tattva.**

Saṃsāra world, the repeated cycle of birth and death.

Sankalpa a positive inner resolve.

Sannyāsa the final stage in the pilgrimage of life which cuts the threads of all bondages.

Sannyāsin an ascetic who has cut the thread of all bondage with worldly life. The six classes of sannyāsins are: *kuṭicaka*, one who is stationed at one place; *bahudaka*, one who drinks water from many places or one who moves from place to place; *haṃsa*, one who is detached and untainted by the mundane aspects of life. Such an ascetic is likened to a swan (*haṃsa*) who floats in water without getting wet; *paramhaṃsa*, one who has realized the highest truth and voluntarily observes the codes of ascetic order; *turyātita*, one who is beyond the four stages of life; and *avadhūta*, who does not require to live by the norms set by society.

Saṅskāra an imprinted impression or memory trace, fruit of *kārmic* actions.

Sañcita-karma see **Karma.**

Sat-cit-ānanda being, conscious, bliss, as a unity, the peak stage of realization.

Sattva the highest of the *guṇas*, principle of equilibrium, truth, purity, the quality of radiance.

Satyaloka see **Loka.**

Sāyujya one of the four forms of beatitude of being in union with the deity.

Sālokya one of the four grades of beatitude of being in the same celestial abode as the deity.

Sāniddhya one of the four grades of beatitude of being in the presence of the deity.

Sārūpya identifications, similarity.

Siddhāsana one of the most important yogic postures.

Siddhis yogic accomplishments, attainments of spiritual powers, there are 18 *siddhis*, 8 higher and 10 lower, acquisition of paranormal powers, fruits of yogic practices but not their ultimate aim.

Sṛṣṭi creation.

Sphoṭavāda concept of sound.

Śeṣa meaning remainder as the serpent, representing time.

Śrāddha the obsequies to honour the dead.

Śraddhā one of the six virtues, humanity, reverent faith and surrender.

Sthūla gross.

Sudhā nectar.

Śukra male seed.

Sukṣama subtle.

Suṣumṇā the subtle channel in the centre of the spinal column through which the Kuṇḍalinī rises.

Suṣupti a state of consciousness identified with deep sleep.

Sūtrātmā the subtle self threaded together and united with the absolute principle.

Svapna the dream state of conciousness.

Svādiṣṭhāna cakra the centre at the base of the genital organ in the subtle body.

Ṣaṇmukhi is said to be the process of hearing the internal sound by closing the two ears with the two thumbs, the two eyes with the two forefingers, the two nostrils with the two middle fingers and the mouth with the remaining two fingers of both hands.

Ṣaṭa-sampat the six treasures/virtues, quietitude (*śama*), restrain (*dama*), withdrawal from the worldy interests (*uparati*), forbearance (*titikṣā*); faith (*śraddhā*); and freedom from conflicts (*samādhāna*).

Śabda sound; cosmic sound.

Śabdabrahman the Brahman as the primal sound energy.

Śāstras sacred books of divine authority, scriptures.

Śrīvatsa a sacred mark or curl of hair on the breast of Viṣṇu or Kṛṣṇa; an auspicious mark on the breast of Viṣṇu representing the female principle (=Lakṣmī) and the garland of five elements.

Tamas power of inertia, the lowest of the three *guṇas*. See **Guṇas.**

Tanmātra infra-atomic energy potential; subtle elements of Sāṃkhya philosophy. See **Tattva.**

Tantra one of a series of scriptures that emphasize practical ways of self-enlightenment, especially relating to the power of Śakti.

Tapas ascetic observance, austerity, penance.

Tattva one of the twenty-five basic elements of creation according to Sāṃkhya philosophy : 1. *prakṛti*, from which emanates 2. *buddhi*, intelligence (also referred to as *mahat*, the great) 3. *ahaṃkāra*, the sense of 'I' or ego; 4-8. five *tanmātras* (space, air, fire, water, earth); 9-13. five *mahābhūtas*, gross five subtle elements; 14-18. five senses (ear, skin, eye, tongue, nose); 19-23. five organs of action (speech, hand, foot, excretory organs, sex organs); and 24. *manas*, intelligence; 25. is *puruṣa*, the conscious principle.

Tala the subterranean regions, consisting of seven planes: 1. Pātāla: the serpent kingdoms of Nāgas; 2. Atāla: the kingdom of Yakṣas and evil spirits; 3. Rasātāla, the abode of demons; 4. Gabhartāla, the kingdom of the ogress; 5. Vitāla, the kingdom of the chthonian people; 6. Sutāla, ruled by Bali and 7. Mahātāla, the kingdom of spectres.

Tāraka is from the Sanskrit root *ṭr*, to cross, as it enables one to cross *saṃsāra*. The higher vision, is said to take place in a subtle centre between the eyebrows.

Trāṭaka to look at the space between the eyebrows, or to gaze without any blinking, concentrating the vision on a single point or object.

Turya the fourth stage of consciousness.

Upaniṣads spiritual doctrines of ancient Indian philosophies composed in their present form between c 1000 BC and 800 BC. The fundamental concepts of Upaniṣads is the identity of the individual soul with Universal Soul, and is essentially an inquiry into the nature of the ultimate Reality.

Uparati withdrawal from worldly interests, one of the six virtues.

Udāna the upward movement of vital life-forces in prāṇāyāma.

Upādhi a superimposed condition,external to the intrinsic nature of an entity.

Vac speech.

Vaikharī the fourth stage of the gross physical sound or vibration manifesting as word.

Vairāgya dispassion and control over desires.

Vajroli-mudrā one of the mūdras by which sexual energy is controlled and reabsorbed into the body. The adept is expected to draw in the female seed through the member into his body during the union, in a process called Sahajoli.

Varṇa-āśrama to integrate both household life and renunciation in the social structure, caste and four life stages. The four stages are—*brahmacarin*, a student of Vedas; *gṛhasta*, householder; *vanaprastha*, forest-dweller and *sannyasin*, wandering renouncer.

Vāsanā imprint of actions (*samskāras*) left in the mind.

Vāyu vital air.

Vedas the original scriptural-books of India, revealed knowledge of the Aryans, consisted of 100,000 verses and are in four divisions, the Ṛgveda (c. 2000-1500 BC), the earliest literature of the world; the Yajur-veda; the Sāma-veda, the Atharva-veda.

Vibhūti example or expression of supernatural powers.

Videha-mukti one who is liberated while still living in the body.

Vidyā knowledge.

Vikalpa differentiated cognition.

Vikṣepa-Sakti the energy that unfolds the process of creation.

Virāṭ cosmic immanent forms of the Absolute.

Viśuddha cakra the throat centre in the subtle body.

Vitrāga one who is devoid of attachments.

Vṛtti mental state, modification of mind.

Vyādhi illness, the imbalance of body constitutions.

Vyāhṛti an 'utterance', one of the sacred words representing the different levels of the cosmos, *Bhuḥ*, *Bhuvaḥ* and *Svaḥ*.

Vyāna one of the five vital airs (*vāyu*) distributed in the body. See **Prāṇa**.

Yama restraints, the first of the eight parts of yoga non-violence (*ahiṃsā*), non-lying (*satya*); non-stealing (*asteya*), control of passions, senses and mind (*bramacarya*) and non-attachment (*aparigraha*).

Yantra a form or symbol, aid to contemplation, geometrical representation of deity.

Yoga union, a system of philosophy; the path on which the individual self is united with the Universal self, teaching about the path of realization; there are four kinds of yoga—the fourth being Rājayoga. Manṭrayoga is one in which perfection is obtained through the pronunciation of manṭras. Layayoga is one in which perfection is obtained through *laya* (absorption).

Yogi one who seeks to action essential identity with the reality.

Yogin a student of Yoga, feminine, yogini.

Yuga aeon, the four yugas are Satya or Kṛta-yuga, Treta-yuga, Dvāpara-yuga, and Kalī-yuga, the present age of mankind.

INDEX

***